MW00989573

THE EMIL AND KATHLEEN SICK LECTURE-BOOK SERIES
IN WESTERN HISTORY AND BIOGRAPHY

Under the provisions of a Fund established by the children of Mr. and Mrs. Emil Sick, whose deep interest in the history and culture of the American West was inspired by their own experience in the region, distinguished scholars are brought to the University of Washington to deliver public lectures based on original research in the fields of Western history and biography. The terms of the gift also provide for the publication by the University of Washington Press of the books resulting from the research upon which the lectures are based.

The Great Columbia Plain: A Historical Geography, 1805–1910 by Donald W. Meinig

Mills and Markets: A History of the Pacific Coast Lumber Industry to 1900 by Thomas R. Cox

Radical Heritage: Labor, Socialism, and Reform in Washington and British Columbia, 1885–1917 by Carlos A. Schwantes

The Battle for Butte: Mining and Politics on the Northern Frontier, 1864–1906 by Michael P. Malone

The Forging of a Black Community: Seattle's Central District from 1870 through the Civil Rights Era by Quintard Taylor

Warren G. Magnuson and the Shaping of Twentieth-Century America by Shelby Scates

The Atomic West edited by Bruce Hevly and John M. Findlay

Power and Place in the North American West edited by Richard White and John M. Findlay

Henry M. Jackson: A Life in Politics by Robert G. Kaufman

Parallel Destinies: Canadian-American Relations West of the Rockies edited by John M. Findlay and Ken S. Coates

Nikkei in the Pacific Northwest: Japanese Americans and Japanese Canadians in the Twentieth Century edited by Louis Fiset and Gail M. Nomura

Bringing Indians to the Book by Albert Furtwangler

Death of Celilo Falls by Katrine Barber

DEATH OF CELILO FALLS

KATRINE BARBER

CENTER FOR THE STUDY
OF THE PACIFIC NORTHWEST

in association with

UNIVERSITY OF WASHINGTON PRESS

Seattle and London

© 2005 by the University of Washington Press
Designed by Pamela Canell
Printed in the United States of America
12 11 10 09 08 07   5 4 3 2

All rights reserved. No part of this publication
may be reproduced or transmitted in any form or
by any means, electronic or mechanical, including
photocopy, recording, or any information storage
or retrieval system, without permission in
writing from the publisher.

Center for the Study of the Pacific Northwest
P.O. Box 353587, Seattle, WA 98195

University of Washington Press
P.O. Box 50096, Seattle, WA 98145
www.washington.edu/uwpress

Library of Congress Cataloging-in-Publication Data
may be found on the last page of the book.

The paper used in this publication is acid-free and
90 percent recycled from at least 50 percent post-
consumer waste. It meets the minimum requirements
of American National Standard for Information
Sciences—Permanence of Paper for Printed
Library Materials, ANSI Z39.48–1984.⊗ ◉

Title page image: "Powers That Be,"
linoleum block print by Jonnel Covault

FOR MY TEACHERS, LIBERATORS ALL

CONTENTS

ACKNOWLEDGMENTS

At Bonneville now there are ships in the locks
The waters have risen and cleared all the rocks
Shiploads of plenty will steam past the docks
So roll on, Columbia, roll on

—WOODY GUTHRIE,
ROLL ON, COLUMBIA, ROLL ON (1941)

When they get us all pushed off the river, maybe
they can build more places for the tourists and
windsurfers. Maybe they can put up a nice little
museum here with statues and pictures, so the
gawkers can see what Indians once were like.

—WILLIS, AN ELDERLY INDIAN FISHER
IN CRAIG LESLEY'S *RIVER SONG*, COMMENTING
ON THE REMOVAL OF INDIAN PEOPLE FROM THE
COLUMBIA RIVER AS A RESULT OF DAM-BUILDING

I grew up in Portland, Oregon, at the confluence of the Willamette and Columbia rivers, where I learned in grade school to sing Woody Guthrie's anthem to a rapidly changing Columbia. He wrote *Roll On, Columbia, Roll On* in 1941, along with twenty-five other songs, when he was briefly employed by the Bonneville Power Administration to sell the region on public power. A classroom visit from novelist Craig Lesley complicated my view of the river and its dams when I was a student at Jefferson High School. Lesley had just completed *Winterkill*, a novel that addresses the inundation of Celilo Falls (he would later publish *River Song*, which also deals with dam-building). This experience introduced me to the importance of Indian treaty rights and the many ways in which they have been challenged and prompted me to begin what became a decades-long research and writing project.

I was fortunate to have high school teachers who believed their students could understand the nuances of Indian treaty rights and who wanted us to understand the historical complexities of our shared home. Bill Bigelow and Linda Christensen raised my initial interest in this topic, provided me with crucial historic questions, and introduced me to a *real* author. Friends and teachers have continued to guide this work with considered criticism and timely encouragement. I must especially thank Professor William Robbins, Emeritus Distinguished Professor of History at Oregon State University. He provided me with convincing evidence that a working class kid could become an academic historian. Bill Robbins, Sue Armitage, Paul Hirt, Bill Lang, Peter Boag, Donna Sinclair, and Andrew Fisher read and commented on the entire manuscript, some of them repeatedly. I took much of their advice; of course, all errors are mine.

I was also assisted by Bob Kingston, Clark Hansen, Donna Sinclair, and Lucy Kopp, among others, at the Oregon Historical Society; Joyce Justice and John Ferrell at the National Archives and Records Administration, Pacific Alaska Region in Seattle, Washington; Chuck Jones at the Bureau of Indian Affairs, Portland Area Office; and Julie Kruger, the City Clerk at The Dalles. Barbara Mackenzie generously shared her time and stories of her experiences in The Dalles with me. Her son, Thomas Mackenzie, prompted her memory and shared family documents. My colleague Jan Dilg and I wrote a separate article about Barbara Mackenzie that dealt with, in part, her work relocating Celilo Indians. Our collaboration on that project made this book richer.

My colleagues at the History Department at Portland State University have supported this work financially and with their good guidance. Gordon Dodds, whom I replaced at PSU but whose shoes I will never fill, was a generous colleague whose advice and good humor I miss very much. I am especially fortunate to be a faculty member of the Center for Columbia River History, a partnership between Portland State University, Washington State University Vancouver, and the Washington State Historical Society. The center and my colleagues there have supported my research in Columbia River history, especially Bill Lang (founder and director of CCRH until 2003), Laurie Mercier, Mary Wheeler, David Johnson, Garry Schalliol, Candice Goucher, current director Sue Armitage, and Donna Sinclair.

Donna Sinclair has been a reader and sounding board, and shares my love of this place and its history. Our conversations have been especially influential in my understanding of this region. I am part of a circle of Pacific Northwest women historians and writers that includes Donna, Jan Dilg, Eliza Jones, and Jo Ogden. Each has contributed to this work and has ensured that historical research and writing is not always done in isolation. Margaret Sherve, who at this point should be included in family, is another colleague to whom I am much indebted. My families have also supported me financially and in spirit. I am proud to come from them.

Julidta Tarver, acquisitions editor at the University of Washington Press, has guided this project to completion over several years. Editorial help from Kris Fulsaas improved the manuscript, and Pamela Canell gave it a great design. I thank all the Press staff for their efforts in producing this book.

My final and most important thank you is reserved for Donald Croker, who has been there every step of the way.

DEATH OF CELILO FALLS

A transportation network that included roads, a highway, rail-roads, and a canal crisscrossed Celilo Village, drawing outside Indians to the area and often threatening the safety of those who made Celilo Village their home. In this staged image (left to right), Henry Thompson, Joe Skahan, and Louis Ike (with fish) present railroad engineer Tom Rumgay with a steelhead taken at Celilo Falls. Photo by Everett Olmstead, 1940. Photo Research Group, Portland, Oregon.

INTRODUCTION

Dam Dedications

Enormous fishing nets and bright blue Navy flags covered the walls of the junior high school gymnasium in The Dalles, Oregon, on a springtime Saturday afternoon in 1957. The navigational wheel of a stern-wheeler hid the basketball hoop at one end, transforming the gym into the site of one of the town's largest celebrations associated with the building of The Dalles Dam. Dave Cole, program coordinator for the city and the chamber of commerce, had spent months preparing the town of 11,250 people for the Nautical Cocktail Hour and Empire Banquet held at the gym, one of the few rooms in The Dalles that could accommodate the 300 to 400 people expected to attend the $2.50–per-plate dinner. By the end of the evening, nearly 600 enthusiastic development supporters crowded into the school to meet visiting dignitaries, to dine, and to watch a thirty-five-minute narrated slide show about the history of Columbia River navigation. Although the entertainment memorialized the past, the banquet and two-day celebration of The Dalles Dam and Lock were decidedly forward-looking. The locks were the pinnacle of Columbia River navigation history, incorporating the latest engineering technology in service of a future of ever-expanding markets and material wealth.[1]

The Empire Banquet (named in reference to both the Pacific

Northwest's interior "Inland Empire" and optimism for an empire based on a world port at The Dalles) topped a busy day that included an official tour of the dam and socializing over cocktails. Sunday was reserved for the flag-raising ceremony, speeches by the governors of Oregon and Washington, a ribbon-cutting ceremony hosted by the governors' wives, music by the Oregon National Guard band, passage of commercial barges through the locks, and a "flotilla of pleasure craft."[2] The festive weekend marked the official celebration of the new Dalles Dam and Lock with revelry reserved for the visible economic impact of easy commercial passage past what was once a formidable navigational obstacle: the Long Narrows and Celilo Falls. A lake now covered the site that for thousands of years drew Indians from around the region to fish, barter, and socialize at the place they called Wyam.

A week earlier 10,000 people turned out on the Oregon Trail Highway 30 and at vantage points on the Washington shore to watch the rise of the Columbia's newest reservoir, named Celilo Lake in dubious honor of the falls it inundated. The Army Corps of Engineers and the Oregon highway patrol worked in concert to contain what The Dalles *Chronicle* called "bumper-to-bumper traffic" for nearly nine hours on Sunday, March 10. The reservoir filled in four and one-half hours after resident Engineer H. B. Elder gave the "down gates" command at 10 A.M.[3]

Two years later, in 1959, Vice President Nixon inaugurated the dam's second purpose when he pressed a button to start the generation of hydroelectricity. Nixon quipped to a crowd of thousands that he saw the biggest of many things on a recent trip to Texas but that he "had to come to Oregon to see the biggest dam ever built by the Corps of Engineers." Senator Richard Neuberger reminded the crowd that "our Indian friends deserve from us a profound and heartfelt salute of appreciation. . . . They contributed to its erection a great donation—surrender of the only way of life which some of them knew."[4] His words underscored

The Nautical Cocktail Hour and Empire Banquet at The Dalles junior
high school gym likely looked a lot like this celebratory luncheon
in 1959. National Archives—Pacific Northwest Region.

the transfer of the river's abundant wealth from Native to non-
Native people.

Celebrations and commemorations reveal what a people consider important. As these celebrations suggest, most non-Indian
people hailed The Dalles Dam as progress. The ceremonies that
accompanied the various phases of construction celebrated a
remade river, a "highway" upon which goods transported to and
from The Dalles would be accompanied by the hum of electrical generators. In contrast, the region's Indians mourned the loss
of fishing sites and a core way of life. Rosita Wellsey remembered
that as a child she watched the floodwaters behind the dam inundate Celilo: "As the little islands disappeared, I could see my grand-

Vice President Richard Nixon speaking at the dedication of
The Dalles Dam, 10 October 1959. U.S. Army Corps of Engineers.

mother trembling, like something was hitting her . . . she just put
out her hand and she started to cry."[5] Jay Minthorne recalled
Indians "crying and singing the religious songs that they sang at
funerals" that day.[6]

With the building of The Dalles Dam, Pacific Northwest
Indians—the Yakama, Warm Springs, Umatilla, Nez Perce, and
unenrolled River Indians—lost a cultural and economic center
that had supported Native cultures for thousands of years.
Indeed, the economic center that The Dalles residents hoped
would result from dam construction was developed over an
Indian site that had existed as long as anyone could remember.
Poet Elizabeth Woody, an enrolled member of the Confederated
Tribes of Warm Springs, wrote that the dam "destroyed a major
cultural site and rent a multi-millennial relationship of a people
to a place."[7] It also pitted Celilo Village Native people against
non-Indians in The Dalles in a struggle over access to resources.

The history of The Dalles Dam illuminates the transformation of Indian-owned resources (salmon) and space (Celilo Falls) into primarily non-Native owned resources (hydroelectricity and transportation) and space (the dam and Celilo Lake) through the building of a large federal work. This particular event was part of a larger battle felt throughout the nation in the mid–twentieth century as reservoirs flooded Native communities in the Pacific Northwest and the Midwest.

But progress and loss are not easy to measure, and one often accompanies or is transformed into the other over time. The Dalles Dam and the inundation of Celilo Falls are at the center of a historic debate about human uses of the Columbia River and past decisions that created what historian Richard White calls an "organic machine," a waterway in which salmon no longer thrive, commercial fishers are largely absent, and the Army Corps of Engineers maintains river levels to optimize hydroelectric production.[8] Contemporary debates about dam construction, drawdowns, wild-versus-hatchery salmon, and Indian fishing rights too often only reference the complex decisions made in the past. It is difficult to recall the original flow of the river, just as it is to conjure the individual acts that have collectively created a new Columbia River. The drowning of Wyam is a symbolic event that marks the dramatic physical and cultural transformation of the Columbia River. It also symbolizes a series of events with specific histories.

The Dalles Dam represents human control over the West's most important resource. Water, or the lack of it, is the most significant defining feature of the American West, even in the unusually damp northwestern corner of the region. Human ability to control the flow of rivers and streams, to divert, dam, and store water has shaped the relationship between westerners and the land. The desire to control water has created a remarkable society in the West, according to historian Donald Worster, who refers to the twentieth-century West as a "techno-economic order" that is "increasingly a coercive, monolithic, and hierarchical system, ruled by a power elite based on the ownership of capital and expertise." Worster's argument belies the myth of the West as a locale of economic and social individual freedom.[9]

Worster's story of a West in the grip of powerful prodevelopment factions—the Army Corps of Engineers, the Inland Empire Waterways Association, The Dalles Chamber of Commerce, and The Dalles *Chronicle,* in this instance—is apt but, as with most generalizations, does not tell the entire story.[10] A sense of loss tempered even the most fervent celebrations of progress on the mid–Columbia River. Senator Richard Neuberger noted the sacrifice of the area's Indians in his 1959 speech at The Dalles. The prominent Seufert family, owners of the largest cannery at Celilo Falls, joined Indian voices in lamenting the changes to the river. More recently, Native and non-Native residents alike have weighed the destruction of aesthetic value and the environmental costs against the benefits of hydropower and flood control. Grief and celebration, loss and progress interact in a complex dialectic.

The historic details of the inundation of Celilo Falls, the story told in this book, are supplemented by a plethora of recent studies that address the history of the Columbia River and the contemporary salmon crisis in the Pacific Northwest.[11] These books range from journalistic treatments of the entire basin to explorations of a single dam and the complex theoretical discussions of the managed river.[12] The region's contemporary salmon crisis has spurred another burst of publications that address the decline of this significant and symbolically weighted animal.[13] With the notable exception of Roberta Ulrich's *Empty Nets: Indians, Dams and the Columbia River,*[14] however, most existing studies do not put the sacrifices made by Indian people at the core of the pursuit of a tamed riverscape. Neither do these studies focus on the small communities that lined the Columbia River and boosted the building of the dams. Instead, most of the scholarship of the twentieth-century Columbia River asks questions about the transformation of the river and the results of that transformation. Because those questions have been so keenly answered, this book does not closely examine the contours of the history that led up to dam construction. Instead, it asks what the effects are on The Dalles and Celilo Village and what impact the dam had on the relationship between the two communities.

The history that follows does not subvert or challenge the arguments that historians such as Donald Worster and others have made about the massive power of the federal government in the West or the ways in which an American culture bent on controlling nature has reshaped the region. Rather, this book examines what happened to two neighboring communities when a large public dam was built adjacent to them. Intertwined in this exploration are issues of the federal West: treaty rights and federal Indian policy, the environmental transformation of the river, and ideas regarding progress and opposition to the dam. This is not a story about an impersonal federal force swooping down to rearrange two defenseless communities: it explores relationships between federal representatives and local residents, as well as between residents of The Dalles and Celilo Village. It is a story about desire and loss—desire for progress by some, of productive fish runs by others. It is also an account of lost sacred space and unrealized economic potential.

Instead of a sweeping view of the river, this story finds its contours in the cracks and crevices of a nine-mile stretch known as the Long Narrows. It hones in on the 1930s, 1940s, and 1950s to explore how environmental and social change interact and how traditional river resources were discarded for a modern river. With the assumption that ordinary lives provide compelling history, this book asks seemingly modest questions—What happened to elementary schools in a town that rapidly doubled in size? How was compensation for fishing sites negotiated?—that assist in addressing larger historical themes such as growth in the postwar West and midcentury federal Indian policy.

This account relies on archival materials such as the records of the Army Corps of Engineers, Portland District, and the Bureau of Indian Affairs, Portland Area Office; both sets of materials are housed at the National Archives' Pacific Northwest regional base in Seattle, Washington. The Bureau of Indian Affairs, Portland Area Office, also gave access to files that had not yet been archived. Newspaper accounts, particularly from The Dalles *Chronicle* and the Portland *Oregonian,* made it possible to trace what was considered newsworthy and the way in which local communities defined and tackled problems related to dam construction. Information from The Dalles *Chronicle* was augmented with and verified by extant Dalles City Council records, but the rich materials from the newspaper became indispensable when it became evident that many of the city's records from the period were missing as a result, ironically, of a 1996 Columbia River flood.

This narrative could have benefited from a lengthy oral history project to record the individual stories of river residents. Originally, the vision for this project was modeled after Roberta Ulrich's rich use of interviews in *Empty Nets* (none of which she can make accessible to other researchers per her agreement with her narrators). I proposed such an oral history project to Wanapa Koot Koot, an intertribal cultural-resources committee comprised of the four Columbia River treaty tribes, in 1999 with the intent that the histories would be widely accessible to future researchers. The committee referred me to the Warm Springs cultural committee, which, in an effort to protect aging elders, urged use of materials already available. Out of respect for the tribal process, I decided not to go forward with interviews even with willing narrators, instead culling from the interviews available through the Oregon Historical Society's oral history collection located in its library in Portland. Nonetheless, given the cultural significance of Celilo Falls to Native and non-Native residents of the region, a broadly conceived oral history project is still warranted.

Both Indians and non-Indians identified with and revered the Columbia River's power; but, whereas Indian residents considered much of the mid-Columbia a sacred place, white residents built a massive tribute to their own ability to manipulate nature. The communities of The Dalles and Celilo Village share a river environment but also present separate histories that reflect divergent and often incompatible values. However, when whites settled the region in the mid- to late 1800s, they did not simply replace Native cultural values with their own, but entered a region in which physical and cultural space was contested among Indian groups and eventually between Indians and whites. Differing cultural and economic strategies coexisted and vied for prominence on the Columbia River even into the mid–twentieth century. The events surrounding dam construction in the 1950s reflected and continued earlier conflicts over the river, embedded in such things as the treaties that delineated fishing rights and the court cases that refined those rights.[15]

In 1946, by the time of the Army Corps of Engineers' first public meeting regarding a dam in the vicinity of Celilo Falls, the agency was certain that the project would be built. Nonetheless, resistance to the project continued even after congressional appropriations in 1952. Various groups protested the dam. From white commercial fishermen to supporters of Indian rights and Indian representatives of tribal governments, people protested the altering of the river, from many perspectives with a variety of purposes. None were successful at stopping or even significantly slowing construction, but all reveal the fissures in the overwhelming rhetoric of industrial progress tied to national security so prevalent at midcentury.

The Dalles Dam simultaneously represented potential commercial development and economic decline for residents of the mid-Columbia. Most residents of The Dalles anticipated tremendous economic growth with the opening of the dam. City leaders promoted the dam and highlighted their ability to manage the changes the small city would undergo but were also frustrated by the lack of financial support from the federal government, even while they endorsed government-to-government cooperation. Concerned for decades about the poverty and conditions at Celilo Village, many non-Indian Wasco County residents viewed the inevitable partial inundation of Celilo Village as a potential opportunity to remake the community. These efforts were matched and encouraged by a Bureau of Indian Affairs that valued assimilation and sought to control the off-reservation site. In contrast, Celilo residents fought to control their village and the relocation of residents who lost their homes to Celilo Lake.

Finally, Indian–Army Corps negotiations for compensation demonstrate the ultimate lack of influence that Native people had as they confronted federal officials intent on settling with them quickly. Negotiations continued even after the federal financial settlement, as tribes decided how to distribute funds and struggled to protect recipients from state and local welfare offices eager to take Indians off their rolls. Although some tribes and individuals benefited financially from the settlement (while also suffering the loss of sacred and productive fishing sites), the experiences of other individuals calls into question whether they could be considered compensated at all.

This book describes two communities that experienced tremendous change in a brief period. Nonetheless, the changes were ultimately limited. Although The Dalles witnessed a population boom accompanied by an increase in industrial and commercial activity, the town never achieved the economic successes that its leaders envisioned. Celilo Village was partially dismantled and its economic base destroyed, but it survives to this day as Oregon's oldest continuously inhabited town.

When Army Engineer H. B. Elder gave the "gates down" signal to twenty-two employees, who then pressed twenty-two buttons to close The Dalles Dam, he concluded a series of events that transformed the environmental, social, and cultural landscape of the mid–Columbia River. It is telling that the reporter who covered the occasion for The Dalles *Chronicle* likened it to the detonation of an atomic bomb. Although it was conceived in the 1930s, The Dalles Dam was a project steeped in the rhetoric of the cold war. Moreover, the fallout from the dam would be far-reaching and long lasting. Despite the decline in Columbia Basin salmon runs, the benefits of the dam reach into the present generation. The loss of Celilo Falls also touches many in the region. The dam is a tangible reminder of the complexity of Indian-white treaties and their ongoing negotiation, the simultaneous promise and destruction of progress, the loss of a natural river and the life it sustained, and the transformative power of the market economy. The river and those living by it would never be the same.

1

VILLAGE AND TOWN

The Communities Transformed
by The Dalles Dam

This is a story of two communities located twelve miles apart on the Oregon banks of the mid–Columbia River and the ways in which a federal dam transformed them. The ancient Native fishing community of Celilo Village existed near the treacherous Celilo Falls and Long Narrows for millennia as a hub in a regional network of trade and cultural exchange. Recent emigrants comprising the city of The Dalles settled in the mid-1800s to sell goods to miners, plow bunchgrass into orchards and wheat fields, and, eventually, create a modern American town complete with an international port that would transport goods to and from the interior Pacific Northwest.

In the mid–twentieth century, as the U.S. Army Corps of Engineers set its sights on the development of the mid–Columbia River, these two communities would clash over the use of local natural resources and the future of the river. The Dalles confidently celebrated the modernity and economic security that a federal dam and professional river management promised. Celilo Village and the wider network of regional Indians who fished at Celilo Falls recognized the dam project as yet another reallocation of resources used by Indians. A dam would transform prime fish habitat into a slack-water reservoir that would support transportation and power production to the detriment of salmon populations. In addition, the reservoir would inundate the abundant basalt outcroppings and islands that provided excellent fishing sites but thwarted river transportation at Celilo Falls and the rapids of the Long Narrows. The dam, completed in 1957, did not simply alter the riverscape of the Columbia; it transformed river communities and the relations between them.

Although The Dalles Dam would negatively affect a relatively small group of Indian people in a still lightly populated region removed from the centers of national power, it represented a continuing history of federal Indian removal and the appropriation of Indian wealth by non-Indian people. Despite the federal reservation policies of the nineteenth century, the stretch of the Columbia River known as Celilo Falls and the Long Narrows and the community of Celilo Village were recognizably non-reservation Native areas in the midst of a region that had progressively "whitened" over the previous several generations. However, Native control over fishing sites and the village were not without conflict. The Bureau of Indian Affairs[1]; Oregon State and Wasco County governments; The Dalles City Council and Chamber of Commerce; the tribal councils of the Warm Springs, Yakama[2], Umatilla, and Nez Perce; and local governing structures at Celilo Village itself all vied to control and, in some cases, dismantle the community. Furthermore, whites consistently attempted to encroach on treaty-protected fishing areas by blocking access to the river, harassing Native fishers, and even claiming the sites themselves. Nevertheless, Indian fishers and their families successfully remained on the river and claimed it, like the generations before them, as the center of their economic, social, and cultural world.

The proposed dam, championed by The Dalles, threatened to remove Indian people from the river by destroying the fishing stations and salmon runs that sustained Native activity there. It was a threat as significant as that posed by earlier federal policies of removal. In addition, river development, particularly in The Dalles, paralleled the mid–twentieth century federal policies of termination and relocation that sought to end the treaty relationship between the federal government and Native people throughout the country. Relocation supported the removal of Indians from reservation communities to urban areas, a federally funded migration that was meant to sever tribal ties. Termination policy would dissolve Indian reservations, remove federal recognition of Indian tribes, liquidate tribal land holdings, and eventually dismantle the Bureau of Indian Affairs. The federal government's treatment of Indian people with a claim to Celilo Falls and property at Celilo Village is unsurprising when placed in this context of termination policy and the longer history of removal. The reallocation of wealth from Indian people to non-Indian residents of the region was, for many, an acceptable, even predictable, outcome of national development.[3]

However, when the U.S. Army Corps of Engineers began its series of public meetings regarding the construction of The Dalles Dam in 1945, it must have seemed both to those who supported the project and to those who hoped to defeat it that anything was possible. Would the federal dam create an economic and cultural gateway that linked the resources east of the Cascade Mountains to the economic centers west of the mountains? Would the city of The Dalles play a key role in the nation's ability to fight the cold war successfully? Would Indian people put aside intertribal conflict to wage a battle against construction and the pending loss of the region's most significant fishing area? Would the federal government, after reviewing the protests of both Indian and non-Indian people, reverse the damage done to Columbia River salmon runs and the fishers who relied on them? These were the kinds of issues discussed from the mid-1940s until 1957, when the dam was closed and the reservoir began to rise over Celilo Falls.

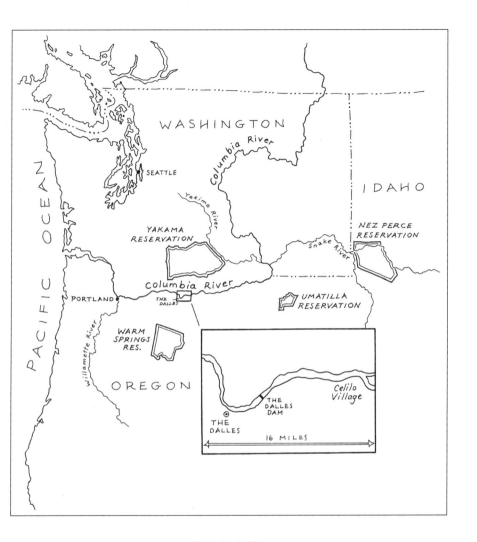

THE PLACE

The Columbia River originates in the cool reaches of the Canadian Rockies, from where it winds through the great basalt plateau of eastern Washington, creating the border between Oregon and Washington. It empties a basin of 259,000 square miles, unifying a culturally and environmentally disparate region. The Columbia River Gorge, an east-west corridor characterized by steep basalt formations on the south side of the river and gently undulating hills to the north, dramatizes a rich, diverse river environment. Dominating the western gorge, verdant growth of invasive English ivy, dew-laden five-fingered ferns, and trillium form the undergrowth of Douglas fir forests. Waterfalls, from springtime flushes of unnamed rivulets to the year-round rush of Multnomah Falls, surge over the steep cliffs on the south bank of the river. In areas of the western gorge, rainfall, heaviest in winter and spring, reaches more than ninety inches annually.[4] However, to the east, in the rain shadow of the Cascade Mountains, the vegetation dwindles with the decline of annual precipitation. Browns replace the greens of the western gorge as lush vegetation gives way to expanses of dry grasslands. It is a striking transition that journalist Robin Cody likens to "driving over a Rand McNally road map with different colored states."[5]

The Columbia River Gorge is a labyrinth of craggy rock formations composed of Yakima basalt deposited ten to sixteen million years ago when fissures along what is now the Idaho-Oregon border released hot magma. Where the river now travels through Wasco County in Oregon and Klickitat County in Washington, these ancient basalt formations were once largely exposed, cloaked with just a shallow layer of loose soil that still supports vegetation such as bluebunch wheatgrass. Then as now, westerly winds matched the ferocity of the river's course through the gorge. The air was gritty and, in the summer months, hot. Winters brought snow, more wind, the bleakness of overcast days. The Columbia River fought its way through the gorge basalt, smoothing sharp surfaces over millions of years. The rocks constrained the river's course, creating black eddies, whirlpools, and crashing falls.[6]

The river, which was severely constricted as it passed through a series of rapids at Celilo Falls, was as violent and unforgiving as the landscape. When William Clark traveled along the mid–Columbia River in October 1805, he described it as "agitated in a most Shocking manner . . . Swels and boils with a most Tremendous manner" as it flowed nearly nine miles westward through the horseshoe-shaped Celilo Falls, Tenmile Rapids, Fivemile Rapids, and Big Eddy.[7] A few years later, Alexander Ross described the topography of the rapids as "a broad flat ledge of rocks that bars the whole river across, leaving only a small opening or portal, not exceeding forty feet, on the left side, through which the whole body of water must pass." The river coursed with "great impetuosity; the foaming surges dash[ing] through the rocks with terrific violence."[8] Rapid currents and exposed rocks created a navigational nightmare. The rapids, backwaters, and eddies also constituted what many considered the best nine-mile stretch of fishing sites on the continent.

Because of a 900-foot drop in elevation from its headwaters to its mouth at the Pacific Ocean, the Columbia River was identified shortly after World War I as a potential hydroelectric source. However, it was not until the Great Depression, when the federal government turned its attention to large, labor-intensive public projects, that a system of dams began to transform the wild river into what historian Richard White calls an "organic machine." The Dalles Dam is a cog in that machine. Constructed less than 100 miles from Portland, Oregon, at river mile 192, the one-mile-wide Dalles Dam stretches across the river like an enormous concrete "Z" at the eastern end of the Columbia River Gorge.

THE SALMON

An ancient story tells of the introduction of salmon to Native people of the mid–Columbia River. Coyote, disguised as an infant, ingratiates himself to two old women who have selfishly hoarded salmon by damming the Columbia River. When the old women leave to pick huckleberries, Coyote destroys the dam, releasing the salmon into the Columbia River for all the people to share.

According to archaeological records, salmon preceded Native fishers in the Pacific Northwest by at least one million years. Pacific salmon thrived in significant numbers in Asia and nearly every Pacific coastal stream extending into the interior of Oregon, Washington, Montana, Idaho, and British Columbia. Indians of the region have fished for chinook (*Oncorhynchus tshawytscha*), coho (*Oncorhynchus kisutch*), chum (*Oncorhynchus keta*), pink (*Oncorhynchus gorbuscha*), and sockeye (*Oncorhynchus nerka*) for thousands of years.

Salmon are anadromous, migrating from freshwater mountain streams to salt water (a transformation that science writer Joseph Cone compared to a human suddenly being able to breath carbon dioxide) to head for the rich resources of the sea, where they feed on microbes and small sea life. They return to the freshwater of their origins when they are ready to spawn. This life cycle is special (only 1 percent of all fish species are anadromous), and it has drawn both storytellers and scientists to salmon. Indians and non-Indians alike have rendered the salmon's life cycle as magical: it embodies the determination to survive, the annual replenishment of a natural resource, and the completeness of nature and its seasons.[9]

AN ANCIENT COMMUNITY

Abundant Columbia River salmon runs as well as roots, berries, and game from Mount Adams to the north and Mount Hood to the south drew Indians to The Dalles region at least 11,000 years ago.[10] At Celilo Falls, where the horseshoe-shaped precipice demanded portage, dozens of villages scattered about the shorelines. A maze of islands separated the small communities and provided fishing sites in the spring and fall. The villages, each an autonomous political unit, faced the rapids or the mouths of tributaries—anywhere the fishing was excellent and accessible. The Indian population may have reached as many as 10,000

Indians fishing at Celilo Falls in 1954.
Gladys Seufert photo, Oregon Historical Society, neg. 61313.

in this nine-mile stretch of the river before postcontact disease devastated the tribes.[11]

This land of basalt and wind perched between the foothills of the Cascade Mountains, the Columbia River, and the semi-arid plains of the Columbia Plateau was the meeting place of two Native cultures: the Sahaptins of Celilo and the upper Chinook of the Long Narrows to the west. On their voyage to the Pacific Ocean, Meriwether Lewis and William Clark distinguished between the "E. nee-sher Nation" to the east and the "E-che-lute Nation" to the west. They were following the lead of their Nez Perce guides and interpreters, Twisted Hair and Tetoharsky, who left the expedition once it entered upper Chinookan territory.

The Nez Perce would have been no use as interpreters to the expedition; "Sahaptin" and "Chinook" denote language classifications. Clark recorded that the captains "took a Vocabulary of the Languages of those two chiefs which are very different nonewithstanding they are situated within six miles of each other."[12] Sahaptin speakers rarely learned the Chinookan language of their western neighbors. They often did not have to; enough Chinooks, who were both savvy and wealthy middlemen, were conversant in many languages because it was essential for trade.[13]

Although language was an audible difference between the two groups, there were visible ones as well. Houses near Celilo Falls were tule-mat dwellings, elongated beehive structures cloaked in woven grass mats. Fish drying in similar shelters filled the air with their smell. Because they were easy to move, the shelters met the needs of a people who participated in the seasonal rounds of food gathering. At the falls below Celilo, Indians built vertical plankboard lodges, similar to those found on the North Pacific Coast. The upper Chinook were fishers who used trade to supplement their catches. Their permanent structures suited their more permanent ways and exemplified their coastal roots. Both types of structures were warm in winter and cool in summer, also providing shelter from the persistent wind.

Before white settlement, Indians traded salmon in what an Army Corps report described as a "sizable commercial trade."[14] Anthropologists David and Katherine French claim that "the importance of trade in earlier times can hardly be overstated. The Dalles was one of the most important trade centers in Aboriginal America."[15] The Dalles was an integral part of a continental trade network that extended west from the Pacific coast east to the Plains, north from what is now Alaska south to present-day California. The marketplace extended well beyond material goods to include languages, social systems, technologies, and mythologies. Cultural intermixing, borrowing, and exchange characterized the area. The intermixing of Sahaptin and Chinook speakers diminished the "distinctiveness of participant peoples," creating a hybrid space, one in which coastal and plateau traits thrived.[16]

The busiest times at the Long Narrows coincided with the spring and fall salmon runs.[17] Entire bands from throughout the Northwest traveled to the mid-Columbia to trade, socialize, and fish with local residents. Both women and men traded goods and strengthened their relationships with neighboring tribes through marriage and renewed friendships. From the south came obsidian and slaves;[18] from the north, dentalia, blankets, and beads; from the east, pipestone, buffalo meat, and horses; and, hailing from the west, wappato, an important root food.[19]

Central to this network was the abundance of salmon. Clark observed stores of an estimated 10,000 pounds of dried and pounded salmon in 1805. A few year later, trapper and explorer Alexander Ross estimated that 3,000 Indians gathered at the river to trade, gamble, and socialize.[20] In his often repeated words, The Dalles was "the great emporium or mart of the Columbia."[21]

Work was seasonal, mirroring the cycles of the river and nature. From May through October, much of the labor centered on the salmon runs. When salmon migrated, fishers waited on scaffolds that hung from cliffs above the roaring water of the falls or on platforms that reached out over the river like pointed fingers. From these cantilevers, Indians lowered mobile and stationary nets deep into the water where millions of salmon forced their way up the river. The rushing current pushed fish backward, stunning them and allowing Indians to skillfully scoop up the fish in their dip nets. Women collected the catch, then gutted and filleted the fish to dry. Migrating birds shadowed the women, swooping down to feast on the entrails.

The river was supermarket, highway, and defense barrier. It was the center of a seasonal journey through fishing and gathering grounds that included netting and spearing salmon; gathering wild carrots, camas bulbs, and berries; and hunting deer and elk. Salmon shaped Native labor practices, and its significance was woven into language, ceremony, and story. In turn, Native cultures transformed the mute fish into cultural symbols, salmon beings that represented the connections between human cultures and nature. One need only look to the First Salmon ceremony as evidence of the importance of salmon in the social, economic, and political lives of Columbia River Indians. The ceremony marked the break of the long winter and meals of dried food by welcoming the coming of the first salmon runs in the spring. Tribal members distributed morsels of the "first salmon" as part of a meal of thanksgiving and celebration "based on a reverential attitude toward the fish and a desire to treat it in such a manner that it will come in great numbers."[22]

Fishing people as far north as Alaska and south to California practiced First Salmon ceremonies. Most tribes ceased the ceremonies as salmon became harder to catch and played a less-significant role in the Native diet. Indians at Celilo Village still hold annual public First Salmon ceremonies, sometimes bringing salmon in from Portland to feed the crowds. Army Corps writers recognized this interplay of social and economic significance when they wrote "the Celilo fishery has some religious significance to the Indians."[23]

By the 1950s, Celilo Village was, as one contemporary put it, Oregon's oldest town.[24] It consisted of about thirty permanent households built on sand-covered basalt. The small village did not support agriculture, had no rangeland, and did not contain stands of timber, but it lay adjacent to the best fishing sites along the Columbia River. It was also a community long under siege as whites encroached on Native land and limited Indians' access to the river. Bureau of Indian Affairs (BIA) officials also hatched numerous plans to modernize the village and assimilate residents. The community was a tourist attraction that drew people from around Oregon and outside of the state to watch Indians fish in the way of their ancestors. Beautiful collections of photographs by amateurs and professionals alike attest to the popularity of the place among non-Indians. The old black-and-white photos also attest to the "Indianness" of Celilo Village, Celilo Falls, and the Columbia River. Even after the federal government removed most Indians to the Warm Springs, Umatilla, Yakama, and Nez Perce reservations, the falls remained a landscape used and prized most by Indian people.

A NEW COMMUNITY

The Dalles lies just above water's edge, an oasis in a dry and dusty environ. Founded in 1856, the Euro-American town developed on the foundations of the Methodist Wascopam Mission and a U.S. military fort adjacent to the Columbia River, the only east-west route through Oregon in the mid-1800s. Both institutions—the mission and the fort—were established to coerce or convert Indian people into a new cultural milieu that would eventually dominate the region. Both institutions facilitated the intrusion of non-Native settlements in the mid-Columbia region.

First to be established, in 1838, was Wascopam Mission, a one-acre compound of four buildings surrounded by a picket fence. By 1841 the mission had become "an important stopover spot for travelers." The U.S. Army manned Fort Dalles, beginning in 1850, to provide a military presence along the Oregon Trail and to protect white immigrants from Indian attack. The fall of 1853 brought 7,000 people along the Oregon Trail, a sure sign of the resettlement of the Oregon Country. When treaty negotiations in 1855 and the subsequent discovery of gold in eastern Oregon brought on Indian wars in the latter half of the nineteenth century, Fort Dalles came into prominence.[25]

As with the nearby Indian trade mart that preceded it, the American city of The Dalles was a trade center, in its case for immigrants and miners. The discovery of gold brought would-be miners to The Dalles, where some purchased supplies before heading for the interior; however, many stayed to work, as the need for laborers in The Dalles elevated wages that became less a gamble than what could be wrought from the goldfields.

Encroaching whites who made their homes in Indian territory, regardless of requirements that they settle on the west side of the Cascade Mountains, threatened mid–Columbia River Indians. So too did road building—which promised even more traffic—for which the U.S. Congress allocated money in the 1850s. But most important, waves of disease, such as smallpox and malaria, frayed the social and economic fabric of Native life. Although epidemics cleared the way for resettlement, historian Priscilla Knuth describes the development of the city of The Dalles as cyclical: "More whites passing through Indian country caused more clashes with the Indians; more troubles with the Indians brought more soldiers to the fort, and more civilians to the nearby settlement."[26] By 1857 the city of The Dalles had incorporated and become the county seat of Wasco County, an enormous stretch of country that once reached into Idaho.

The Dalles was the hub in a transportation network that included Indian foot and horse trails, white immigrant trails, U.S. military roads, railroads, a highway, and, of course, the river highway. The Columbia River and its banks still provide the easiest route through the Cascade Mountains. The county's wool, cherries, apricots, and aluminum were sometimes processed and always shipped through the city.[27] While much of Wasco County is unsuitable for cultivation because of low rainfall and poor soils, orchardists have made productive use of the gently sloping lands directly above The Dalles, where today cherry, apricot, and peach trees bloom in spring. Dryland wheat farming is also important in a county where most farms are not irrigated. Farms are expansive, averaging among the largest acreage per individual farm in the state of Oregon. Not surprisingly, the value of Wasco acreage is among the lowest in the state.[28]

By the 1950s, The Dalles was a respectable midsize town of a bit more than 7,500 people. It supported a daily newspaper, a high school, a hospital, and a small but promising port.[29] It was also a community on the verge of expansion and growth that most residents supported. Boosters celebrated the possibilities of a large federal dam in the vicinity, a county-built bridge that would connect Klickitat County in Washington State with the city (replacing an outmoded ferry system), and port facilities that would make the city the "gateway" between Portland and the cities of the interior Northwest. Harvey Aluminum, drawn to The Dalles by its proximity to low-cost electricity, would begin processing billets and ingots by 1958, employing more than 600 people.[30]

NEIGHBORS: INTERACTIONS BETWEEN
CELILO VILLAGE AND THE DALLES

The city of The Dalles originated in the federal need to simultaneously protect westward migrants and to control Indian behavior. Perched at one end of a portage, it became the economic center through which goods and people traveled between east and west. Essentially, this is what the upper Chinook had been doing for hundreds of years: using their geographic location to control trade along the mid–Columbia River. As such, The Dalles and its non-Native residents displaced older Indian communities, both economically and culturally. Some river Indians moved to reservations after the 1855 treaties, but many stayed, much to the chagrin of their new white neighbors. Reversing an earlier period in which interracial relationships included social and economic cooperation, by the mid–twentieth century, The Dalles was a segregated community. Sinews of racism and discrimination tied The Dalles to Celilo Village and shaped interactions between the two communities.

Racism took two primary and related forms: social and economic. Socially, Indians were made to feel unwelcome in The Dalles, where they were often harassed when they traveled the

social & econom. racism

twelve miles to town. A Dalles druggist told BIA employee H. U. Sanders in 1940 that he welcomed Celilo Indians only if they were "clean, well-behaved, and did not 'smell of fish'."[31] Ed Edmo, who lived in Celilo Village as a young child from 1946 to 1957, recalls signs in The Dalles announcing that dogs and Indians would not be served. During a family visit to Johnny's Café, one of the few establishments open to Indians, Edmo remembers his mother "pointing out which stores I could go into, which stores I couldn't go into."[32] Barbara Mackenzie, a white social worker, had a similar experience in 1956 when she wanted to stop for lunch with Teemingway Moses, an elderly Indian woman who lived on the Washington side of the river:

There was a restaurant on the Oregon side and I said, "You know, Teemingway, I think we'll both be hungry and it will be a long day." "They won't let me in." I said, "Yes, they will let you in." And she said, "No, they don't let Indians in there." But I marched in with her. We walked in and sat down at a booth. No one said anything to us. The waitress came and served us.[33]

Not only were Indians made to feel unwelcome in The Dalles, non-Native residents of the area challenged Indian rights to fish, even though these rights were spelled out in federally negotiated treaties. They did so by limiting access to traditional fishing sites, threatening Native fishers (sometimes at gunpoint), calling for the dismantling of Celilo Village (which they considered unsightly and poorly managed), and developing a mythology in which Indians misused fish resources and the material wealth they accumulated. This mythology was born out of initial Indian-white contact when the region's first settlers justified the relocation of Native people by arguing "that [whites] practiced superior methods of cultivation and represented a more advanced civilization." From the dawn of Euro-American presence on the Columbia

River, non-Indians have accused Indians of having an unfair and privileged access to resources that they did not deserve.[34]

Some strands of this mythology are evident in the way non-Indians describe how Indians use material goods. White fisherman Frederick Cramer revealed some of his assumptions about local Indians and how they differed from local whites in an article published in the *Oregon Historical Quarterly* in 1974:

> One Indian I knew bought three used cars in one spring salmon season—he wrecked the first, drove the second into The Dalles–Celilo Canal while drunk one night, with the third lasting him, to my knowledge, at least through the huckleberry season on the slopes of Mt. Adams. . . . And what did it matter if the slime from freshly caught salmon ran over the rear seat upholstery and out under the doors—cars were for transportation![35]

Francis Seufert echoed Cramer's description in his 1980 memoir, *Wheels of Fortune.* He remembered two Indian women who filled the backseat of a new Buick with salmon heads they purchased from the Seufert Cannery. Seufert reflected that "Indian fishermen loved cars" but that "cars were just a means of transportation to an Indian."[36] These descriptions of Indians too drunk or irresponsible to care for their limited material wealth may have been rooted in individual experience, but they also pandered to old stereotypes and were projected onto an entire group as part of a racist mythology that shaped Indian-white relations in the Pacific Northwest.

This attitude pervaded the conflicts between local whites and Indians in the 1940s and 1950s and into the present day. But it was interwoven with complexity made visible in the ways that non-Native residents of The Dalles celebrated the "Indianness" of their region. The Dalles High School football and basketball teams were known as the Indians; Brady's, a local grocer, celebrated "Indian summer specials" with "heap big values"; and the Edmo family danced in traditional regalia as part of an Easter ceremony for a 1950s non-Native audience.[37] The "Indian" who graces Brady's advertisement is a smiling white businessman in suit, tie, and Plains-style headdress.[38] He, like the high school athletes of The Dalles, were "playing Indian." Both are sanitized versions of the "Indian," versions that might have been welcomed at the druggist's shop included in Sander's BIA report.[39]

Nonetheless, some local whites who supported the rights of Celilo Indians risked friendships and prestige to do so. Although the druggist may have been racist, Indians were welcomed at Johnny's Cafe. Martha McKeown, a Hood River high-school teacher, wrote two sympathetic children's books about mid–Columbia River Indians and aided many village residents. Barbara Mackenzie raised eyebrows by advocating for the Indians at Celilo. Her boss, county judge Ward Webber, was also sympathetic of what he may have considered the "plight" of the river Indians. Finally, bank president and *Oregon Journal* editor Marshall Dana supported, in deed and words, efforts to equitably relocate Celilo Indians (Dana later married McKeown after her first husband died). All of these individuals were outraged at the poverty of the Indians around them and sought to ameliorate the worst effects of river development. Yet they also all supported the building of The Dalles Dam.[40]

CREATING A FEDERAL RIVER

The Dalles Dam was part of a multidam project planned by the Army Corps of Engineers for the Columbia-Snake river system. Congress authorized the Corps to survey the nation's rivers in 1925, in part to document their hydroelectric capacity. The Army Corps's Portland District submitted its nearly 2,000-page report in 1932, supporting proposals for ten large dams on the Columbia River. The "308" Report and subsequent reports marked a turning point in the history of the Army Corps of Engineers, spurred on by the great Mississippi flood of 1927. Instead of haphazard development based on individual proposals, the Corps began an effort to systematically develop entire watersheds.[41] More important, the report assumed the development of the river would be done by the federal government, not private efforts. The "308" Report described the numerous benefits that dams could bring to the region, including improved navigation routes, power, irrigation water, and flood control. This kind of benefit analysis was a shift from a nineteenth-century focus on transportation networks to multiuse projects that could be justified from several angles because they benefited a variety of interest groups.[42] Because the Columbia River "308" Report embodied this shift in the type of projects proposed, William Dietrich calls it "the most decisive in Columbia River history" and a "blueprint [that] would be followed closely" for the next three decades.[43]

At the outset of the 1930s, Oregon and Washington were home to just 2 percent of the nation's citizens. The region's economy depended primarily on extractive industries, and it seemed there was little need for the enormous amounts of electricity that the proposed dams could generate. Under these circumstances, the Army Corps and its supporters found it difficult to justify an extraordinary expenditure of public money to support hydroelectric and irrigation development. However, the events following the report's release spelled its eventual success: population and economic changes as a result of World War II, an especially destructive flood year in 1948, and the advent of the cold war.[44]

Boosters promised that the electricity generated by dams would transform the culture of the Pacific Northwest and even make it more democratic. Electricity would free people of the darkness of night, bring new and innovative industries to the region, liberate women from the worst drudgery of housework, and allow people to live in independent, decentralized centers of commerce.[45] William Dietrich reminds his contemporary read-

benefits

region
change
yes

ers that, even though "it is difficult to realize today how extraordinary" electricity was for boosters, it promised no less than "to change the world." Electricity "would pump, it would heat, it would cook, it would clean, and it would banish the tyranny of the solar day." Just as important, "it would give to anyone the kind of physical luxury only the rich had ever experienced."[46]

In order to achieve this new society, the region's residents would have to put nature—particularly its rivers—to work. The population and economic growth during and after World War II and the great Columbia River flood of 1948 that affected cities such as Portland, The Dalles, and Vanport strengthened this rhetoric. A general nationwide trust in technological advances among average Americans and policy makers alike accompanied these events.[47] Even so, it was the emergence of the cold war in the 1950s, described by one booster as a "national emergency created by naked aggression in Korea and the international threat of imperialism," that provided the most compelling justification for mid-century development of the Columbia River.[48]

According to historian William Robbins, early promoters of dams built upon a Progressive Era ideal of the greatest good for the greatest number and turned concrete into a symbol of modern virtues such as "efficiency, the elimination of waste, and the development and scientific management of resources."[49] In the Pacific Northwest, this meant promoting the development of resources so that the region reached its "fullest potential" within the capitalist marketplace; rooting out and eliminating waste (such as the water "wasted" as it flowed, unused, out of the region and into the Pacific Ocean); viewing the Columbia River as a natural "river highway"; and seeing the river's potential in providing the region with navigation and hydropower production. Ultimately, boosters saw Celilo Falls as an obstacle to clear passage to the Pacific Ocean, a view that would justify the flooding of the falls. Although the Army Corps initiated construction of the dams during the Great Depression, World War II and the cold war ensured that the agency would view the region's hydroelectric output as an integral component of national security.

The Great Depression inspired President Franklin Roosevelt to support Grand Coulee Dam as a make-work project. World War II—and its effects on the region's economy and population—further influenced how average Pacific Northwesterners as well as the federal government approached postwar development.[50] War-related industries in the West attracted many Americans to the region, and the population of the Pacific Northwest grew by 25 percent in just seven years (between 1940 and 1947). Boosters hoped the increase would extend beyond the war years, a hope realized as the region's population continued to grow into the 1950s.[51]

The Second World War brought high employment, new industries, and wealth to a region that historically experienced the boom-and-bust cycles typical of economies based on natural resources. Boosters touted river development as a way to move the region away from its singular reliance on extractive industries to more stable and diverse industries. Charles McKinley, a political scientist as well as a booster in his own right, claimed in the 1950s that electricity was a renewable, clean energy source and the nation would neglect its development at its peril. McKinley argued that "to use our rapidly shrinking oil resources to generate electricity in a region with so vast an unused supply in inexhaustible water power would . . . be a tragic blunder from the standpoint of national welfare."[52] In addition, the war brought new power-dependent industries to the region, such as the aluminum plants that dotted the shores of the Columbia River. By the end of World War II, the region enjoyed the nation's lowest energy costs *and* the highest per capita usage.[53]

Furthermore, the 1948 flood confirmed for many in the Pacific Northwest that the success of the region was dependent on dams that would regulate river flow. In the spring of that year, both the Columbia and the Willamette Rivers breached their banks, spilling water into low-lying cities. The wartime city of Vanport, built by shipping magnate Henry Kaiser to house incoming war workers near Portland, Oregon, was totally destroyed. Throughout the Columbia Basin, flooding claimed fifty-two lives and destroyed approximately $1 million in property.[54] The flood reminded the region's residents that flooding could destroy all that they developed if they did not control the area's rivers.

Dams promised flood control, water for irrigation, and inexpensive electricity that would fuel economic growth in the Pacific Northwest. The series of dams of which The Dalles was just one would create a new kind of Pacific Northwest. The region would become one in which its inhabitants put nature to work to realize its highest potential for the betterment of the people. Decentralization and a realized and meaningful democracy in which women and men could find productive work at livable wages would characterize this new society. Water from the Columbia would enrich potential farmland and generate enough electricity for its booming population. Cheap electricity would attract innovative nonextractive industries so that the region could lessen its reliance on natural resources. Dams would also protect new factories and homes in the region from flooding.

The Dalles Dam was part of a complete revisioning of the river that could only be carried out in the twentieth century, but the roots of such change extended into the nineteenth century and reflected a tradition of struggle over control and access to the Columbia. The river was always contested water, wherein whoever controlled access also controlled regional wealth. The modern concrete structures that suggest a "managed" river today are only the most recent and dramatic evidence of a river long managed to benefit humans.

2

A RIVERSCAPE AS
CONTESTED SPACE

On any given sunny mid-June Saturday, the rock out-croppings at Celilo Falls teemed with fishers who sat two to a platform. One man sat on an upturned fruit crate, a rope tied around his waist to guide a rescuer to him should he fall off the slippery ledge, a half-empty Pepsi bottle at his right foot, his hands loosely cupping the end of a twelve-foot dip-net handle. The other man was there to help the first pull a dip net out of the rushing water once a fish was caught. When three or four salmon were caught, he would load the fish into a cable-car box, swing himself into the box, and pull it through the air hand over hand or wait for the fish buyer at the other end to pull him in. Both men wore Levi's and a white T-shirt, their Converse sneakers soaked with river spray. They could barely hear one another over the roar of the falls, and if either looked up to scan the Oregon shoreline, the gaze of tourists would greet him.

If they were brave, tourists scampered along the narrow foot-bridges between scaffolds to get a closer look at the Indians' work. Otherwise they perched on the rough basalt rocks above the com-motion and drank soft drinks or ate sandwiches they bought at Hemlick's, a gas station and convenience store overlooking the falls that provided a parking lot for tourist cars. Russell Jim (whose father was a signatory on the settlement compensating the

Yakamas for the Celilo Falls inundation) remembered selling pop to tourists and fishermen when he was a child, earning enough over the course of a summer for his school clothes. Some visitors came to take pictures of the falls, Indian fishers, and Indian children, to whom they paid a few quarters. But most were there to buy fresh salmon, which they packed in ice and loaded into the trunks of their cars for the drive to The Dalles or Hood River or Portland.[1]

Tourists at Chinook Rock saw what might have seemed a reenactment of ancient practices, perhaps even a reminder of a presumably simpler time when humans caught or gathered the foods they ate. Yet the Celilo Falls landscape was hotly contested, shaped as much by political and social factors as environmental ones. The Long Narrows was a social landscape marked by human labor and the regulation of that labor. Indian dip netters, non-Native gillnetters and seiners, the owners of the Seufert cannery, the fish commissions of Oregon and Washington, and the Bureau of Indian Affairs all vied to determine who should have access to the mid–Columbia River. Quarrels for control of the falls would be reflected in and exacerbated by the construction of The Dalles Dam.

Mid-Columbia conflicts were every bit as divisive as the jutting rocks that interrupted the river's flow. To place into context the negotiations over river space brought on by The Dalles Dam, one must understand the history of the contested river. The conflicts over river space can be examined through three sets of relationships: the intertribal and federal relationship as revealed by the Celilo Fish Committee and the Bureau of Indian Affairs (BIA); the economic relationship between the Seufert canning family and Indian fishers; and the competitive relationship between the Cramers (white fishers) and Yakama fishers. Each relationship reveals the limits of a public "commons." Despite sharing a respect for the river and mourning the inundation of the falls, the Seuferts, Cramers, and Native fishers battled one another to control the fishery—battles that would eventually be reflected in the negotiations related to building the dam. The Celilo Fish Committee negotiated the conflicts between Indian fishers; the Seufert family and local Indians were business partners often wary of one another; and the Cramers competed directly with Indian fishers for productive sites. The individual strands of these relationships have been pulled from a knot of overlapping and simultaneous confrontation and conflict in the 1930s and 1940s for closer examination. However, each collision, regardless of parties, informed subsequent contests. Moreover, lurking behind these relationships were the state and federal agencies that managed the river.

REGULATING THE INDIAN FISHERY: THE CELILO FISH COMMITTEE AND THE BIA

The mid-Columbia Indian fishery, which extended from May to October, supported approximately 5,000 Indian fishers at about 480 separate fishing sites at midcentury. As many as sixteen different fishermen would fish from a single scaffold at sites passed on to sons or nephews. Fishermen also shared sites with distant relatives and friends and sometimes with strangers. Two or three fishermen commonly formed what Indians called companies, allowing a group of fishermen to use a site even as individual members became too exhausted to fish. Company members could fish the site nearly continuously, then sell the fish to buyers and divide the profit. In other cases, the owner of a site might exact a sort of rent—up to half the catch—from a fellow fisher who needed a site. The fishery comprised an annual catch somewhere between 2.3 million and 2.6 million pounds, which were sold to fish buyers and tourists and dried for winter consumption.[2]

From a tourist's perspective, the human activity over Celilo's wooden platforms may have seemed picturesque. From a fisher's perspective, the platforms likely seemed overcrowded, a reflection of the growing popularity of the falls among "outside" Indians and even whites. In the twentieth century, indigenous fishery regulation responded to overcrowding. The BIA formalized these regulations within agency structures. The four primary groups who used Celilo Falls—the Yakamas, Umatillas, Warm Springs, and unenrolled Wasco and Wishram Indians—established the Celilo Fish Committee (CFC) in 1935 under Bureau of Indian Affairs supervision, which had grown tired of refereeing fishing disputes.[3] Three members from each reservation and three members representing the year-round residents (commonly referred to as river Indians) comprised this representative group, which developed out of an earlier intertribal fisheries council. According to Richard Schifter, attorney for the Nez Perce, "these meetings grew out of an old traditional custom of the Shehapatin [sic] Tribes who met at Celilo Falls in the Spring."[4]

The establishment of the Celilo Fish Committee was local Indians' response to regulations imposed by the state and federal governments and to the increasing numbers of out-of-area Indians and whites who came to fish from the falls in the 1930s. The growth in newcomers was a result of two developments: heightened profitability in the fishery and the decline of fisheries elsewhere. The rise in profitability coincided with the introduction of effective refrigeration processes that allowed canners to buy more than they could quickly preserve, thereby increasing the demand and the price paid for salmon. Moreover, the Depression of the 1930s made fishing the falls economically attractive.[5]

Local Indians established the Celilo Fish Committee to ensure that they retained a measure of control over their own fishery. Salmon chief and leader of the Celilo Village Wyams, Tommy Thompson, enforced conservation measures and organized fishing activity by determining when fishers would start each morning and leave each evening. In an interview after his death, Thompson's wife, Flora Cushinway Thompson, recalled that

Indians at Celilo did not fish at night, to allow for escapement. But self-imposed conservation measures began to break down during the 1930s and 1940s when more whites and Indians without traditional fishing rights began to fish commercially at Celilo Falls. Committee members found that they had little power over non-local Indians or whites when enforcing their own restrictions.[6]

From the committee's inception, its members were concerned with limiting who could fish at Celilo. Although the CFC fought to get rid of white interlopers, the committee was also involved in efforts to keep nonlocal Indians such as Buck Towner from fishing. Towner was a Siletz Indian whom many local residents identified as "the seat of all the trouble" between local and nonlocal Indians.[7] At a Celilo Fish Committee meeting in April 1935, Isaac McKinley made a successful motion to restrict fishing at the falls to only those Indians represented by the committee. Even so, outside Indians continued to be a problem, as evidenced by a resolution passed in September 1939 to restrict the fishery to Yakama, Umatilla, Warm Springs, and Celilo Indians.[8] Then in 1949 Alex Saluskin, a Yakama member of the committee, asked the BIA whether it could keep Nez Perce Indians from fishing the falls. Edward Swindell, an attorney with the BIA, responded that anyone could fish at Celilo "whether they be an Indian from some other part of the United States, a white man, or a Chinaman" as long as they "did not interfere with Indians fishing there under reserved treaty rights."[9]

Swindell's statement undercut the CFC's authority to evict unwanted fishers, and local Indians were dependent on BIA employees to protect fishing stations, unless local Indians were willing to act subversively, as some would during conflicts with white fishers. The BIA frequently supported efforts to protect local fishers with long-standing recognized rights when those rights were encroached upon, but despite the importance of the Celilo fishery to Columbia River treaty tribes, it was not until the end of the 1930s that a BIA employee was stationed at the site. The Bureau of Indian Affairs formed a "sub-agency" at The Dalles in 1939 under the jurisdiction of the Yakima Agency and appointed Clarence G. Davis to the post until the government closed the office in 1950.[10]

The appointment of C. G. Davis symbolizes the pinnacle of BIA support for mid–Columbia River Indian fishers. Davis, the only employee in the office, spent eleven years traveling throughout the mid-Columbia region, providing Indians with personal, legal, medical, and financial assistance. Davis acted as an advocate on behalf of the local Indians in disputes with the Seufert fish buyers, white fishermen, and nonlocal Indian fishermen. He attended meetings organized by the Indians, most notably those of the Celilo Fish Committee, and took copious notes that he saved in his files. H. U. Sanders, another BIA employee, claimed that Davis's appointment was "a great step forward in handling the problem of that area because he immediately began to learn and understand the people and their problems and is now in position to render valuable assistance to others who may be added to the personnel there." One such person added to the personnel at The Dalles was an Indian policeman, Dave Saluskin. Again, according to Sanders, "the value of Mr. Davis and Dave Saluskin in this area can hardly be over-estimated."[11]

But the value afforded by a subagent at The Dalles was not long-lived. In response to congressional support for termination policy, William Brophy, Bureau of Indian Affairs commissioner (1945–48), reorganized the BIA into five area offices in the late 1940s, with Portland as one of the headquarters. This reorganization allowed the BIA to eliminate forty offices nationwide. One of the offices closed in the Pacific Northwest was the field office at The Dalles. When C. G. Davis relocated from his post in 1950, he left at precisely the moment when he was most needed and could have contributed to guiding river Indians through the complex bureaucracies of the BIA and the Army Corps of Engineers during the negotiations for compensation. With Davis's removal from the area, the effectiveness of the Celilo Fish Commission diminished in the 1950s.[12]

Internal pressures in the CFC matched those from outside the small committee and were made worse during dam construction. The attorney for the Warm Springs Indians, T. Leland Brown, warned E. Morgan Pryse, the regional BIA director, in September 1950 that the Umatilla and Warm Springs Indians had decided to withdraw from the Celilo Fish Committee. They complained that Yakama Indians dominated the committee, preventing the Umatilla and Warm Springs Indians from getting a fair hearing. Brown also warned that the exclusion of the two tribes would likely lead to bloodshed, and he asked that the BIA dissolve the committee until they could resolve the issue.[13] (The withdrawal of the two tribes prevented the committee from having a quorum to vote on resolutions, but it continued to regulate the fisheries.)

Warm Springs superintendent Jasper Elliott also warned that the Yakamas would soon claim exclusive rights to Celilo. The Yakamas argued that the Umatillas fished at Celilo Falls only after they signed the 1855 Walla Walla treaty. This assertion put Celilo Falls outside of the Umatillas' "usual and accustomed" off-reservation fishing sites. In regards to the Warm Springs' claim, the Yakamas pointed to a disputed 1865 treaty in which the Warm Springs supposedly relinquished their off-reservation fisheries. Even federal agencies suspected that this "Huntington Treaty" was procured under false pretenses, and most knowledgeable observers considered it illegitimate. Nonetheless, the Yakamas claimed exclusive rights to Celilo Falls in a council resolution passed in May 1951.[14]

This conflict arose as the Umatillas, Warm Springs, and Yakamas were embroiled in negotiations with the Army Corps of Engineers over a cash settlement for the fishing sites at Celilo Falls. The Corps put a set value on the Indian fishery at Celilo, to be divided among those tribes that had reserved rights at the area. Therefore, the Yakamas' move to claim exclusive rights can be seen as an extension of an ongoing struggle to determine who had rights to fish at the falls, and the Yakamas also stood to claim the entire $26 million if they could prove that the Umatillas and the Warm Springs did not have a legal claim to the Celilo fishery. In other words, the conflicts among Indians over fishing sites played themselves out in the negotiations with the Army Corps, and vice versa.

THE SEUFERT CANNERY AND THE NATIVE COMMERCIAL FISHERY

Threemile Reef, Grave, Wasco, Rabbit, Kiska, Big, and Chief were bare basalt islands scattered over a nine-mile stretch of the Columbia constricted by a narrow riverbed. The islands diverted the river's rushing waters and sent the current spiraling into black eddies and whirlpools large enough to swallow a railroad tie, with quiet backwaters where salmon rested on their journey upstream before they attempted to propel their way through the numerous rapids and falls. Most did not make it on the first try and were momentarily stunned as the current swept them downstream until they tried again.

The salmon's upstream journey led to several likely outcomes. If a salmon did not reach its natal stream and found itself trapped in a dip net instead, an Indian woman might deftly gut and fillet the fish, hanging the meat in the rafters of a drying shed. Or a tourist or Portland-area fish buyer might pack the salmon in ice and take it west on the Oregon Trail Highway 30 (now Interstate 84). Or the salmon might end up at the Seufert cannery a few miles downstream.

Although fish buyers representing several canneries vied for Indian-caught salmon, the Seufert family's was the largest local cannery. The prominent, wealthy family had roots in The Dalles that extended to the 1880s when Francis A. Seufert first opened

The Seufert cannery in about 1930.
Gifford photo, Oregon Historical Society, Gi 12400.

the cannery operation. The relationship of the Seuferts to Indian fishers went beyond purchasing fish to include advancing money to Indians, occasionally hiring Indian men and women at the cannery, and attempting, somewhat ironically and unsuccessfully, to keep Indian fishers from traversing Seufert land to reach their fishing sites. Despite the thread of conflict that ran through the dealings between Indians and the Seuferts, the Seufert Brothers Company Salmon and Fruit Cannery made every attempt to ensure that fishers would sell their salmon to the Seuferts' business.

Toward that aim, the Seufert cannery built its first cableway in 1907, which connected fishing sites to shore. Other fish buyers followed suit, and eventually cable-car lines maintained for Indian use crisscrossed the skyline. The cableways guided small motorized or hand-cranked cable cars that could hold the weight of four adult men or the equivalent weight in fish. The three-by-five-foot cars replaced cedar canoes that earlier Indians had used to ply the river. Fish buyers built cableways as an inducement to fishers to sell their harvest to the buyer whose cable they used to cross the river.

Indian women often used the cableways and large burlap sacks to collect the fish caught by their male relatives and then delivered them to the fish buyer's weigh station. The buyer would throw the salmon one at a time on the mobile scale, recording its weight in a notebook. If he did not buy the salmon with cash, the buyer would tear off a slip of paper to create a fish ticket, which would stand in place of currency, with the weight, the name of the fisherman, and the name of the cannery. The Seufert cannery always had at least one fish buyer at Celilo to purchase salmon as the Indians unloaded it from Seufert cableways.[15]

Francis A. Seufert established the area's largest cannery when, at the turn of the twentieth century, he bought up the four competing canneries and two salteries in The Dalles. The Seuferts' two-story white warehouse that housed the canning equipment, as well as outbuildings such as the cook- and bunkhouses, sat on a cliff overlooking the mouth of Fifteenmile Creek just short of its confluence with the Columbia River. During the off-season the cannery turned to prunes, cherries, asparagus, and other local produce, but from November to May it hummed with the butchering and cooking of salmon. The cannery purchased as much of the Indian catch as it could and then augmented that with two cannery-operated horse-drawn seines as well as purchases from the white gillnetters who traveled up the Columbia every season to harvest the midriver runs. There was no means of garbage disposal, so salmon waste, old cans, packing labels, and other odds and ends cluttered the creek bed until semi-annual floods washed the waste out to the Columbia and eventually to the Pacific Ocean. At times Fifteenmile Creek ran red with the blood of salmon.[16]

The Seufert cannery presents an intriguing study of the intersections of labor and race on the mid–Columbia River. The cannery's extended labor force consisted, until the 1930s, of four principal groups of men: white gillnetters, Indian dip netters (who also occasionally worked on the canning crews), white men who supervised canning crews or held other management-level positions, and Chinese men who flayed and packed salmon into tin cans. Francis Seufert recalls that racial categories defined labor positions, social activities, and living quarters:

> In those days the relationship between Indians, Chinese and whites was very clear cut. Each man tended to his own business and didn't interfere with the rights of others. The Indians all stayed at the Indian camp, the Chinese all stayed down at the China house, and the whites all stayed at the white bunk house.[17]

Portland-area Chinese labor contractors sent groups of male Chinese laborers to The Dalles by rail each April for the salmon season. The Seuferts used Chinese labor, as did much of the Pacific Coast fish-canning industry, from as early as the 1890s through the onset of World War II. According to Francis Seufert, the cannery used Chinese labor exclusively at first except in the positions of steam engineer, foreman, bookkeeper, and machinist, positions reserved for white men.[18]

Originally the canneries turned to Chinese labor because, according to anthropologist Courtland Smith, whites "proved to be too transient and too unreliable." Attracted to The Dalles at first by railroad work, the Chinese labor force in Wasco County became increasingly reliant on the Seufert cannery after 1900. In 1910, the Seuferts employed 40 percent of the Chinese men who worked in The Dalles. Beginning in the 1930s white women, as well as Japanese, Mexican, and Filipino workers, began to replace Chinese men. With better work available to them, Chinese laborers at the cannery dropped off considerably during World War II. Although Francis Seufert blames the decrease on the Americanization of Chinese youth, the cannery ultimately could not compete with the high-paying jobs in war-related industries along the West Coast.[19]

Until the 1930s, whites on the canning crews were mostly single and, like the Chinese workers, lived at the cannery, which also provided them with meals. During that decade, the habits of the men changed as more of them commuted to the cannery from homes in surrounding towns. Cannery workers brought their own lunches and were less likely to be single. The gillnetters who sold their fish to the Seuferts were "professional fishermen" (in contrast to Indian dip netters, whom non-Native fishers often considered "subsistence" fishers even while they sold a majority of their catches to canneries).

Race dictated the kind of work a laborer performed, and white gillnetters used violence to keep Chinese and Indian men from joining their ranks. The San Francisco *Chronicle* claimed in 1880 that Chinese men "never venture on the [Columbia] river, for the [white] fishermen are not the class to tamely submit to such competition." When some Chinese men attempted to break into the trade, "their boats were broken to pieces, and their nets cut up and scattered on the beach. The fishermen made no attempt to conceal the fact that they had drowned the intruders."[20] Indians sold their salmon catches to the Seuferts during the fishing season but did not work in the cannery itself except in the offseason. The cannery hired Indians, according to Francis Seufert, only if the cannery was "busy and short-handed" because "when you hired [an Indian] you could never be sure he would come back the next day."[21]

Francis Seufert describes a segregated workforce in which there was little, if any, interaction between white, Chinese, and Indian

workers (except that mediated by white management). Historian
Richard White describes this kind of system as a "dual labor" or
"two-tiered labor" system in which people of color comprise a
bottom rank of low-paying and low-skilled positions, whereas
whites have access to the upper rank of skilled and high-paying
work. Seufert claims that Indians were inherently unreliable,
which was why they were not hired to work inside the Seufert
cannery. He also reports that the hands of Chinese men were "as
nimble as a woman's" but as powerful as a man's, physically suit-
ing them to long hours of packing salmon into tin cans. These
kinds of assertions had a significant impact on labor practices
and indicate the complexities and intersections of race and
gender in labor practices on the Columbia River. For example,
Indian women were unlikely to work as fishers because they were
women and often did not work in the canneries because they were
Indians.[22]

The Seuferts and the Indian dip netters regarded one another,
from the position of their conflicting interests, as buyers and sell-
ers, respectively, of salmon. Fishermen were intent on garner-
ing the best possible prices for their catches; the cannery was
equally intent on paying as little to the fishermen as possible.
Seufert describes a "natural" distrust between fishermen and fish
buyers: Buyers could "never fully trust what a fisherman told you
about fish prices" offered by other buyers, because Indians did
their best to keep prices high. Seufert claims that Indians tried
to increase the weight of fish by forcing gravel or railroad spikes
down the throats of salmon.[23]

Francis Seufert and members of the Celilo Fish Committee
met with attorney Carl Donaugh in 1938 to discuss several local
Indian-white conflicts. During the meeting an Indian claimed that
"Seufert has robbed Indians by paying low prices." Moreover,
"some Indians will protect [Seufert]" and his attempts to maintain a monopoly on fish buying. Other buyers who visited the
falls to buy fish from the Indians occasionally offered higher prices

than the Seuferts were willing to pay. Francis Seufert complained that prices were raised by the "noble packer who was pious and prissy who just thought the fishermen deserved more money." And some Indians trucked their catches to Portland fish markets in the hopes of earning more. But for the most part, Indian fishers sold to the Seuferts, who tried their best to ensure they would.[24]

The Seufert cannery and the modern commercial Indian fishery developed in tandem in the mid–twentieth century. The Seuferts hoped that the Indians who used the cannery's cableways would feel obligated to bring their fish to the Seufert buyer before going to others. This practice undercut the competition and, the Seuferts hoped, encouraged loyalty to their company. To ensure that local Indians would sell their catch to the company, the Seuferts loaned Indians money during the off-season. The practice of borrowing money from the Seuferts reveals two economic realities for Indian fishers: their commercial fishery was financially precarious and did not always provide adequate wages; and Indians subsisted in an economically hostile world in which banks would likely deny them credit. Seufert recalls that Indians would retain a measure of economic freedom by selling the cannery their fish under another name to avoid paying off their debt right away. Although Seufert depicts Indians as economic "tricksters," the cannery would not have continued to loan money to Indians if they did not repay their debts.

Relationships between the Seufert family and local Indian fishers were often rocky, even though Francis Seufert remembers them as mutually respectful. In his 1980 memoir, Seufert carefully explains that Indians had a legal right to traverse Seufert-owned property to reach "usual and accustomed" fishing sites. What Seufert does not mention is the fact that Indians won the right of easement in an 1887 court case. Then the Seuferts attempted to restrict Yakama Indians to the northern shore of the Columbia River, claiming that they had no traditional rights to fishing sites accessed from Oregon. In 1919 the U.S. Supreme

Court upheld Yakama fishing rights that were threatened by the Seuferts. Describing the river as a "great table where all the Indians came to partake" of the harvest, the court recognized the Yakama's "usual and accustomed" sites. This is no small omission; it reveals the length to which Indians actively protected their rights even when it pitted them against a business "partner."[25]

Seufert also omits the continuous battle that Indians and C. G. Davis, the Bureau of Indian Affairs employee at The Dalles, waged against the Seufert cannery to retain the right of easement. At a Celilo Fish Committee meeting in August 1945, Davis claimed that the Seuferts farmed some strategic strips of land "with evident financial loss to them—and that they had fenced off certain areas under excuse of farming." The real purpose of doing so, he remarked, was to prevent Indians from enjoying passage across Seufert land to reach the river.[26]

When The Dalles Chamber of Commerce voted to pass a resolution to support the development of The Dalles Dam, however, Francis Seufert, the chamber's president, was the only member to cast a "no" vote. Seufert adamantly opposed a dam that would flood the cannery and destroy his family's business.[27] Eventually, the Army Corps compensated the Seufert family with more than $1 million, but twenty years later Francis Seufert's bitterness at his loss is palpable as he recalls life and work on the river. In his 1980 memoir, Seufert bluntly states that when the Army Corps dammed the Columbia, the salmon "were doomed. No amount of propaganda nor money will ever bring them back."[28]

Just as the Army Corps envisioned a reservoir at the ancient fishing sites around Celilo Falls, when the agency viewed the Seufert cannery it saw large buildings conveniently situated near the river that could be converted into office space. More than five years before the dam was completed, Army Corps representatives negotiated with the Seufert family so that the agency could use cannery buildings as its construction headquarters. It was not a reshaping of the landscape that sat well with the Seuferts. The real estate division of the Corps met with Arthur Seufert in 1951. According to one observer, "During the course of the first few minutes of our visit Mr. Seuffert [*sic*] took pains to point out that this friendship with Mr. Rucker [a Corps representative] was not extended to the balance of the engineers of the Portland District." Despite the animosity felt by the Seuferts, the Army Corps honored the family by naming a park established at the cannery site Seufert Park. The name is a reminder of the site's original function and how much the landscape has been altered.[29]

Francis Seufert was raised with the rhythms of the fish runs and intimately knew the ways of the river, just as the Indian men and women did. By the 1950s, Francis Seufert and the Indians who fished at Celilo found themselves in a similar position: they all faced the alteration of the wild river that supported their livelihoods. That shared fate evidently overrode the earlier "natural" distrust between the canner and fishermen—at least, that was Seufert's view in later life. However, the dramatic shift in uses of the river that came about with the construction of the federal dams is part of a longer history in which Indian uses of the Columbia increasingly gave way to non-Indian uses of the river.

DIVIDING THE RIVER: INDIAN AND NON-INDIAN FISHERS

When European and American traders explored the Columbia River beginning in the early 1800s, they entered an established system of indigenous commerce. European and American contact enormously altered Native economic, cultural, and social systems that were dependent on both the Columbia River salmon fishery and trade networks. Author Charles Wilkinson calls the arrival of Lewis and Clark to the Columbia Basin "a crackling, lightning-bolt event" for local Indians.[30] Not only did the expedition mark the onset of written Columbia Plateau history, it also initiated a period of fundamental transformation for both Indian peoples and the river environment. The white settlements that followed, including missions and trade stations, distorted the fabric of relations between Indian cultures and the Columbia River landscape that were already fraying due to exogenous diseases. Lewis and Clark's arrival marked the onset of a period in which the region's white settlers increasingly shaped the river and its surroundings, making the river progressively incapable of supporting salmon. Simultaneously, treaties removed the river from Indians, who would, in turn, embark on an arduous and lengthy struggle to retain access to the salmon.

In the treaty with the Yakama; the treaty with the Walla Walla, Cayuse, and Umatilla; the treaty with the Nez Perce; and the treaty with the tribes of Middle Oregon—all signed in 1855—Indians reserved the right to retain their salmon fisheries. Indians retained exclusive rights to reservation fisheries and "the right of taking fish at all usual and accustomed places, in common with all citizens of the Territory." In a prophetic passage in an annual report written prior to treaty negotiations, Indian agent (and territorial governor) Isaac Stevens indicated that he was concerned about possible legal conflicts between the territories and their citizens, on the one hand, and the Indians who retained their fishing rights: "the subject of the [Indian] right of the fisheries is one upon which legislation is demanded."[31] Historian Kent Richards claims that Stevens conceded off-reservation fishing rights because he thought they were transitional and would be needed only until Indians learned to farm.[32] Fay Cohen refers to earlier Puget Sound treaty negotiations during which tribes made it clear to Stevens that they would not enter into treaty negotiations without assurances that their fishing rights would be protected.[33] Whether Stevens agreed to reserve salmon for Native peoples in the interest of rapidly liquidating tribal territory or whether salmon had little economic value to whites, who thus were willing to let Indians retain their rights to them, remains debated today.[34]

The 1855 treaties marked initial efforts at codifying who and where people could fish for salmon in the Pacific Northwest. Instead of marking the end of negotiations regarding Indian fishing rights, treaties marked the onset of more than a century of debate between federal, state, and tribal governments about who has rightful access to the salmon of the Columbia River and its tributaries. In that sense, treaties and subsequent court decisions reconfigured the traditional Native fishery. Treaties were the first signs of non-Native regulation of the Columbia River fishery, and they provided the foundation for the contours of the modern Indian fishery.[35]

The modern fishery brought with it a deepening need for regulation. White settlement forced Indians to fish their most productive and most unambiguously traditional sites; increasingly, however, even those sites came under attack. White settlement and industries such as farming and logging precipitated a decline in both the salmon runs and in productive, accessible fishing sites. The rise of the commercial fishery exacerbated these problems as Indian fishers found themselves competing with whites for the resource. By the turn of the twentieth century, Indians had far fewer off-reservation places from which to fish than they had had a mere fifty years earlier, and their access continued to diminish. With increased competition between Indian and non-Indian fishers, the states of Oregon and Washington stepped in to regulate the fisheries.[36]

By the 1920s, both states attempted to bring Indian fishers within their jurisdictions, often singling them out for racially based harassment. In 1915 the state of Washington made it illegal for Indians to fish without a license—and it was impossible for Indians to even buy licenses because the state Legislature did not recognize them as citizens of the state. Throughout the Northwest, but particularly in Washington, Indians found that the states would arrest them for fishing and hunting without a license, even on their own reservations. Eventually, the federal government overturned rulings that supported the rights of states to regulate the Indian fishery, but not before many people suffered the social indignities and the financial costs of being jailed. As legal scholar Felix Cohen points out in *Handbook of Indian Law*, the federal courts have "never developed a consistent theory about the legal rights" Indians have to the fishery. Instead, what has developed is a patchwork of well-defined and -supported rights pieced together with rights that are still open to interpretation.[37]

Because of the treaties, Indian fishers comprised a separate category of river users. State agencies and their non-Indian constituents often regarded Indians as "rogue" fishers who operated outside of any regulatory authority. This assumption disregarded the regulations that Indians placed on themselves through organizations such as the Celilo Fish Committee. Property owners, non-Indian commercial fishermen, and state regulatory agencies proved to be enemies of Native fishers who fought to protect their treaty rights through a series of court cases.[38]

On a hot, dusty August afternoon in 1946, several Yakama fishers forced two white fishermen, Earnest Cramer and his nephew Ernest Cramer, off the Cramers' scaffolding. The Yakamas threw the timber into the rushing Columbia, perhaps pausing just a moment to watch it vanish, before running the Cramers off what most people regarded as Indian fishing sites. The Portland *Oregonian* reported that "the Cramers suffered a mauling," though neither was seriously injured and the police made no arrest.[39]

The Cramers later pressed charges against three men, Louis Barker and brothers Lawrence and Alfonse Gowdy, for the destruction of property. A Wasco County court acquitted the young men. Almost one year later, Columbia River Indian fishers Jobe (Job) Charley, Lawerence Gowdy, Seymore Gowdy, Tommy Thompson, Henry Thompson, Sampson Tulee, and William Yallup testified in *United States v. Earnest F. Cramer and E. R.*

Cramer before Judge James Alger Fee of the District Court of Oregon, to prevent the Cramers from fishing commercially at Celilo Falls.[40]

Although *United States v. Earnest F. Cramer and E. R. Cramer* was not a legal landmark case, it was significant for local Indians who had engaged in protracted battles to reserve the falls for themselves. The Cramers competed directly with Indians for fishing sites and for a portion of the salmon harvest. As a result, Indians asked the court to decide just what it meant to have "usual and accustomed" fishing sites reserved for use "in common with other citizens of the Territory." Could whites fish those sites? If so, under what circumstances? More important, did whites or Indians have a *superior* right to the salmon when fishermen clashed over access to the fish?

At the heart of the matter was the division of the Columbia River into specific places for white and Native fishers. The hundred years from 1855, with the signing of the treaties, to 1957, with the closing of The Dalles Dam, brought a consistent pattern of diminishing access among Indian people to the mid–Columbia River—even at their renowned traditional fishing site, Celilo Falls. Indeed, the negotiations between the U.S. Army Corps of Engineers and Indians surrounding the development of The Dalles Dam was a continuation of this longer struggle to maintain a Native presence on the river.

In the 1940s and 1950s, when tourists flocked to Celilo Falls to watch Indians fish, they journeyed to a river that was increasingly less a Native place as non-Native transportation, irrigation, hydroelectric production, and recreation displaced Indian people. By the mid–twentieth century, Indian fishers had engaged in a hundred years of struggle to maintain a place at the river.

The midcentury Indian fishery shared characteristics with its precontact predecessor in that it included trade and a subsistence harvest and embodied spiritual practices. Although those threads connecting the past to the present were evident to even casual observers in the 1950s, Indian practices were not dominant on the river then.

The Native fishery itself underwent modernization as well, presenting a pastiche of ancient and modern elements. Indians adopted the use of new materials to construct tools of ancient design, such as scaffolds and dip nets. Fishermen now built their scaffolds each season from cut lumber, not from driftwood. Scaffolds were mobile; they were easily dismantled and moved to another location or stored for the winter. This was essential because only some fishing sites were above water's reach during any given month. During the spring, Indians fished at the west end of The Dalles–Celilo Canal and at Spearfish on the Washington shore. During the fall, they clustered around the spectacular falls at the head of nine miles of rapids. During the winter, fishers constructed or repaired dip nets, their steel hoops and nylon netting an indication of twentieth-century industrialism.

Events on the river in 1946 were the culmination of conflict—spread out for more than a decade—between Native fishers and the Cramers. The conflict was rooted in the treaty negotiations of 1855 and the ways in which the Indian fishery had changed over nearly one hundred years.

In 1974 Frederick Cramer recollected that his father and cousin began fishing at Celilo Falls at the onset of the Great Depression.[41] The economic desperation of the 1930s drew many whites and Indians to the fishery, where they sold salmon to canneries for as little as half a cent per pound. Indians often took at least some of their catch to surrounding farmers and bartered for fruits, vegetables, and eggs, waiting out the Depression. The Cramers also bartered for "smoked hams, bacon, eggs, and potatoes," even a live turkey that they kept until butchering it for a Thanksgiving feast.[42]

Despite the Depression, fishing was sufficiently profitable that the Cramers formed a partnership in 1931, and over the next eleven years they extended the sites from which they fished to three scaffolds on two different islands. A young Frederick Cramer joined his father and cousin in what he called a "priceless experience" between 1930 and 1937 during his summer vacations (later, Frederick would marry his high school sweetheart, Edna Mae Seufert, sister of Francis Seufert, the last president of the Seufert cannery).[43]

The Cramers claimed they fished from areas that local Indians did not use. In fact, Earnest Cramer reported that he had told Indians he thought they should fish at these sites but, failing to recognize that they were prime locations, the Indians refused to use them.[44] Indians claimed the Cramers kept them from these sites, sometimes forcefully.

The conflict came to a head in September 1938 when the Celilo Fish Committee voted to deny the Cramers fishing access. The decision prompted Walter Sheldon, a BIA property clerk at the Umatilla Reservation, to visit the Cramers. The Cramers told Sheldon that the state of Oregon authorized them to fish their sites and had even sent out members of the state police to protect them, much to the disbelief of the clerk. Sheldon reported that "this indicated that they knew they were taking away from the Indians some of their accustomed fishing places and expected opposition, otherwise they would not have asked for police protection." Cramer insulted the BIA employee, saying, "The Government had made reservations for the Indians and that a lot of the trouble was caused by the various Superintendents failing to keep the Indians within the confines of the Reservations." Sheldon found that "there is just grounds for the complaint of Indians" and described the attitude of the Cramers as "one of bullying or bluffing the matter through."[45]

In the fall of 1938, Carl Donaugh, U.S. District Attorney for Oregon, along with a BIA employee from Washington, D.C., the Yakima BIA superintendent, and BIA employees from the Umatilla Reservation, conducted a series of informal meetings with local Indians and the Cramers. After these meetings, Donaugh arranged a formal meeting in October. At this point, the Cramers fished from three scaffolds and had hired out-of-area Indians to fish from two others. The BIA was particularly concerned that the Cramers were intent on increasing the scope of their operations. The Cramers were represented by their attorney, a man identified only as Mr. Brown, who stated that "Kramer [*sic*] wants to fish there in harmony with the Indians."[46]

Charles Johnson, Job (Jobe) Charley, and Sampson Tulee all testified that the Cramers interfered with their ability to fish.[47] The Indians who met with Donaugh were active in their communities and in the protection of Indian fishing rights. Many were members of the Celilo Fish Committee, and Sampson Tulee would defend his right to fish before the U.S. Supreme Court in 1942 in *Tulee v. Washington*. Andrew Barnhart, who often acted as an interpreter at meetings between government officials and older Indians, was described by Wilerton Curtis, a former resident of the Pacific Northwest, as a man who "fought a good fight, though mostly a losing one, against the encroachments and treaty violations of the white man."[48] Even Charles Hopkins, special BIA officer at the Warm Springs Reservation, verified in a letter to Donaugh that the Indians who complained about the Cramers were "very reliable."[49]

All of the Bureau of Indian Affairs employees who intervened in this conflict agreed that the Cramers interfered with the fishing rights of local Indians and that the sites along the Columbia at Celilo Falls should be purchased by the federal government so that whites and non-local Indians could be legally denied access to them. This was an idea that the BIA would begin to advocate by 1944, with local Indians passionately in support of it. An even more expensive solution would have been to create a formal reservation site at Celilo Falls that incorporated Celilo Village.[50]

Stopping short of a land purchase, Carl Donaugh pushed for the installment of a local BIA agent at The Dalles to oversee the protection of local Indian fishermen. Donaugh told the U.S. Attorney General that "part of the difficulty arising at Celilo Falls . . . is due to the fact that no one connected with the Indian Service is on the ground very much of the time during the spring and fall fishing season." Shortly after Donaugh suggested that the BIA establish a subagency at Celilo, the agency appointed C. G. Davis as a field agent at The Dalles. Without the ability to exclude whites from traditional, off-reservation fishing sites, though, when Indians and non-Indians clashed it was up to the courts rather than the BIA to decide whose right to those sites was greater.[51]

The Cramers would continue to compete with Indian fishers until the mid-1950s, but the flare-up of 1938 seemed to be under control by October. Despite initial Yakama success in defending Native fishing sites from encroachment by the Cramers, the Cramers continued to have run-ins with Indian fishers. In 1945 and 1946, as soon as the commercial season ended, young Yakama Indians removed the scaffolds owned by the Cramers so that the Yakamas could install their own scaffolds and fish the sites for their subsistence catch.

At this point, Carl Donaugh filed a suit on behalf of the local Indians against Earnest Cramer and Ernest Cramer, to keep them from fishing from the falls altogether. It remains unclear why the BIA waited so long to take legal action against the Cramers; perhaps the arrests and escalating violence galvanized the agency. C. G. Davis wrote, "It was fortunate that no deaths occurred" as a result of the lack of action taken by the government to prevent whites from fishing at traditionally Native sites.[52]

From the beginning of this conflict, extralegal action by both white and Indian fishers shaped the contours of the struggle over access. The Cramers held their fishing sites under tremendous pressure from Indians to abandon them. Lawrence Gowdy recalled in *United States v. Earnest F. Cramer and E. R. Cramer* before Judge James Alger Fee of the District Court of Oregon that the Cramers were known to have run Indians from the river with a .30-.30 rifle, and Indians complained that the Cramers repeatedly destroyed Native-owned fishing gear. As the Indians became increasingly frustrated by delays in what they saw as a simple case of justice, they also turned to extralegal action, by removing the Cramer scaffolds in 1946. In his testimony, Lawrence Gowdy remembered that the Yakima BIA superintendent promised the Indians that the BIA would seek an injunction against the Cramers, but when it was not forthcoming, a "fight took place."[53] Wyam chief Tommy Thompson pleaded with Donaugh: "I ask you, if you are to help us, to do it right, and exclude the whites. The fish are all we have." A growing number of Indian fishers joined Thompson in asking that the BIA purchase the rocks at Celilo Falls so Indians could legally exclude non-Native fishers.[54]

After two days of testimony, Judge Fee found in favor of the BIA and "its Indian wards." Fee decided that Indians had a superior right to fishing sites reserved by the treaty as "usual and accustomed," even though the treaty also included language about fishing "in common" with non-Indian citizens. Fee granted temporary restraining orders against the Cramers and ordered them to permanently remove their scaffolds located at traditional sites. The decision legally ended the conflict between the Cramers and local Indians, although it did not preclude whites from fishing at the falls as long as their activities did not prevent Indians from enjoying their treaty rights.[55]

One striking thing about this case is both the generational distributions among the Indian plaintiffs and the experience that nearly all of the older Indians had with the court system. In many ways, United States v. Earnest Cramer and E. R. Cramer symbolizes the protection of young Native fishermen by their elders. Those who testified could be divided into two groups: the older men (ages sixty-seven to eighty-one), who testified to the importance of the contested sites, and the young men (ages sixteen to thirty), who wanted to fish them and had participated in the direct confrontations with the Cramers. When asked whether these sites would fall under the "usual and accustomed" sites protected by treaty rights, elders such as William Yallup and Tommy Thompson spoke of all the Indians who had fished the sites but had passed on. In a very real sense, the young Gowdy brothers represented a new generation of fishers who needed protection.

Furthermore, William Yallup and Jobe Charley had both been witnesses in the *Unites States v. Brookfield Fisheries* case in 1938 (also heard by Judge Alger Fee), and Thomas Yallup had also testified in a case brought against the Seuferts. Experience in protecting fishing rights went beyond the courts: John Whiz, an Indian who interpreted for Tommy Thompson, reportedly camped outside the doors of the Oregon Senate to remind legislators of their duty to protect the Indians who resided within their state.[56]

The case of the Cramers also illustrates the difficulty that Indians had in enforcing legal decisions, even when the courts found in their favor. There is sporadic evidence of an ongoing struggle between Indian fishermen and the Cramers even after Oregon's U.S. District Attorney Carl Donaugh and the Yakamas decided to take the Cramers to court. In 1948, BIA subagent Clarence Davis wrote a letter to Kenneth Simmons, the lawyer retained by the Yakamas, suggesting that Earnest Cramer had hired Indian fishers to use his platforms. This would indicate that the Cramers skirted the law by using Indians to fish for them while getting a cut of the profits. Earnest Cramer also complained to Davis in 1948 that Indians had removed one of his scaffolds during the night. Davis claimed to know nothing about the incident but also admitted that some of those involved in the dispute believed that Davis was aiding the Indians.[57]

The Yakamas, and the other Indian fishers who joined them in fending off the encroachment of the Cramers, were engaged in a protracted struggle to retain a measure of power and visibility on the Columbia River. This was no easy task. It must have seemed to the young fishermen that nobody save other Indian fishermen appreciated the rights that Indians held to traditional sites on the river.

There were other problems. Property owners sought to keep Indians from traveling through their fields to reach the river; the state hounded fishers for proof of license; and the Bureau of Indian Affairs was only as responsive as its best employee. Furthermore, the fishing industry had divided the river into the rich non-Indian commercial fisheries of the lower Columbia River and the Indian and sports fisheries of the mid-Columbia. In terms of economic clout, the fishers of the mid-Columbia could not compete with those of the lower river. For the Indians who continued to fish at places such as Celilo, the struggle was to maintain cultural and economic integrity. But for the agencies that regulated midriver fishing or sought to develop the river, the mid-Columbia was an expendable fishery that could not stand in the way of progress.

ENTER THE DAM

Because of the industrialization of the Pacific Northwest, the places from which Indians could fish—as well as their salmon runs—declined sharply between the 1880s and the 1950s. In that context, dams exacerbated a salmon fishery already in decline. This era of fishery deterioration paralleled the period in which Indians successfully defended their treaty fishing rights through the state and federal court systems. Because the right to fish became increasingly hard to fulfill, it is not surprising that Indians galvanized to protect their treaty rights even while fish stocks were declining. Between the year of the first Pacific Northwest Indian fishing case, in 1887, and the 1950s, local Indians protected their right to river access. They did so by traversing private property, fighting for the right to use new technologies, seeking protection against state interference, and attempting to limit the use of Celilo Falls by non-Native fishers and Indian fishers from outside the region. Finally, local fishers attempted to defeat the damming of the wild river so important to their culture and economy.

Protecting their treaty right to fish was no easy task for the mid-Columbia Indians. Oregon and Washington consistently complained that there was no definition of "usual and accustomed" sites and that Indian fishing remained unregulated, despite the existence of the Celilo Fish Committee. Although nearly everyone accepted some sites—such as Celilo—as traditional, individuals and the states challenged other places. Moreover, identifying traditional sites could be difficult if one worked at a state agency. Indians passed that information down from one generation to the next and often under names not recognized by state governments and courts. It was not until the federal government had to compensate Indians for their submerged sites that any federal agency conducted a survey of surviving traditional sites.[58]

BIA Commissioner John Collier sent BIA attorney Edward Swindell Jr. to the mid-Columbia region in 1941 to survey the impact of Bonneville Dam (completed three years earlier, in 1938) on the Native fishery and to document remaining sites. Swindell's extensive report provided background material for the Indians and the Army Corps of Engineers as they negotiated a settlement for the sites that The Dalles Dam would obliterate. But according to historian Donald Parman, the report had little effect: "Evidently preoccupied with the [Second World] war and resulting dislocations in his office, Collier thanked Swindell for his 'careful research' and 'painstaking work,' but did little more than note that the 'report will be filed for future reference purposes'." As Parman points outs, the BIA did not release the report until a decade had passed.[59]

Furthermore, when in 1946 Judge Fee granted Indians a superior right to fish at Celilo Falls, the real threat to Indian fishing was not from white fishers but from the development of the

Columbia River. Although the federal government defended local Indians when the states of Oregon and Washington threatened their rights, it was the federal government itself that struck the crucial blow against Native fishing in the region. Through the authorization of dams, Congress decided that Indians *did not* have a superior right to fish the Columbia when that right competed with economic progress. Congress and the Corps assumed Indians at Celilo Falls would lose their fishery to a reservoir. In doing so, the federal government effectively exchanged the Indian salmon resource for improved transportation, inexpensive electricity, and plentiful irrigation, resources that benefited white communities.

Yakama Indian Moses Squeochs pointed out in 1998 that the damming of the Columbia River was a matter of cultural significance as well as of economic importance to Indians. It was every bit as devastating as the implementation of the Dawes General Allotment Act nearly eighty years earlier, in which Indians across the nation lost about 60 percent of tribally held land. The allotment policy and dam building meant the enormous loss of resources among Indians and placed them at risk of losing the cultural structures that sustained the use of those resources. Furthermore, underlying the cultural and economic loss was the threat to treaty-protected rights. What did it matter if Indians retained the right to fish in "usual and accustomed places" if those places (and the fish themselves) could not survive regional progress?[60]

3

DEBATING THE DAM

"A Serious Breach of Good Faith"

"There is no feeling on the part of any members of
Congress to destroy a natural resource, a natural
resource of food supply. On the other hand, we are
face to face with the necessity for electrical energy....
It makes it a very difficult position if we sit here
and decide these momentous questions."

U.S. REPRESENTATIVE LOUIS RABAUT, 1952[1]

"Must these feats of engineering stand as monuments to our injustice and broken word?"

**SAM HUNTERS, LETTER TO HIS CONGRESSIONAL
REPRESENTATIVE AND THE BIA PROTESTING
CONSTRUCTION OF THE DALLES DAM[2]**

Colonel Ralph Tudor stood before a crowd of The Dalles
residents and local Indians in September 1945 and promised that, after contributing to victory in World War II,
the rivers of the West would now be "utilized for peace time purposes."[3] Tudor was the chief engineer of the U.S. Army Corps of
Engineers, Portland District, a local boy raised by an engineering
contractor who moved his family from town to town in Oregon
following work on causeways and railroads.[4] Tudor visited The
Dalles frequently as he oversaw dam building on the Columbia

Aerial view of The Dalles Dam, 8 October 1956.
U.S. Army Corps of Engineers.

River. After retiring from the Army Corps and starting an engineering firm, he would be hired to design and build the Wasco County Bridge across the Columbia. He eventually became an important figure in The Dalles, especially when President Eisenhower appointed him as undersecretary of the Department of the Interior. But in this initial 1945 meeting, Tudor acted as Corps spokesman and meeting facilitator.

The Dalles Dam and its navigation lock, Tudor promised, would "be the gateway of the Empire. . . . Through this dam will move all the waterborne commerce of the Empire, inbound and outbound." With the project's promise of abundant power and its ability to efficiently link the city of The Dalles to farms in the interior and to Portland markets, it is no surprise that the barging industry and city developers found the project attractive. Area farmers also supported the dam because it would irrigate upland orchards and lower costs of transporting their crops. Boosters viewed the proposed dam as essential to future regional growth. In the words of the Army Corps's official statement, "industry follows power."[5]

Fifty-four witnesses spoke before the large general audience at this meeting, choosing sides for or against the project and laying out arguments regarding the dam. In its coverage of the event, the Portland *Oregonian* declared that only those associated with the fishing industry opposed the dam. The newspaper ignored the diversity of the fishery: Indian fishermen, state fish and game agencies, commercial fishermen's unions, sports fishing groups, and the U.S. Fish and Wildlife Service. All of these groups, to varying degrees, expressed concerns about the construction of a dam near The Dalles. Furthermore, the *Oregonian* did not anticipate the opposition that would come from white supporters of Indians rights or the Bureau of Indian Affairs in the years to come. On the other hand, representatives from the chambers of commerce at The Dalles and Goldendale, Washington, the Inland Empire Waterways Association, and the Walla Walla Farm Bureau joined most mid-Columbia residents in support of the project.[6]

The protests of The Dalles Dam are examined here in the context of the overwhelming support the dam received from most segments of the regional and national population. Opposition to The Dalles Dam came from three camps: non-Indian fishers, Indians, and non-Indian supporters of Indian treaty rights. Resistance to the project is evident in public meetings organized by the Army Corps of Engineers, resolutions passed by Indian people in their tribal councils, congressional committee hearings, and a collection of letters written to government officials. Non-Native fishermen and whites who supported Indian fishing rights demanded that the dam be stopped. Friends of the Indians asked that Congress consider relocating the dam to save Celilo Falls when it became apparent that the dam would be constructed. The motives of these two groups, one financial and the other born out of a concern for social justice, were quite different. Nonetheless, both groups protested the dam out of the same misgiving: they feared that it would irrevocably destroy the salmon and steelhead runs that flourished in a wild river system. Furthermore, both groups wanted to protect the rights of all Pacific Northwesterners to wrest a living by fishing from the Columbia River whether they were white or Indian.[7]

The parallel protests of Indian and white fishers and their supporters against The Dalles Dam are a significant part of the history of the Columbia River. The efforts of opponents were ultimately unsuccessful, but their protests made cracks in the rhetoric of progress that saturated the Pacific Northwest in the mid–twentieth century and threatened what critics referred to as the iron triangle in water development: the collaboration of water agencies, Congress, and local boosters. The rhetoric used by the Army Corps and other proponents of the dam promoted a radical transformation of resources in which salmon runs would literally be traded for hydroelectricity. These oppositional narratives questioned the pace and design of development and asked developers to contemplate what would be lost when dams were built. Moreover, some protesters asked the nation to address treaty responsibilities that would be threatened by economic development benefiting white residents at the expense of Native people.[8]

GAUGING DISSENT

Testimony before congressional committees followed on the heels of local public meetings organized by the Army Corps. The process the Army Corps and Congress used to gauge public views on river development relegated opposition to the dam to the periphery. Daniel Mazmanian and Jeanne Nienaber studied the changes in the U.S. Army Corps of Engineers as a result of environmental activism in the 1960s and 1970s. They describe the traditional means by which the Army Corps developed a public project as a method dependent on "political accommodation among the Corps, Congress, and local proponents." Throughout a typical process, "principal local proponents, their congressmen, and the Corps were in constant communication, exchanging information and lobbying one another . . . to the almost total exclusion of real and potential project opponents."[9] An exchange between Oregon Senator Wayne Morse and Herbert West, the vice president of the Inland Empire Waterways Association and a witness before the congressional appropriations committee in 1951 and 1952, captures this kind of close joint participation between The Dalles Dam boosters and congressmen. Morse sent West a telegram in 1945 assuring West: "I heartily endorse the project and shall do everything I can through my position to secure its approval."[10]

Even more representative was the relationship between Wasco County Judge Ward Webber, U.S. Army Corps District Engineer Ralph Tudor, and Bureau of Indian Affairs employee Barbara Mackenzie (Tudor's sister). It is likely that Tudor met Webber sometime in the mid-1940s, when both became interested in the dam project and attended meetings in The Dalles. Webber and Tudor would subsequently work closely on both the dam and then a county bridge that Webber approved and Tudor's private company designed. Tudor hired his sister's husband, Tom Mackenzie, to oversee the construction of the bridge in 1953. When Barbara Mackenzie, a former Red Cross executive secretary in Lincoln County, arrived in The Dalles, she learned that volunteers ran The Dalles chapter of the Red Cross and began to hunt for a paid position.[11] She also met one of those volunteers, Mrs. Ward Webber, and shortly thereafter Judge Webber hired her as the county's first juvenile officer. She later worked as a liaison between the Bureau of Indian Affairs, Wasco County, and Indians at Celilo

Village during the relocation of families. She collected her paycheck from the BIA while holding meetings in the judge's office. There is some evidence that the county benefited from its connection to Tudor when he was the undersecretary of the Department of the Interior. It is also likely that Mackenzie benefited from her brother's positions and friendship with the Webbers, although she denied that many years later in oral history interviews.[12]

Despite these close informal ties among dam boosters, opponents found room for dissent at initial public hearings and at congressional hearings. The Army Corps typically held preliminary public hearings before passing its recommendations up the chain of command for authorization. At its meetings, the Corps would define a problem (such as the demand for electricity) and then suggest one or more solutions, to gauge public opinion regarding them. The Corps' Portland office held a number of meetings concerning The Dalles Dam, from 1945 to 1949. The district office sponsored a meeting with local Indians to discuss plans for the dam on 25 April 1945 and a second meeting for local non-Indian residents on 22 September 1945. Finally, the Corps held a meeting in Portland in 1949 to record public response to the comprehensive plans for the Columbia River.[13]

The problem with these meetings, according to Mazmanian and Nienaber, "was that the public seldom knew anything about the proposed project or had any concrete ideas about what the Corps should or should not be doing."[14] In addition, the Army Corps proposed no alternative solutions. Thomas Yallup (a Yakama Indian of the Rock Creek band) described one of these meetings, in which "most of the talks made were by the agencies, which seemed to me to be like a group of friends, with a pat on the back—'You might say this,' and so on." He continued: "There was no opposition at the hearing. All the talks were made so as to back one another in regard to the building of The Dalles Dam."[15] Because they opposed the dam, opponents appeared to oppose growth and development.

Following this process of limited public participation, the Portland district of the Army Corps made its recommendations for building the dam to the chief of engineers, who supported the proposal. The Army Corps asked the governors of Oregon and Washington to weigh in with their support for the project and then passed the proposal on to the executive branch. Although President Truman approved The Dalles Dam in 1950, it still needed funding approval from Congress. At this point, proponents and opponents of the project were testifying before Congress about a proposal that had already been approved. This system benefited the tight network of congressmen, regional Corps districts, and local boosters to near exclusion of opponents of the project. According to the Corps' Colonel Howard Sargent Jr., "The traditional way engineers go about planning a public works project leaves little room for the citizen to be heard."[16]

STRANGE BEDFELLOWS: WHITE FISHERS
AND THEIR OPPOSITION TO THE DAM

White fishermen and the agencies that supported them worried that the eight large dams slated for the Columbia River would lead to a severe reduction in fish populations. The U.S. Fish and Wildlife Service, at the behest of the Army Corps, developed a Columbia River fisheries plan in 1949 that focused salmon restoration on the lower Columbia. Because of dam construction, Fish and Wildlife expected a considerable decrease in fish populations on the mid– and upper Columbia River. By addressing the river and its tributaries as a unit, the agency could feasibly argue, as it did before the U.S. House of Representatives in 1951, that dams would not harm Columbia River salmon runs.[17]

In contrast to dam boosters, opponents of the dam were viewed as naysayers complaining about the *possible* negative effects of the project. To combat the glowing assessment of dam development advocated by the Army Corps, the Columbia Basin Fisheries

Development Association prepared its own statement. Its president, William Seufert, a senior partner at the Seufert cannery, warned that the "economic justification of the Dam is open to serious question in the light of the public value of the river." He was referring to the Columbia's commercial and sports fisheries and businesses such as the Seufert cannery. The association focused on the potential impact the dam might have on the fisheries and claimed that the Pacific Northwest was a region with a power surplus, thereby contradicting booster claims that the region faced a power shortage. Seufert warned that the new dams might be obsolete in a few years, when atomic power plants were expected to come online.[18]

The Yakama Nation, Warm Springs, and Umatilla confederated tribes, as well as Indians from Celilo Village, also weighed in against the project, using their experiences with Bonneville Dam to anchor their protests against additional dams on the Columbia. The Yakama Nation subsequently demanded that the federal government investigate relocating the dam in order to preserve the fishery at Celilo Falls.[19]

The initial 1945 public meeting set the tone for later arguments for and against the proposed Dalles dam. Apart from the Army Corps's later inclusion of cold war rhetoric, the agency's arguments did not change significantly. As the 24 September 1945 *Oregonian* article suggests, support or opposition to the dam was largely contingent on how closely one depended on the fisheries. Whereas the proponents of the dam seemed unified in their support, those who fought the project were often divided. The most significant division among opponents was between Indian and non-Indian fishers who competed for the same dwindling resource. That historically antagonistic relationship, while mitigated somewhat in their shared opposition to the dam, was not easily erased by a mutual enemy. White fishermen objected to The Dalles Dam almost solely on economic grounds: the dam would eliminate or greatly curtail their ability to make a living by reducing fish populations. Indians and their supporters used several arguments to oppose the dam, only one of which was economic. Beside the loss of livelihood, Indians and their white supporters viewed the project as a direct threat to Indian treaty rights as well as a threat to Columbia River Indian cultures.

Most people in the Pacific Northwest and around the nation supported the development of the nation's river systems. Even those who opposed The Dalles Dam did not object to the general idea of building dams. Instead, opposition rested on two issues: long-standing arguments about who would benefit from the resources of the Pacific Northwest, and a challenge to the spirit of American democracy. Protesters who claimed that dams destroyed salmon runs did not root their opposition in environmental values that would become popular in subsequent decades. Instead, fishermen claimed, in an effort to preserve the runs for use by commercial and sports fishermen, that the dams would destroy salmon runs. Likewise, social justice protesters who addressed their concerns about The Dalles Dam to their congressmen were less concerned with the environmental effects of development than with destroying a traditional Native fishing site and thus abrogating treaties. These protesters asked that the United States uphold the highest standards in honoring the sanctity of its word as an example for other nations during the cold war.[20]

White fishermen opposed river development on two fronts. Both Indian and white fishers united in their dislike for river development that threatened the fish runs of the mid-Columbia (even if those losses could be mitigated by bolstering the fish populations of the lower river). At the same time, white fishermen also disliked the competition they faced from Indian fishermen, and some of them simultaneously protested any actions that furthered the rights of Indian fishermen at Celilo Falls.[21]

Like Indian fishers, white fishermen viewed The Dalles Dam as one part of a larger system of dams that would slowly destroy the Columbia River fishery. They often pointed to the effects the Bonneville Dam had had on fish populations, claiming that it eliminated "90 per cent of the Upper Columbia River fisheries from Bonneville to Big Eddy."[22] White fishers feared that Oregon and Washington agencies would close commercial fishing for a stretch of fifty miles above Bonneville Dam on completion of The Dalles Dam (as the agencies had recommended in a report to Congress).[23] When Robert Jones, Oregon's commissioner of the fisheries, agreed to file a protest against The Dalles Dam, he also "expressed the opinion that such a dam might not possibly be as destructive to fish life as are the Indians" at Celilo.[24] Nearly a year later, the same agency went on record opposing The Dalles Dam and the establishment of a reservation at Celilo Falls, fearing that the latter would strengthen Indian fishing rights.[25]

These actions clearly indicate that the Oregon Fish Commission did not consider Indians among their citizen constituents. In this view, river development and Indian fishermen threatened the ability of white fishermen to use the river. Representatives of the state fisheries agencies and the U.S. Army Corps of Engineers repeated this assumption in congressional hearings, as did the media in its coverage of the dam construction. In retrospect, it is surprising that Indian fishing would be labeled a more significant threat to the survival of salmon than a concrete barrier that would funnel the fish through ladders on their way upriver and through turbines on their way to sea and that would generally slow and warm the river. Jones's 1946 statement reflects the long-standing animosity between the state regulatory bodies and Native fishers in Oregon and Washington.

There is some evidence that all white fishermen did not view Indian fishers as a dire threat to their own livelihoods. In a formal protest against The Dalles Dam submitted to the Army Corps of Engineers at the September 1945 meeting, the Columbia Basin Fisheries Development Association cited the destruction of the treaty-protected Native fishery as one of the many reasons the dam should not be built. The association also pointed to the promise of alternative energy, challenged the navigationists' claim that the dam was necessary for improved transportation, and cited the value of Celilo Falls as a tourist attraction. The organization's submission mentioned the rights of Native fishermen only on the final page of its twenty-eight-page packet:

> A dam which cost the people of the United States a hundred millions to construct, cost the Nation its integrity in the breaking of an unmistakably clear commitment to a racial minority, a dam which the rapid progress of science rendered obsolete within a short time after its construction when the salmon industry and the natural grandeur of Celilo Falls had been irrecoverably lost— such a dam would indeed contribute little either to the social or economic progress of this region.[26]

The location of this argument suggests that the association employed all of the available grounds for opposing the dam and used Indian rights as a rhetorical tool rather than as an indication of actual support. In his 1951 congressional testimony, Nez Perce James Blackeagle complained that non-Indian fishers "below Bonneville, around Astoria, are somewhat perturbed over these things, and they exploit the Indian to put him in front to protect the industry."[27]

Some of the alliances between Indian fishers and the broader industry are confirmed by the history of the Seufert cannery. The proposed dam threatened both the Seuferts and the Indians who fished near the cannery, prompting Francis Seufert and William Seufert to meet with C. G. Davis, the BIA employee at The Dalles in 1945. In an effort to join the BIA and Indian fishermen in their opposition to the dam, Francis Seufert told Davis that opposition among white fishermen and businessmen in The Dalles was growing.[28] In a letter to Senator Wayne Morse that same year, Seufert reminded the senator that flooding Celilo Falls would "deprive the tribesmen of an age-old fishing place," which would be "in violation of a solemn treaty and unconstitutional."[29] This was a dramatic turnabout in attitude. Richard Grace, the Army Corps's land appraiser, warned E. W. Barnes in the Portland District Office that "after years of quarreling with the Indians, [Francis Seufert] is now advising them as to the value of their fishing rights."[30] Seufert also sent Jasper Elliott, BIA superintendent at the Warm Springs Agency, a copy of his brief opposing the dam.[31] In his 1980 memoir, Seufert continued to draw parallels between his family and the Indians who fished at Celilo when he explained that "the government, in paying the Indians for destroying their fishing sites at Celilo, was doing no more for the Indians than the United States government did for Seufert's when they bought Seufert's shore lands that were flooded out by The Dalles Dam pool."[32]

There is no evidence that any group of Indians believed they were allied with the Seuferts. As did the Columbia Basin Fisheries Development Association, it appears that Francis Seufert put aside old animosities with his Indian neighbors, knowing that the issue of Indian fishing rights would be the biggest obstacle to the construction of the dam. As canners rather than fishermen, the Seuferts were never in direct competition with Indian fishers and therefore could perhaps risk an alliance with the Yakama, Umatilla, and Warm Springs Indians. In contrast, white fishermen could not do so as easily.

TESTIMONY BEFORE THE HOUSE AND SENATE APPROPRIATIONS COMMITTEES

The potential kilowatts of the Columbia River's hydropower rested "like sleeping giants, awaiting only the summons of man to rouse them from their river beds to the Herculean task of all-out production," according to Herbert West, whose overblown language matched his enthusiasm for river development. The executive vice president of the Inland Empire Waterways Association warned the congressional appropriations committee in 1951 that the United States faced a potentially devastating power shortage as it battled international cold war enemies. A strong industrial economy, he argued, would prevent the spread of communism at home. He described without equivocation the benefits that Columbia and Snake River dams would bring: increased industrial and agricultural output; an uninterrupted power supply for Pacific Northwest cities, farms, and defense installations; and the potential to manufacture energy-intensive and militarily significant materials such as titanium. When he was questioned about the impact of river development on fish populations, West described an imperfect science that produced contradictory conclusions. He reminded congressional leaders that salmon stocks had been in decline for more than fifty years and that "you have the inroads of industry and stream pollution, and that has also created that particular problem." The dams, in his view, would be only one influence among many in the decline of salmon populations; the industries they supported would harm fish as well. Although the science that supported development was infallible, West contended, the science that described negative impact was questionable and possibly unreliable. West likely saw no irony in his logic and quickly moved away from the discussion of the "fish controversy" that surround The Dalles and others dams.[33]

The day after West's testimony, William Minthorne of the Confederated Tribes of the Umatilla Reservation spoke to the same committee. Congressman Louis Rabaut of Michigan mistakenly asked, "I suppose you are in favor of building the dam?"[34] Minthorne corrected the committee members and described why the Umatillas opposed the dam. Unlike boosters such as Herbert West, Minthorne had come to Washington, D.C., to talk about fish, tradition, treaty rights, and the obligations the most powerful country in the world had toward Indian tribes. Appropriations hearings from 1951 and 1952 illuminate what was essentially the culture clash of Indian and non-Indian perceptions of the river.

Although Congress had appropriated some funds for building the dam, 1951 and 1952 were seminal years because of the level of Native protest. As a consequence, Congress threatened to halt construction until the Army Corps of Engineers negotiated a settlement with Indians who would lose their fishing sites. Non-Indian witnesses, like most residents of The Dalles, extolled the benefits of development, whereas Indian witnesses warned of the cultural and environmental costs of the project. Questions and comments from the congressional committee, overly imbued with the ideals of progress, reflect a nation grappling with the indirect costs of development, generally misunderstanding the issues at stake for Native people.

The hearings before the House of Representatives appropriations committee in 1951 and 1952 reveal the ways in which the Army Corps justified the development of The Dalles Dam as part of a hydropower network in a national defense system. According to one witness, The Dalles Dam was vital to supplying the nation with energy to produce much-needed defense materials such as magnesium, aluminum, steel, and titanium. The Army Corps argued in 1951 that the additional power generated by new dams was necessary if the defense industry was to meet the needs of the nation in the cold war. The Corps appealed to congressional authority to address the issue of treaty rights, concluding that "where we infringe on the rights of Indians or any other people, those negotiations will be effected either by ourselves or through congressional action."[35] This statement suggests that the Corps did not consider Indian treaty rights any different from the rights of non-Native citizens. This attitude was in keeping with the congressional policies of termination. However, several Congressional representatives felt that the Army Corps did not treat Native and non-Native interests equally, pointing out that the Corps dealt with non-Indian interests more expeditiously than it had Indians'.

JUSTIFYING THE COST OF DEVELOPMENT

Most Pacific Northwesterners were enthusiastic about river development, and people who questioned the pace or scope of Columbia River development had little effect. Ultimately, the federal government did not have to negotiate the terms of development with the citizens of the region. Even if local residents had questioned development, "the project itself contain[ed] no requirement for local cooperation" because the city of The Dalles did not lie in the path of the reservoir.[36] The Army Corps had to justify only the expense of river development to often-friendly congressional committees that wanted to determine the national benefits of regional projects.

While the Army Corps justified its work to Congress in 1951 and 1952, representatives from Yakama, Umatilla, Warm Springs, and Nez Perce confederated tribes testified that the proposed Dalles Dam would rob them of their fishing sites. Because treaties reserved traditional sites at Celilo for Indians, the federal government had to negotiate the terms of the federal "taking" of those sites, preferably prior to the onset of construction of The Dalles Dam. As a result, Indian fishing rights became an issue during the appropriations hearings at the beginning of the 1950s.[37]

When the Army Corps of Engineers testified before the congressional appropriations committees in the early 1950s, it argued that hydroelectric dams would provide a competitive edge in the cold war. Witnesses supporting The Dalles Dam pointed to the significance of hydroelectricity in winning World War II: "How this great giant of the West rose to the task and delivered constitutes one of the brightest pages in our Nation's history," claimed one booster.[38] If the United States was to win the war against communism, the nation needed the hydropower of one of its most powerful rivers.

The Korean War (1950–52), the first of the cold-war conflicts, galvanized the prodam rhetoric. The testimony of the Army Corps, Oregon Representative Lowell Stockman, and the Inland Empire Waterways Association intertwined neatly, providing a clear example of what Daniel Mazmanian and Jeanne Nienaber call "political accommodations" among the groups supporting development.[39]

Herbert West of the Inland Empire Waterways Association warned that "our nation is faced with an emergency of almost global proportions . . . the national defense of our country, and the economy of the Pacific Northwest is [sic] now being threatened through the shortages of electrical energy in a district where potential hydroelectric power is the greatest in the Nation."[40] The Army Corps echoed West's sentiments in 1951, reporting that "substantial amounts of additional power are needed to meet the increasing requirements of defense industries . . . at the lowest possible cost."[41] Congressman Stockman told the committee that "The Dalles project will make a large amount of low-cost power available at a location close to major load centers and defense industries and is an essential unit in present plans for overcoming the existing power shortage in the Northwest."[42] Charles Baker, president of the Inland Empire Waterways Association, warned Congress that "the demands of national defense, in trying to avert World War III, make this program imperative."[43]

The Army Corps used the cold war and national-defense needs to shore up its arguments in support of Pacific Northwest dams; these requirements would far outweigh the costs to the region's fisheries or to area Indians. By 1951, the Army Corps had spent $800,000 on the project, mostly on exploratory drilling; it would ask for more than an additional $326 million over the next decade. Colonel W. H. Potter went before the subcommittee in April 1951, asking Congress to appropriate an initial $18 million so that the Army Corps could commence actual construction of The Dalles Dam in 1953. Potter assured the committee that he did "not think that there is any group in the Nation that is more anxious about maintaining the present fishing capability on the Columbia River than the Corps of Engineers."[44]

Later in the month, Dr. Lloyd Meehan of the U.S. Fish and Wildlife Service went before Congress to explain how the Department of the Interior intended to develop the Columbia River *and* save its salmon populations. According to Meehan, the agency would concentrate its efforts on the lower Columbia, thereby compensating for the losses bound to occur in the mid- and upper Columbia because of dam building. Meehan was able to allege that the dams would not cause "any major losses" to the commercial fisheries only by viewing the Columbia and its tributaries as a system. In Meehan's words, "The maximum increase of populations in the lower river streams will compensate in part for the anticipated loss of the valuable middle and upper river populations."[45]

Congressional members did not debate dam building on the basis that it would be detrimental to the mid- and upper river fisheries, but they were concerned when Colonel Potter revealed that "the cost of negotiations" with local Indians had "not been included in the cost estimate" the Army Corps submitted to Congress.[46] It was one thing to claim that fish declines could be mitigated by relocation of populations and hatcheries; it was quite another not to have even estimated the price of settlement with the region's Indians for the loss of their fishing grounds. Like Fish and Wildlife's plans to save salmon, this settlement could prove expensive, which would make it impossible, in the words of U.S. Representative Christopher McGrath of New York, to "determine the total cost of this project."[47]

Assistant Secretary of the Department of the Interior William Warne's cavalier attitude concerning the Indian treaty fishing rights at Celilo also worried members of the committee. Warne initially assured Congress that the department had "carefully considered the effect of the construction of The Dalles Dam on the Indian fisheries at Celilo Falls," but added that "provisions . . . to compensate these Indians" would be made "at the proper time."[48] This prompted Michigan Representative Louis Rabaut to ask when might be a proper time for the Department of the Interior to negotiate provisions. In an eloquent speech on behalf of Indian compensation, Rabaut asked, "How would we get along with the railroads if we said in proper time we will take care of this relocation, or if we said to a State in proper time we will take care of this highway, or in proper time we will do something about clearing this area or some other matter?"[49] Congressman John Kerr of North Carolina joined Rabaut in asserting that the Corps would have to settle with the local Indians quickly in order to do justice by them. Representative Glenn Davis of Wisconsin reminded Warne that the nation was "moving in on land which is a very sacred thing to these people."[50]

The Army Corps admitted in 1951 that although it had given "considerable thought" to the issue of compensation, nothing had "yet been negotiated" with the Indians.[51] The House committee found that lapse unacceptable by 1952 and demanded that the Corps take steps to settle with the affected Indians. The agency immediately began negotiating with the Yakama, Warm Springs, Umatilla, and Nez Perce. In this way, Indians successfully used the opportunity to testify before Congress to promote one of their objectives: compensation.

TRIBAL TESTIMONY

Indian fishing rights and protection of the fishery were both obstacles to the allocation of construction funds. The U.S. Army Corps's proposal to construct a dam eight miles downriver from Celilo threatened to destroy the falls, to endanger salmon, and to abrogate one of the key components embodied in federal treaties: traditional off-reservation sites commonly understood as "usual and accustomed places." The federal government did not protect fishing sites during the dam-building spree between the 1930s and the 1960s, and the loss of those sites forced Indians and whites to reconsider the Native fishery and how it should be protected in the future. The tribal councils of the Yakama, Umatilla, Warm Springs, and Nez Perce, as well as the Celilo Fish Committee, passed annual resolutions beginning in 1945 to protest the loss of the falls.

Indians argued that their needs deserved consideration on two levels. First, Indians argued that the United States had a legal obligation to uphold its treaties. Tribal testimony before Congress always began with a careful reiteration of treaty negotiations and the rights Native people reserved for themselves with them. The Yakamas pleaded, "Let it be known that this great United States lives up to its promises."[52] After stating that they were "violently" opposed to all dam construction in the Columbia-Snake river system, the Nez Perce delegation claimed that "the United States government in its treaty with our tribe is legally bound to protect these rights."[53]

Second, the record of Native people within the military and war industries during World War II had earned them consideration equal to that of non-Native citizens. Indians had registered for the draft during World War II at a higher percentage than any other racial or ethnic group in the United States. In addition, Native men frequently enlisted rather than wait for the draft. Because Indians had established citizenship through military and war-related service, the federal government should not ask them to once again forego treaty-derived benefits for a "greater good." This argument, which carried considerable clout, is reflected in a recent interview with Louis Pitt, a Warm Springs enrollee who linked the World War II fight for freedom from totalitarianism to the contemporary struggle for treaty rights.[54] Historian Kenneth Townsend writes, "The extent of patriotism among

Native Americans was impressive," with nearly total compliance with the draft across the country.[55] Townsend suggests a number of reasons why Native men responded to the call to service, including a desire to prevent a *second* conquest. Although Indians in the Pacific Northwest had relinquished most of their land holdings in the nineteenth century, the land was "ceded" territory and continued to represent a homeland that required protection. The Army Corps addressed this peripherally by suggesting that the Columbia River had proven *itself* in time of war and that the federal government could use its power potential even more heavily in the postwar era.

The first tribal group to testify before the committee was the Yakamas, represented by Thomas Yallup, Alex Saluskin, Eagle Seelatsee, Watson Totus, and tribal attorney Kenneth Simmons. The Yakama delegation submitted a prepared statement that claimed that the "United States must foot the bill and compensate the Yakima Tribe for property taken by the United States."[56] Despite the request for compensation, the Kah-Milt-Pah, one of the fourteen bands that comprised the Yakama Nation, submitted a tribal resolution stating that "the mere substitution of a monetary settlement" would not be adequate compensation because "money is easily spent and will become exhausted, whereas our fishery provides means of livelihood for us year after year without interruption."[57]

Thomas Yallup addressed the religious importance of Celilo Falls to the area's local Indian population. "Fishing at the falls water is held sacred to the Indians," according to Yallup, who described Celilo as a site where Indians caught "sacred fish" for "their customary religious practices, which have been practiced for centuries and are protected now." Congressman Rabaut asked if another site on the river could substitute for Celilo Falls, perhaps misunderstanding that the site was as sacred as the salmon. When Yallup responded that an alternate site "would not be a substitute to our beliefs," Rabaut retorted that "they would be the same salmon." Yallup carefully stated that "[I] should be talking to you through an interpreter, but I am doing the best I can, and I hope you people will understand."[58] Yallup then returned to the argument that Celilo Falls was a revered site that ought to be protected as such:

> The Christian people of the States of Oregon and Washington have recognized our holding the [salmon] ceremony for each year, and throughout the country I believe that the other religions, including the Christian religion, have also backed us up in asking the Government not to take a sacred place, a place that is held sacred by the Indians.[59]

Even while Thomas Yallup entered into the record the centrality of the notion of the spirituality of Celilo Falls, Indians fought against the rhetoric of progress, the fish-versus-hydropower values promoted by the Army Corps and Congress. In their effort to assess the monetary costs of the dam, Corps employees neglected the cultural costs of their project, a strategy that made it simpler for the government to determine a figure for compensation by reducing the value of the falls to the number of fish caught. By not incorporating the spiritual value of the site into a compensation package, however, the Army Corps left open whether its settlement was equal to the spiritual value of the falls.

The following day, William Minthorne and Ed Forest Jr. of the Umatilla Reservation raised the issue of national defense and its connection to river development. Minthorne, a veteran of World War II, assured the congressmen that "we, too, believe in national defense." Like other Indian leaders in a variety of venues, Minthorne argued that the patriotic duty performed by Indians during World War II should secure for them treaty rights in the postwar world. He reminded his listeners that "our sons made fine records as soldiers in World War II, and many of us worked in shipyards or ordnance depots. But we do not know that it is necessary for national defense to destroy our centuries-old salmon fishery at Celilo."[60] Ed Forest suggested that "the moment for making the decision [to fund The Dalles Dam] has come at a very inopportune time, as it may do an injustice to our people because of the pressure brought on by world conditions."[61]

Tribal leaders were forced to take a defensive stance in their opposition to the Corps's insistence that the dams were needed to win the cold war. However, it was an argument that relied entirely on the sympathies of the congressmen before whom they spoke. It also relied on the ability of those congressmen to imagine the significance to a small population of Indians of an area the legislators had never seen. T. Leland Brown, tribal attorney for the Warm Springs confederated tribes, assured the congressional committee that "the Indian does not want to do anything to injure the national defense." He then asked what would be a reasonable request for "an adequate compensation for the loss of their fishery."[62]

After Representative Rabaut congratulated William Minthorne on a "very good statement," Minthorne's testimony concluded with a fascinating exchange between the Umatillas and committee members. Committee chairman Representative John Kerr of North Carolina asked Minthorne where he had been educated. Minthorne responded, "I have been educated in government reservation schools and graduated from Haskell Institute. I am an ex-serviceman, with an overseas record. I am now going to Gonzaga University in Spokane, Washington." When Representative McGrath inquired about Minthorne's subject major, the Umatilla responded impatiently: "Civil engineering. But that is hardly important." He proceeded to redirect the exchange back to larger and less-personal Native issues. After a few questions, Representative Gerald Ford complimented Minthorne, saying, "In my estimation you have made a most sincere statement, and I think a statement with the deepest feeling of most any witness we have had before us."[63]

Because the transcript cannot convey the tenor of the exchange, it is impossible to know with certainty whether it smacked of paternalism. What is evident is that no other witness was singled out for such probing questions or unusual compliments. The committee seemed to dismiss the Warm Springs delegation later in the day when Representative Rabaut asked for their prepared statement and a brief verbal description. Attorney T. Leland Brown responded that the delegation had "come a long way, and would like to have a little time. It is a very important matter to us."[64]

At the hearing described above, most Indian witnesses vacillated between asking for adequate compensation (which remained undefined) and claiming, as Watson Totus did, that "no compensation could be made which would benefit my future generations, the people still to come."[65] The problem tribal leaders encountered was how to simultaneously demand that Congress save Celilo Falls *or*, in the face of rising uncertainty, ask for proper compensation. This was especially true as witnesses argued that because of Celilo Falls' spiritual and cultural significance, the federal government could never sufficiently reimburse Indians for the losses they would experience if the Corps built The Dalles Dam.

Although each of the tribal groups affected by the proposed inundation of Celilo incurred the expense of a trip to Washington, D.C., in 1951 to speak before Congress, the Yakamas were the only group to send representatives the next year. Alex Saluskin, Eagle Seelatsee, Thomas Yallup, and Watson Totus once again made the journey to the nation's capital, bringing with them fish biologist F. A. Davidson and their new attorney, Paul Niebell.[66] Davidson spent much of the time arguing that there was no real energy shortage in the Pacific Northwest. He pointed to the number of generators at preexisting dams that were not in use and to a report released by the Atomic Energy Commission that claimed nuclear energy would replace hydroelectricity within fifty years. Davidson also claimed that funds earmarked for Columbia River dams might be better spent fighting communism: "The materials that would go into The Dalles and some of the other dams in the Columbia River might well be used by our Armed Forces to save [the] lives of our men fighting in Korea."[67] Finally, Davidson pleaded with Congress to save Celilo Falls as a national monument in order to uphold the treaties between the U.S. government and Indian nations and to save the river's salmon.[68]

THE ARMY CORPS'S RESPONSE

When congressional representatives asked Assistant Secretary of the Interior William Warne and Army Corps of Engineers Colonel Potter about these issues, both suggested that the Corps and the Department of the Interior were concerned about the problems but that these problems would not impede development. Warne suggested to the subcommittee, "There comes a point where you must determine as to how the river is going to be used."[69] For his part, Potter argued that the proposed dam would "interpose no more obstruction to the passage [of salmon] than will the Bonneville Dam."[70] Moreover, it would *remove* a major impediment to the upstream passage of salmon at Celilo Falls. Both men even suggested that the dam would be beneficial to the salmon runs and to local Indians.[71]

William Warne compared the development of The Dalles Dam to Grand Coulee Dam. Indians lost their fishery at Kettle Falls in eastern Washington but successfully negotiated for fishing rights in Lake Roosevelt behind the dam. Ignoring the cultural significance of Celilo Falls (or Kettle Falls), Warne told the congressmen that "the existence of the lake there and access to it and the ability of the Indians to use the reservoir may be worth a great deal more to them, from the economic standpoint, than the rights at Kettle Falls to take a few fish."[72] Supporters, therefore, imagined the dam as an environmental and economic improvement even for salmon populations and the Indians who relied on them.

THE DECISION TO FUND THE DAM

Although congressmen such as Louis Rabaut raised concerns about the disadvantages of river development, the arguments of the Army Corps and the Department of the Interior eventually persuaded Congress to allocate money for The Dalles Dam, but not until the Corps compensated the tribes for the fishing stations that would be lost. Even more influential than the proponents' rhetoric was the list of contracts negotiated by the Army Corps of Engineers for drilling, concrete, steel, excavation work, and office space. Colonel Potter stated that the Corps had invested about $800,000 on The Dalles site up to 1951, but the actual expenditure on the proposed dam was likely much higher. The dam had been under development, at least on paper, since 1928. Furthermore, the momentum toward final construction was enormous and very powerful. Opponents of the dam had to persuasively argue that construction was more destructive than beneficial, a nearly impossible task in 1951 and 1952.[73]

Even so, Representative Rabaut's statement cited at the beginning of this chapter points to the ambivalence among some congressional leaders about the costs of river development. Although there is no indication that Congress might have opposed funding The Dalles Dam, the evidence suggests that lawmakers wanted to force the Army Corps to speed negotiations with local Indians. At the same time, congressmen were concerned that the region's fisheries would not survive intensive development and that Indians such as Alex Saluskin and Watson Totus continued to pay for white incursions into their homelands. Most problematic was the way the Army Corps and Congress measured dissent. It was a system that recorded opposition but, as environmentalists would argue in later years, did not incorporate dissent into the decision-making process. After the onset of construction, protests continued. The section that follows examines the last-ditch efforts to save Celilo Falls.

Until the spring of 1953, white protests against The Dalles Dam were limited primarily to those affiliated with the fishing industry. But during the spring and summer of 1953, people as far away as Minnesota and Texas wrote letters to congressional representatives, Secretary of the Interior Douglas McKay, and President Eisenhower opposing The Dalles Dam. What provoked these letters remains unclear, but the campaigns probably stemmed from events just prior to the summer of 1953. Some of the letters were clearly part of a campaign to encourage the U.S. Senate to follow the House of Representatives, which had denied an Army Corps request for $18 million for The Dalles Dam until the agency negotiated a settlement with Indians.

When the House and Senate eventually granted the funds for the dam in early 1953, Yakama Indians requested, in an attempt to save Celilo Falls, that Congress consider relocating the dam to the mouth of the Deschutes River (thirteen miles upriver from its original location). Thomas Yallup's challenge that the dam be relocated "at some other place, rather than destroy the place which we have held sacred,"[74] was never fully considered by the Corps or Congress. White fishermen adamantly opposed a move that would preserve Indian fishing rights but still limit their own ability to harvest salmon. Conversely, white friends of the Indians from across the country supported the Yakama's relocation efforts.

Regional civic and religious groups used the relocation request as an opportunity to shape the treatment of Indians in the Pacific Northwest. Declaring that "it is only through such charitable-minded organizations as The Women's Forum . . . that [the Indian] side of the question can be given to the public," Gertrude Jensen headed the Save the Columbia Gorge Committee, which supported the relocation of the dam.[75] Members of the Women's Forum hoped to make Celilo Falls a national monument and the

Columbia Gorge a national parkway. Jensen went to Washington, D.C., in February 1953 to meet with congressional representatives on behalf of the Indians (though it is not clear whether she had tribal permission to do so). In addition, Charles Castner, whose association with the Women's Forum remains unclear, wrote a flyer titled "Help Save Celilo Falls," asserting that the "people of Oregon do not want the dam built at The Dalles." Castner claimed that 70 percent of Oregonians agreed that the dam should be relocated. He concluded by asking concerned citizens to write to President Eisenhower: "Every letter is a voice calling for justice."[76]

Nothing did more to publicize the potential for relocation, however, than an article published in the April 1953 issue of the *Christian Century* magazine, a nondenominational Protestant weekly. The headline asked, "Are Indian Rights Again Being Betrayed?" and introduced readers to the Reverend Malcolm Norment of the Yakima Indian Christian Mission in White Swan, Washington. According to Norment, relocation of the dam would preserve the rights of Indian fishers "and the power and irrigation interests of the government [would be] equally served" because a dam would still be built in the vicinity.[77] Readers were encouraged to write to Norment for more information regarding relocation and Indian fishing rights. Massachusetts Congressman Angier Goodwin wrote to Secretary of the Interior Douglas McKay in September 1953 complaining that he had received so many letters regarding the construction of The Dalles Dam that he was requesting information on the issue. He explained, "Apparently the letters I am receiving are inspired by an editorial in the *Christian Century*. The point involved seems to be that the government, in going ahead with the project, is breaking faith with the Yakima."[78]

Nearly all of the letters included concerns about the breach of the Yakima treaty, the treatment of minority populations in the United States, what that indicated about the nation's role in the cold war, and the larger scope of injustice toward Indians, including termination policy. Above all, letter writers emphasized the government's breaking a binding treaty. In the words of a respondent from Unadilla, New York, "Our concern . . . is not with compensation to the Indians for losses but for keeping our treaty promises to them."[79] According to protesters, the violation of a treaty would damage the relationships the United States had with friendly nations around the world and would provide fodder for the propaganda machines of its enemies.

More than other commentators on Columbia River development and its effects on Indian fishing rights, letter writers connected the breach of federal Indian treaties with the cold war. One writer warned New York Senator Irving Ives that "we certainly cannot afford to give [the Russians] any true grounds for destroying our reputation throughout the world."[80] Another letter argued that "we, as a free people, should be an example to the rest of the world."[81] Letter writers often suggested that the United States needed to pay special attention to how it treated its minority citizens in this case, because the United States stood as a beacon to oppressed people around the world who carefully watched how the nation treated its own citizens. Moreover, a denial of Indian rights would provide fodder for the enemies of the United States. In this way, writers connected the impact of regional development to international politics, reversed the arguments presented by the Army Corps, and insisted that The Dalles Dam might prevent the United States from successfully fighting the cold war.

Although the cold war provided the political context for these letters, protesters also placed the plight of the Yakama Indians within a larger context of the violation of Indian rights due, in part, to the policy of termination. Sam Hunters wrote Iowa Senator Guy Gillette that "a few years ago it was the Indian group at Ft. Berthold, North Dakota; last week we found that Montana interests were trying to take advantage of the Flathead Indians; recently it was reported that the Navajo Indians have a life span of 20 years in contrast to the white man's 68.4 years. Do we have a national conscience?"[82] It is likely that many letter writers were knowledgeable about and critical of termination policy but, thanks to occasional articles in *Time* and *Life*, also knew that Indian groups often lost land or other resources when river basins were developed.

Life magazine published a short piece in 1946 about the Arikara, Hidatsa, and Mandan who were protesting the Garrison Dam, the key structure in a flood control plan for the Missouri River.[83] The development of the Missouri River basin "caused more damage to Indian land than any other public works project in America," according to historian Michael Lawson, so it was no surprise that Indians in North Dakota, Montana, and Wyoming resisted the massive project.[84] Three years earlier, *Time* magazine printed a short article that explored the resistance of Pueblo Indians in New Mexico to the mapping of a series of dam sites on the Rio Grande by the Army Corps of Engineers. "Indian governor" Don Sanchez led the resistance by denying permits to cross Pueblo land and warned, "We would rather die" than permit the mapping. "After they have killed us they can take our land and do what they want with it."[85] Although the popular press often ridiculed Indian resistance to these public projects by describing Indians in "war paint," traveling on the "war path," and shouting "war whoops," they did publicize a pattern in which Indian resources were destroyed for what was considered the larger good of the western United States. This pattern was not lost on Columbia River Indians or on their white supporters.

FEDERAL AGENCY AGAINST AGENCY: RESISTANCE FROM THE BIA

For many years, the Bureau of Indian Affairs supported Columbia River Indians' protests against The Dalles Dam. The agency cautioned that hasty development on the river could topple the foundation of Indian rights in the Pacific Northwest and lead to the economic dependence of mid–Columbia River Indians. The BIA objected to the Columbia-Snake dams in 1946, claiming that the dams would "destroy the Indian fisheries on the Deschutes, the Yakima, the Klickitat, and other tributaries." BIA Commissioner William Brophy recommended that "the installation of dams which would destroy the fisheries should be postponed until all other sources of low cost power which will not affect the salmon runs have been fully developed."[86] He suggested that the Army Corps commission a survey on the effects of dam building on Native health, noting that salmon comprised a significant part many Indians' diet. In his study of Yakama death records, historian Clifford Trafzer addresses the connection between river development and Indian health. When the federal government funded dams that destroyed fish habitat, it ignored the importance of traditional foods in the Indian diet, with "the ultimate consequences of such actions" being "the ill health of Yakama people."[87]

In *Justice Delayed: A Sixty Year Battle for Indian Fishing Sites,* journalist Roberta Ulrich documents the way in which Indians were "almost an afterthought" in the development of Bonneville Dam.[88] As a result of that experience, both the BIA and its Indian constituents demanded that the protection of Indian fishing rights was central to any further river development. But the early support that the BIA provided the Indians began to erode as both The Dalles project and termination policy proceeded.

Termination policy, which by the early 1950s was popular with Congress, was a reversal of the Indian New Deal of the 1930s. By the late 1920s, the BIA had begun to replace assimilationist assumptions—which had held sway in federal policy since the mid-1800s—with an affirmation of Indian rights to self-government. The *Meriam Report,* published in 1928, symbolized and inspired this new federal policy.[89] The report recorded the poverty in which many Indians lived and listed solutions to the

"Indian problem." It called for the support of education, economic development, protection of Indian lands, settlement of Indian claims against state and federal government, and strengthening Indian governments. As commissioner of the BIA from 1933 to 1945, John Collier attempted to implement these suggestions under the revolutionary "Indian New Deal."[90]

One of the unique characteristics of the BIA under Collier was its reliance on cultural pluralism as its "working philosophy." Collier defended the practice of Indian religions, increased the number of Indians employed by the BIA, affirmed the cultural heritage of Indians (particularly those residing in the Southwest), and worked to extend New Deal legislation to reservations. On the other hand, Collier focused so much of his energy on the Southwest that his administration was slow to recognize the significant Indian fisheries jeopardized by New Deal projects.[91]

The ideological assumptions embedded in Collier's policies were directly attacked by termination policy.[92] Termination required that the federal government relinquish its responsibilities to Indian nations and shift those to state and county governments. Terminationists hoped to dismantle the reservation system and get the federal government "out of the Indian business." Downsizing the Bureau of Indian Affairs left the Portland Area Office unable to respond to threats to Indian fishing rights. The appointment in 1950 of Commissioner Dillon Myer, who was sympathetic to termination policy, meant a shift in policy away from support of treaty rights.[93]

During this same period, the BIA was under attack for abandoning the river Indians. Wilerton Curtis from the University of Missouri wrote to his congressman that what was happening at Celilo Falls was "a sorry story of Federal officials, supposed to represent the Indians' interests, apparently conniving with other white men to defraud their wards." Myer answered curtly that "Mr. Curtis has been misinformed regarding the treatment of Indians at Celilo."[94] The BIA issued a statement claiming that "while the affected Indian tribes were originally opposed to the construction of the dam, objections were withdrawn by all interested parties, except the Yakima Indian Nation, in favor of the national defense aspects of the project."[95] The agency over-simplified a complex decision and the myriad ways in which Indians resisted river development. Although Indian opposition is an important component of the history of The Dalles Dam, those who supported Indian treaties could not compete with the dominate narratives of progress.

4

NARRATIVES OF PROGRESS

Development and Population
Growth at The Dalles

"We have motored past Celilo falls and observed the
tremendous store of potential hydro-electric energy
going to waste here and have remarked to ourselves
that 'some day' it would be developed."

THE DALLES CHRONICLE EDITORIAL, 1933

"To me the dam means a better price for everything
I grow and ship away and for everything I receive."

WASCO COUNTY ORCHARDIST[1]

M en sporting hats that read "Best dam town in the
U.S.A." mingled over a dinner of salmon and cherry
pie at The Dalles Elk Temple in the spring of 1952.
Earlier they had watched as H. B. Elder from the Army Corps of
Engineers orchestrated the first blast in the construction of The
Dalles Dam, a "Hiroshima-like" eruption "of rock and mist . . .
lingering in the sky, as if reluctant to return to earth."[2] The blast
was for show, with the Corps using dynamite along the Washington shoreline for added sound effect to impress the hundreds
of people who gathered to watch this first step in permanently
altering the river environment. Parades and banquets accompanied dam building just above The Dalles, celebrating the per-

sistence of local developers and politicians who were optimistic about the effects of river development on the local community. Dignitaries from Portland, surrounding towns, and the Corps periodically flocked to the town to praise local leadership and to extol the benefits of a managed river.

The Dalles *Chronicle* and the Chamber of Commerce were the two major dam boosters in The Dalles. Members of the Chamber of Commerce represented the business community in both public and private meetings with the federal government, compiled reports about the city, and met with other organizations to orchestrate river development. While the Chamber of Commerce sponsored banquets and parades, The Dalles *Chronicle* saw the changes as evidence of modernity and growth. The newspaper did its utmost to shape how those events were interpreted by The Dalles residents. Reporters and editorial staff lent cohesion to the massive changes associated with dam construction; the newspaper also pointed with pride to a new county bridge and a Harvey Aluminum plant with a boosterism reminiscent of the nineteenth century. Growth symbolized progress. At every opportunity, leaders in The Dalles represented the community as the very epitome of a modern American town on the verge of tremendous economic expansion.[3]

In the narratives presented by The Dalles *Chronicle* and the Chamber of Commerce, growth and development were orderly, measured by their cost effectiveness; furthermore, orderly development, facilitated by trusted community leaders in concert with the federal government, was good for The Dalles. Extant records reveal that the physical transformation of the town was a central objective. The social transformation of the community—with the huge influx of new workers and the visible influence of the federal government—warranted fewer comments. What historical records do not reveal is how ordinary people responded to the rapid transformation of their community.

The narratives of The Dalles *Chronicle* and the Chamber of

Commerce present development in its most positive light, smoothing over pressures and conflict. The one exception is the newspaper's treatment of one of the town's most pressing concerns: who would pay for the effects of growth—new teachers, affordable housing, and the building of a new county bridge. Simultaneous with the celebrations was a growing concern over the tenor and cost of growth, as well as tensions between federal and local control. The city's leaders looked beyond temporary growth—represented by Quonset huts, trailer parks, and transient dam workers—to permanent development represented by new residents, new buildings, and new housing. This comprised the primary conflict between local governmental representatives and boosters, plus a federal government that wanted to consider growth in The Dalles as temporary and manage it with short-term solutions.

W. S. Nelson, manager of The Dalles Chamber of Commerce since 1925, was one of the leading proponents for development.[4] Nelson joined forces with men such as Ward Webber, former owner of a dry-cleaning business who served as president of the Chamber of Commerce for four terms before being appointed to the Wasco County judgeship in 1948.[5] These were men who, in the words of Webber, believed that "the dam is the greatest thing ever to happen to The Dalles."[6]

The celebration of the first construction blast was the culmination of nearly two decades of lobbying by Nelson. A "short, graying, rather rotund and raspy-voiced" man who was born in La Grande and came to The Dalles in 1913, Nelson energetically pursued the dam with statistical details, compiling fact-filled reports about The Dalles, river and railroad traffic, and industry and labor potential.[7] He courted other chambers in small river towns in Washington and Idaho, partnered with the Inland Empire Waterways Association, and helped found The Dalles Industrial Club. The city commended his dogged pursuit of the dam by naming him Man of the Year in 1952, announcing that

Nelson "did the most locally to bring the project to reality."[8] The Bonneville Power Administration claimed that the "information [Nelson] gave us was so thorough and complete that we used it as a model for other communities."[9] In meetings with the Army Corps of Engineers, in congressional hearings in Washington, D.C., and through his official position as manager of the Chamber of Commerce, Nelson helped to shape the public narrative of The Dalles as "the best dam town in the U.S.A."

The constructed narrative followed two main themes: that mid–Columbia River development was part of the effort to control the entire river system, and that those efforts would benefit future generations. Both arguments alleged that the benefits of the dam would be far-reaching geographically and temporally, justifying the costly federal project near a population center that, at its height during this period, did not surpass a population of 12,000. It was a narrative that downplayed the effects of construction as citizens endured traffic congestion, filled-to-capacity classrooms, and housing shortages. Federal-state cooperation in municipal planning had its roots in the Great Depression, but because dam construction followed World War II, the community's response to dam-related growth reflected the strategies of communities that had earlier experienced wartime upheaval. Federal solutions to local problems also paralleled World War II–era responses to shortages and problems endemic to communities earlier transformed by munitions factories and shipyards. As the nation became embroiled in the cold war, the wartime framework that gave shape to change in The Dalles took on even more importance, as did the dam project itself.[10]

While positioning The Dalles as the only city in the Pacific Northwest with "such a tremendous potential development program ahead of it,"[11] leaders in The Dalles claimed that the dam would benefit all the river communities above it. Taking a page from Corps reports, the Chamber of Commerce claimed that Celilo Falls was the last great obstacle to upriver transportation.

The dam would help to eliminate "sectional advantage, resulting in the advocacy of projects unrelated to and establishing no economic relation with any other development in the region or nation." Not to be confused with local pork-barrel projects, the dam would bring regional and national benefits because it was just one piece—albeit a significant one—in a river *system*.

Boosters argued that the dam would benefit the present generation by providing "men with purpose," a project that would bring men of disparate paths together in a common goal that benefited the entire community. It would also benefit future generations because the "results will not vanish in a day, or a year or a decade."[12] Colonel T. H. Lipscomb of the Army Corps of Engineers promised that "when the workers leave there will be a monument, a million watts of power parked on the edge of your community." The cost-benefit ratio of dams relied on future electricity consumers to move these large public projects from the expense side to the profit side of the ledger. But who would pay for the dam and for how long was not something often addressed.

ASSURING A NORMAL, ORDERLY DEVELOPMENT

The Dalles *Chronicle* printed its largest edition in April 1952, a hefty sixty pages devoted to a town bursting with change. Part news and part boosterism, the edition presents a snapshot of a town undergoing great economic, physical, and social transformation. The "progress edition" was not unique to The Dalles or the *Chronicle*, following as it did in the footsteps of an American booster tradition of a town claiming growth as progress. But in postwar The Dalles, growth was accompanied by city planning. The city participated in what historian Mel Scott refers to as a postwar renaissance of city planning to assure orderly development.[13]

Several days before the progress edition thudded onto the porches of The Dalles subscribers, a radioman named R. L. Wheeler took advantage of a mild spring day to drive through

The Dalles High School Booster Girls celebrate the opening of The Dalles Dam in 1959. National Archives—Pacific Northwest Region.

Washington's Klickitat hills (across the river from The Dalles), where he performed some routine maintenance on a radio antenna. On his way back, he stopped at Connie Jackel's farm on a hunch that the farmhouse sat high enough to receive television reception from stations west of the Cascade Mountains. Located in the Columbia Gorge, The Dalles was blocked from clear television reception by the Klickitat hills. Wheeler had been searching the counties on either side of the river for decent reception and always had his television set in the car with him. When Wheeler switched his set on in the Jackels' living room, the sounds and images of Seattle's KING TV station filled the room.[14]

The comforts and distractions of postwar life rushed into The Dalles area simultaneously, providing the city and its surroundings with economic and social opportunities and threatening to rip at the fabric of the community. Like Wheeler's TV experiments, small towns across the country experimented with city planning after World War II. An overriding issue among The Dalles' leaders was how to manage development and growth so that it enhanced the community. The key to development was to find the proper reception, the balance between rapid growth and regulation. City planning would ensure orderly development at a time of potential crisis. Planning was a response to immediate problems and a way to map out the city's future. The city council spent the majority of its meetings in the 1950s discussing one-way streets through the downtown area, reconfiguring street numbers and names, arranging for the town's first stop lights, and organizing sidewalk construction programs. Planning also drew residents' attention to property values and unrestricted growth. It marked the expansion of local governmental activity at the same time that the federal government's regional planning was inserting its influence into the everyday lives of The Dalles residents.[15]

In March 1951, the city organized The Dalles County Planning Commission; voters approved of the commission in November 1952, providing the group with the necessary muscle to shape city growth.[16] This action was the culmination of a movement toward organized growth, not a movement that would regulate growth. Even before the end of World War II, the city adopted its first building codes and put in place a building permit system that would later allow the county to measure development brought on by dam construction. The city adopted basic land-use zoning in 1948, which it revised in 1951, to prevent the remodeling of older homes into "substandard apartments." Housing was in such high demand by the 1950s that many people performed amateur remodeling jobs, transforming a garage or shed into a makeshift apartment, often without running water. The city wanted to put a stop to this trend in an attempt to keep "shanty towns" and "jungle camps" at bay.[17] Undergirding these trends was the desire to protect property values in what was becoming a small city. Although the passage of zoning laws, housing codes, and traffic regulations was reflected in postwar The Dalles, it easily could have described similar activities of wartime communities across the country. And though part of a national planning trend, The Dalles County Planning Commission was a response to postwar growth in The Dalles.

Although dam construction clearly invited a population boom, it merely accelerated a trend in the postwar development of the Pacific Northwest. Between the end of the war and the beginning of dam construction, The Dalles added a new downtown bank building, a motel, a tuberculosis hospital expansion, and a Safeway. The largest increase in building, however, occurred with the dam and bridge construction, with the period between 1951 and 1953 representing the heaviest residential and commercial construction. Those years heralded a new J. C. Penney store, Woolworth's, Payless, and several heavy-industrial buildings.[18]

Apartments, "a sign of the times," were filled nearly as quickly as they were built.[19] In six years, 450 new housing units pushed the boundaries of the city limits. The state of Oregon estimated that the number of available living units increased by 50 percent between 1953 and 1956, for a total of 1,400 new units.[20] Duplexes and single-story ranch houses filled the bluff behind The Dalles; closer in, "numerous other single residences built in the spacious style of the past century were converted into modern multi-unit apartments." New ranch homes boasted large picture windows to capture "the variety of scenic views made possible by the upward slope of the city from the river."[21]

At the same time that ranch homes updated the city's architecture, there is some evidence that the city's elite were also reconceptualizing what constituted blight. Dam construction brought sixteen trailer camps (twelve of them in Oregon) within a short distance of the project. The trailer homes that dotted the outer limits of The Dalles and housed those unable to find more substantial housing had, according to The Dalles *Chronicle,* "progressed from the unsavory position they once held to a place of respectability."[22] This was a necessary step toward reconciling with federal demands favoring temporary housing for dam workers.

Growth was not relegated to homes and businesses alone. The new population included the wives and children of construction workers, creating a significant demand on area services such as welfare, water, and the educational system. Church congregations expanded and updated their buildings; the U.S. Post Office hired new employees to keep up with the larger volume of mail.[23] Even more pressing was the need for additional fire and police services. New houses were located on the outskirts of town, some distance away from the downtown fire station, a situation that threatened to push The Dalles into a higher insurance rating. A proposed uptown fire station promised to reduce insurance costs by cutting response time. One firefighter used his downtime to painstakingly build an exact replica of the new station based on blueprints the city ordered. The fire department and town leaders waited for the federal government to designate The Dalles a critical defense housing area, thus allowing much of the cost of the new structure to be picked up by the federal government.[24]

Police services were also spread thin, especially in unincorporated areas where the county sheriff and state police were responsible for three counties.[25] The city's police staff was also stretched to its limit. In a request for funds submitted to the federal government, the city complained that its jail was inadequate, because it could accommodate only ten prisoners "at a level which would shock even the most hard-bitten of law enforcement officials." Beds were a cramped five feet long.[26]

At the behest of the city council and spurred by visits from the Federal Bureau of Investigation and the American Hygienic Association, city police embarked on a citywide weekend vice cleanup in 1953, collecting punchboards and payoff pinball machines from restaurants and taverns and closing all three brothels in town.[27] Although Mayor Melvin Davidson described it as a raid "seventy-five years overdue," the city council consulted with businesspeople before issuing its orders so "the whole responsibility wouldn't be on the council."[28] The brothels, raided as recently as 1951, had long been a part of downtown life in The Dalles. However, there was growing concern that an influx of male workers to the area would push vice, long accepted by city fathers, out of control. The mayor conceded that despite the raid, gambling and prostitution would likely be on the rise with the population increase. But in 1954 the state hygiene board declared that vice in The Dalles was "definitely under control and that prostitution did not exist." According to Francis Seufert, madams "relocated around the dam site on the Washington shore and outside of any town" and continued to operate.[29]

Growth was a direct result of the number of families who flocked to The Dalles hoping to find work on the dam. The state of Oregon experienced population growth during the 1950s but at a rate far less than that experienced in The Dalles. The state's growth rate of 2.2 percent could not compare with Wasco County's population growth, which expanded by nearly 25 percent in less than four years (13.4 percent of that growth occurred in a six-month period in 1953). Although considerable growth took place outside The Dalles, nearly 50 percent of Wasco County's population lived in the city. The small town of 7,600 residents exploded to the bustling residence of 11,200 people between 1950 and the end of dam construction in 1957.[30]

Population Figures for The Dalles, Wasco County, and Oregon[31]

	1930	1940	1950	1957
The Dalles	5,883	6,266	7,676	11,250
Wasco County	12,646	13,069	15,552	21,500
Oregon State	953,786	1,089,684	1,521,341	1,768,687 (1960)

Dramatic population growth pushed the limits of city services. The city was quickly running out of room at the garbage dump.[32] Traffic congestion, though mitigated by carpooling dam workers, threatened livability.[33] Summer water shortages in the early 1950s prompted city officials to urge residents to conserve water until the water system could be expanded. Unmetered Dalles residents paid just two dollars a month for water and as a result were "almost in a class by [themselves] when it comes to high consumption."[34] The Dalles residents used one-third more water than their eastern Oregon neighbors. Although most water was used for expansive, lush lawns and for orchard irrigation, much was also wasted in leaking plumbing systems because there was little incentive to repair a dripping faucet.

Bordered by the Columbia River and located atop mountain-fed aquifers, The Dalles did not so much face water shortages as it did an inability to keep up with the costly infrastructure necessary to supply water to new homes. Wells, pumps, reservoirs, and new lines were expensive, and the city estimated that upgrades that quickly became a necessity would not have been needed until 1980 had dam construction not brought on additional population. The city prodded residents to conserve water, and beginning in 1951, it imposed a schedule of alternate lawn-watering days.[35] More urgent was the need for additional teachers and classroom space.

"THERE IS NO FEDERAL SANTA CLAUS"[36]

"Gleaming new schools and larger school districts are the two outstanding signs of progress in education in Wasco County," the Dalles *Chronicle* proclaimed in December 1953.[37] The declaration ignored years of struggle for adequate funding to support new facilities and ever-rising enrollment in the area's school districts. Wasco County faced two district-related challenges simultaneously: huge enrollment increases and a short-lived, intensive process of consolidation as several small districts formed or joined larger ones.[38]

The need for new schools was dire, and anxious school board members warned the public that schools were at full capacity and that students might face double shifts or converted classrooms in local churches.[39] It was clear that construction on the dam, the county bridge, Harvey Aluminum plant, and various road projects increased student enrollment. The Army Corps of Engineers estimated that the dam project alone would increase enrollment by nearly 1,200 students during the period from 1953 to 1957.[40] What was less clear was who would be responsible for incurring the cost of those additional students.

In October 1952, District Twelve faced a record student enrollment, with more than 2,000 students. Nearly half of those students were enrolled in the grade school where the worst squeeze was felt;[41] 40 students enrolled late in the month of September, making it difficult to predict how many students would fill the district's schools. Late enrollment and sharp midyear drops in enrollment reflected the transient nature of construction work. Construction work and consolidation of districts increased enrollment, but school boards had not predicted the increase, relying instead on the projections of the Army Corps of Engineers, which factored in only dam-related increases in enrollment.[42] The projected enrollment continued to increase until the 1955–56 school year, when the Corps anticipated a decline as dam construction wound down.

Two hundred junior high school students squeezed into the high school by 1953[43] (overcrowding was even worse for elementary students because most construction families had young children). The district consistently warned that it would turn to split shifts, Quonset huts, and temporary classrooms in churches to accommodate the additional students, though enrollment apparently never necessitated these measures. Districts clamored for federal funding that would allow them to hire additional teachers, build new schools, and meet their rising operating expenses. District Twelve Superintendent Dave Bates needed only to look upriver to the McNary Dam site and the adjacent towns of Hermiston and Stanfield to see the future for local districts. That future promised a prolonged crunch, ill-supported schools, compromised education for the county's children, increased taxes, and voluminous paperwork as the city district appealed to the federal government for aid.[44]

The district required funding in two essential areas: for new facilities and for operating expenses. Bates and the school board were soon to discover that the federal government would cover operating expenses, but only if the district could verify that school enrollment was up by 10 percent on a daily average (another indication of construction transience) and that the rise was due to dam construction. Once the district met those requirements, it might wait up to a year to actually see federal funding, during which time it simply to had to accommodate too many students with too little funding. Bates warned that bureaucratic red tape would make "obtaining federal aid . . . harder than anyone realizes."[45]

It was even more difficult to qualify for funding for new facilities. The federal government was generally opposed to supporting the construction of permanent facilities, believing that community need would be met by permanent facilities and therefore individual districts should pay for new buildings. Paul Jackson, director of the Federal Security Agency for the Pacific Northwest and Alaska, advised school district leaders that temporary facilities were more likely to be funded, spurring the school board to reluctantly consider Quonset huts rather than "permanent buildings which might be empty 'after the exodus'."[46] The Dalles school board did not relinquish its initial desire for permanent facilities, however. In order to qualify for funding for new buildings, the district would have to exhaust its bonding capacity, requiring county residents to "bear extremely heavy local property tax levies."[47] County voters approved school bonds in 1952 and in 1953,[48] but the board was reluctant to place too much of the burden on the shoulders of local taxpayers. The school board preferred transferring the tax burden to the nation by requesting federal subsidies.

The District Twelve school board proceeded with plans for a new joint elementary and junior high school building, despite concerns about funding new construction. Because The Dalles had little undeveloped land within its city limits, when the district decided on a site for a new school, it exacerbated the local housing shortage. The location of the new school building was a site that the federal government had used for "temporary" housing during World War II. Terrace Gardens, a forty-one-unit building, had become a dilapidated eyesore located on land the school district had loaned to the federal government with the agreement that after the war, the housing would be torn down or relocated and the district could reclaim it for a future school. Regardless of its state of disrepair, the potential housing was coveted by the Corps, as well as by other federal agencies.

In December 1952, the Civil Aeronautics Administration asked the Corps to make three units available for families seeking rental housing in the area. Simultaneously, the city attempted to wrest control over the site from the Corps of Engineers. In response, the San Francisco branch of the federal Housing and Home Finance Agency warned The Dalles that "the Department of Defense takes a very stuffy view of federal ownership and control of housing in critical defense areas being relinquished to local bodies."[49] The Dalles officials countered that the federal government was a poor absentee landlord and that "local authorities are more responsive to the immediate needs for housing and can certainly be relied on for improved standards of maintenance because of the pressure of public opinion."[50]

The federal government challenged the city to consider forming a housing authority to manage the complex. Arguing that cities formed housing authorities to provide low-income housing and to eradicate substandard housing, The Dalles refused to organize a housing authority;[51] the federal government responded by refusing to relinquish rights to the site.[52] Eventually, the Army Corps of Engineers promised the school district that the housing would be removed if voters passed a levy to pay for the construction of a new elementary and junior high school.[53] Voters passed the levy overwhelmingly in May 1953, only to find out that the federal government did not consider the Army Corps of Engineers the agency responsible for the site.[54] The city would now have to work with the Public Housing Administration (PHA) to remove the apartments. The Corps's Portland District engineer, Colonel Lipscomb, publicly vowed not to stand in the way of removal of Terrace Gardens, though in a letter to PHA, Lipscomb warned that the city faced a housing shortage brought on by dam construction and that "it is hoped that . . . the Public Housing Administration can be persuaded to relocate the housing units rather than demolish them."[55] The Corps had employees living in twelve of the units by May 1953.

The events surrounding the Terrace Gardens housing complex and the new elementary–junior high school reflected broader problems The Dalles faced in providing services for a growing number of residents. The various needs of The Dalles would continue to overlap and compete with one other for attention, space, time, and money. Providing homes, jobs, schools, and water services to these new residents taxed, both figuratively and literally, the abilities of The Dalles leadership. These issues propelled city managers into close collaborative relationships with the federal government, sent them searching for information from neighboring cities that had also been transformed by dam-building, prompted them to raise taxes, and significantly increased the amount of paperwork and meeting time necessary to run the city.

THE "PROBLEM COUNCIL"

In addition to the city planning described earlier in this chapter, the city of The Dalles formed a "problem council," which was responsible for tackling the myriad challenges that would arise with the construction of the dam and the county bridge. Appointed early in 1951, the "problem council" provided a liaison between community leaders and the federal government. Some of the most prominent men in The Dalles comprised the "problem council," which made recommendations on behalf of the city and hoped to keep from infringing on federal, state, or county agencies.[56]

In part, the "problem council" was instigated by a meeting that city officials had with Colonel T. H. Lipscomb in December 1951 during which the Army Corps of Engineers committed itself to cooperation with the city (the Army Corps of Engineers referred to the "problem council" as The Dalles Community Council). Lipscomb warned city officials that the dam required a steady stream of "good workers, healthy workers, whose minds are not troubled by worries about conditions under which their families are living."[57] Providing those conditions was the responsibility of the federal government only if the municipality did not step in to bridge the gap between services and demand. But, Lipscomb claimed, the Army Corps was not "coming here to take over The Dalles."

Although Lipscomb proved to be a polite and gracious guest, the city of The Dalles and its representatives were about to be overrun by federal engineers and their crews. Despite the federal agency's promises of cooperation, it was the city, not the federal agency, that was at a disadvantage in the partnership to build the dam. Thus, the "problem council" set out to define just what that cooperation entailed. However, the city's success in constructing new housing, providing for schoolchildren, shoring up the police and fire departments, and supporting other services put the city at a disadvantage when requesting money from the federal government. So too did The Dalles' boosterism and claims of being on the verge of great growth that was only partially a result of the dam. The federal government questioned whether it should fund improvements that would be necessary regardless of dam construction. Federal assistance, it believed, should be limited to increased demand resulting solely from the public project.

Like other affected cities, The Dalles found it difficult to claim that population increase was primarily brought on by the dam. Making matters worse was the fact that the Pacific Northwest had sustained considerable growth during and after World War II. The dam certainly accelerated growth; what was unclear was by how much. Concerned that the city could not meet housing demands, in 1952 the Army Corps urged the Housing and Home Finance Agency to recognize The Dalles as a "critical defense area."[58] After months of lobbying, the housing agency replied that the designation was unnecessary, suggesting that the city acquire trailers no longer needed at the Chief Joseph Dam site.[59] After more wrangling, recognition as a "critical defense area" came in November, opening the way for federal assistance.[60] Reasons for the reversal remain shrouded, but the Democratic National Committee weighed in with its support of the designation just weeks before the Housing and Home Finance Agency awarded the coveted designation.[61]

Echoing Colonel Lipscomb's earlier warning, Wasco County Judge Ward Webber, chairman of the "problem council," pointed out that a lack of adequate housing would be costly to the community and to the Corps, which "could be expressed in high turnover of personnel because of unsatisfactory housing, a deterioration of the caliber of the workers, poor workmanship on the project, and other factors."[62] Those worries proved to be baseless when local contractors leaped at the chance to make a profit in providing housing. The Army Corps of Engineers helped local

builders when it announced in June 1953 that it would not provide temporary housing for construction workers, with the possible exception of trailers. In reversing its earlier plans, the agency
saved between $4 million and $5 million.[63] The "problem council" welcomed this because permanent housing was preferred to
temporary housing, which often quickly became run-down and
was not always "temporary," as evidenced by Terrace Gardens.

RELOCATING THE SITE OF THE NEW COUNTY BRIDGE

As permanent chairman of the "problem council," Wasco County
Judge Ward Webber was integral to the negotiations between the
federal government and the county and city. Webber's biggest
challenge—the relocation of the site for the new county bridge
across the Columbia River—illustrates the limits of cooperation
between the federal government and the county, as well as the
strong relationships forged between representatives of the two
entities. Webber worked closely and sometimes at odds with Army
Corps of Engineers personnel such as Colonel Lipscomb.

In addition, Webber's key advisor during the construction of
the county bridge was its designer, Ralph Tudor. Described as "vig-
orously stocky," Tudor, the son of a railroad engineer, had grown
up in Oregon. In 1919 he had been appointed to West Point, went
on to study engineering at Cornell University, and became the
Portland District Engineer for the Army Corps from 1942 to 1947,
years during which the agency developed plans for the dams on
the Willamette and Columbia Rivers, including The Dalles Dam.
As a private engineer (his firm was called Tudor Engineering),
Tudor assisted Wasco County in its negotiations with his former
employer.[64]

The Oregon Legislature cleared the way for bridge construction in 1949 by passing a bill allowing counties to issue revenue
bonds to support the construction of interstate bridges.[65] This
allowed Wasco County to implement plans for a bridge that had

been in the works since the 1930s. Replacing a privately operated ferry system, the proposed county bridge would link the
Oregon Trail Highway 30 with Washington's Highway 830 to create one continuous north-south route linking the Canadian and
Mexican borders. The Secretary of the Army granted Wasco
County a building permit in 1950, though both parties knew of
plans to build a dam in the area. When Congress allocated funds
for The Dalles Dam in October 1951, construction on the new
bridge was already well underway.[66]

The first indication that the bridge might pose a problem to
the Corps came in February 1951 when Judge Ward Webber
announced that designer Ralph Tudor was conferring with federal engineers. Fearing that water released from the dam's spillway would erode the bridge's piers, the Army Corps of Engineers
asked to meet with the county and Tudor Engineering to discuss
a possible relocation of the structure.[67] While negotiations continued, so too did the construction of the bridge as dozens of
workers poured the cement piers. The Army Corps described talks
with the county as "amicable," but a year later the federal agency
condemned the bridge and offered the county less than half the
funds the county estimated would be necessary to relocate the
structure.[68]

Although Colonel Lipscomb described the condemnation as
"friendly" and "in the interest of the public," Judge Webber
stated that the $890,000 offered by the Corps to relocate the
bridge was inadequate. Declaring that the county was "thor-
oughly disappointed" at the turn of events, Webber asserted that
the federal agency should be obligated to compensate the county
for its loses, an estimated $2 million. The county threatened to
contest the condemnation of the bridge, which was nearly one-
third complete.[69]

To avoid a confrontation, Senator Wayne Morse invited a delegation from Wasco County to meet with the Oregon congressional delegation in Washington, D.C. The delegation included

Oregon District Attorney Donald Heisler, Colonel Ralph Tudor, and Judge Webber, who complained that the county did not "feel that it has received sufficient consideration from the Army Engineers."[70] Pressure from Congress pushed the Corps back to the negotiating table, where the agency offered the county $1,994,600. Judge Webber made it clear that the new offer was not the $2 million that the county hoped for but concluded that "the county may be forced to accept that amount."[71] The local newspaper counted the new offer as a victory for the county.

Ultimately, political pundits and engineers seemed to agree that the $1 million fiasco was a result of neglect and poor planning among agencies rather than the fault of the federal or county government. In an editorial, the *Oregonian* claimed that "it will do little good to try to find a scapegoat" because, although those involved acted with "considerable lack of knowledge and with a complete absence of common purpose," they did act "in good faith."[72] During the negotiations that preceded and followed condemnation of the bridge, there was an element of the agencies being hindered in their relationships with one another not by malice but by legal constrictions. A generous reading of the Army Corps's handling of the condemnation would lead one to conclude that the agency defined its legal obligations to the county as narrowly as possible, arguing that it could compensate the county only for labor rendered, not for the actual cost of relocation (hence the initial $890,000 figure). For its part, the county argued for a broader interpretation of the law. This does not suggest that federal and county governments were enemies of one another. It simply indicates that each agency advocated what was most advantageous to itself. Newspaper coverage of these negotiations was balanced, and apart from a few statements by Webber that implied that the county felt ill-treated by the Corps, there was little to suggest that this was an issue that pitted county residents and local government against an indifferent federal agency. This should not be surprising, given the close working relationship between federal and county representatives. Colonel T. H. Lipscomb and Judge Ward Webber pledged to work together on behalf of both entities, and each man likely took advantage of Colonel Ralph Tudor's experience in both the federal agency and in private industry. Furthermore, the county could contest condemnation of its bridge with the backing of the state, an option not open to individuals whose property is condemned by the federal agency. Condemnation was made unnecessary by the intervention of Oregon's senators and congressmen, who convinced the Corps that the additional funds requested by the county for relocation were within the agency's purview.

When Wasco County dedicated its new bridge in December 1953, Ralph Tudor, now Undersecretary of the Department of the Interior, made a special trip to The Dalles to help celebrate its opening. The governors of Oregon and Washington, Judge Ward Webber, Tudor's sister Barbara Mackenzie, and his brother-in-law Thomas Mackenzie flanked the undersecretary. The relationship between Webber and Tudor extended beyond the construction of the bridge. The two had become friendly enough by 1952 that Webber took Tudor's recommendation of his sister Barbara Mackenzie for a county position. Thomas and Barbara Mackenzie had recently moved from Lincoln County to The Dalles so that Thomas could supervise the construction of the bridge. The move left Barbara Mackenzie, an experienced social worker, without work. Webber hired her as Wasco County's first juvenile officer in July 1952, a position she would soon leave at Webber's encouragement when it became obvious that the county would need to negotiate with the federal government again, this time to relocate Indian people living at Celilo Village.

DAM WORKERS

The day-to-day life for workers and residents of The Dalles and the surrounding area is merely hinted at in extant research materials. Construction workers and their families lived on the periphery of town in trailer homes—cramped metal boxes that were probably too hot in summer and too cold in winter—or, if they were lucky, in new in-town apartments. But the housing was temporary, as was their stay in the area, until the job was done and they moved on to find other work. Their children joined scores of newcomers in classrooms filled past capacity and eventually in new schools built for the booming population. Dam workers were overwhelmingly male and young. Seventy-five percent of dam workers and their families lived in The Dalles area. At the height of employment in 1955, construction brought 4,100 workers and more than 3,900 dependents.[73] It is unclear what young wives did, but one imagines them struggling to cook meals in tiny, inadequate kitchens, visiting the Laundromat, and fighting a losing battle against the powdery dust of the Columbia Plateau.

The local newspaper hints at working conditions at the dam site. In December 1952 the paper reported a "wildcat" strike lodged against a construction company.[74] The strike suggests worker resistance to conditions or pay, but the newspaper article does not indicate what strikers were picketing for or how many workers joined the protest. The strike was not mentioned in the newspaper again, so perhaps it was resolved in a single day.

The *Chronicle* also reported the death of several workers. A few days after the strike and just before Christmas, a twenty-five-year-old bridge worker from Kalispell, Montana, suffocated when loose soil engulfed him. The worker had been in the area for just one month and left a young family behind.[75] An even worse accident claimed the lives of two construction workers in May 1954. A boom came loose at the spillway, tipping an eleven-ton bucket onto its side, spilling a load of concrete. In all, six people were injured, two of them fatally. The men who died were both twenty-two and from out-of-state, like many of the workers who flocked to the city during this period.[76] Apart from notices of accidents and progress reports (in which workers were mentioned only in the aggregate), dam workers did not make the news except in one rare article that focused on a James Stewart lookalike who rappelled down the cliffs adjacent to the dam site to pry rock free. The *Chronicle* reporter described the work as dangerous, suspenseful, and exciting; the good-looking construction worker lent the "illusion that a movie was being filmed" just outside town.[77] But most construction work was dirty, noisy, and monotonous, and most workers did not resemble movie stars.

One of the ironies of the period was a rise in unemployment during the construction of the dam. The announcement in 1952 of congressional allocation for construction of the dam spurred laborers from the Willamette Valley and elsewhere to move to The Dalles before contractors began hiring. This movement, coupled with the seasonal nature of dam work, led to a spike in county unemployment figures during a time of general prosperity. By 1953, the city's unemployed hit its highest peak since the close of the Second World War.[78]

The winter of 1954 was particularly bad. A mid-January snowstorm stopped construction and slowed work at area sawmills for two weeks. The layoffs added to the large contingent of unemployed day laborers and increased the number of people on aid to more than 1,500. Unemployment compensation was a paltry $22.50 a month, barely enough to pay for rent and groceries. Families and businesspeople alike felt the pinch, prompting the city to launch a "Do It Now" campaign. Mayor Melvin Davidson urged housewives and farmers to hire out chores to support the local economy. To demonstrate the good sense of the campaign, the *Chronicle* highlighted the story of one man who had meant to have a perilously leaning tree removed from his yard. An estimate given to him the previous summer stood at $80, but a laid-off logger removed it that winter for just $15.[79] It is not clear whether the campaign was a success, but six months later the employment agency was still warning that "the job outlook for newcomers to The Dalles is not good."[80]

Judge Ward Webber's wife appeared before the city council in May 1954 to request support for the local chapter of the American Red Cross to help alleviate the "transient situation," which she described as the chapter's "biggest problem." Wasco County had joined forces with the Red Cross, the Salvation Army, and other civic organizations to provide for the unemployed and their families. The Red Cross believed it was the "Dalles City's obligation to do something" about the situation; the council agreed only to send representatives to future Red Cross meetings. As in so many other areas, dam construction posed both a tremendous opportunity for The Dalles and created crises on a level not before experienced by city leaders.[81]

THE *CHRONICLE* AND CELILO VILLAGE

The city of The Dalles, Wasco County, and the Indian fishing village of Celilo were closely linked in ways that became increasingly apparent as dam construction progressed. Just as The Dalles *Chronicle* made comprehensible its community's municipal growth, it interpreted the neighboring community of Celilo Village for the residents of The Dalles. The newspaper helped to construct as well as commented on the relationship between the two communities, but the newspaper's version of life at Celilo Village was meant for The Dalles city consumption and did not fully reflect the Indian community. The relationship between The Dalles and Celilo Village, which was complicated by racism and regional pride that hearkened to a Native past, echoed in the newspaper's regional coverage.

Celilo Village residents frequently traveled to The Dalles to purchase food, clothing, and shoes; to visit doctors and dentists; and to attend school. Each journey to the city was a risk that could result in a potentially racist confrontation between the white Dalles residents and the Indian visitors. At the same time, citizens in The Dalles celebrated their proximity to such significant Native sites as Celilo Falls. The high school teams were the "Indians," local store owners advertised wares using Native motifs, and "society" women dressed in Indian garb and learned a few Native dance steps. The Dalles residents separated a romantic Native past from what many non-Indians perceived as a destitute Native present in order to foster this kind of celebration.

The Dalles *Chronicle* described Celilo Village as a contemporary community often caught up in alcohol-fueled violence, accidental deaths, and fishing-related arrests. In that way, the newspaper presented a struggling community in stark contrast to the forward-moving Dalles. Although there were exceptions to the *Chronicle*'s portrayal—the annual coverage of the First Salmon ceremony and the struggle to maintain fishing rights—the perceived violence it described at the village hardened stereotypes of Indian people and worried Dalles residents who otherwise celebrated the Native history of the river environment.

Coverage of life at Celilo was most intense during the spring, summer, and fall fishing seasons when the population of the village exploded. Between 1950 and 1952, several instances of accidental death and injury and criminal violence characterized the newspaper's coverage of the community. The *Chronicle* reported a horrific murder of a Navajo railroad worker near a spur track in 1950. Police hypothesized that the thirty-year-old man was crushed to death, perhaps by an automobile. There was also an apparent attempt to emasculate him, as evidenced by a large knife wound in his pelvic area. Police immediately turned to the Indian community to search for the killer and rounded up "all Indians whose appearance showed signs of a fight." Four Indians were taken into custody, but they were eventually released after being questioned, and the apparent murder remained unsolved.[82] Just as in any community, that level of violence was rare at Celilo. Fights, however, were more common. Lawrence Gowdy (whose efforts to rid Celilo Falls of the Cramers are chronicled in Chapter Two) pushed Warm Springs Reservation resident Henry Polk through a plate-glass window at a Dalles furniture store because Polk had taken up with the wife of Gowdy's friend.[83]

In the *Chronicle*'s coverage of Celilo-related violence, police assumed that if the victims were Indian, so were the perpetrators. The exceptions were in fishing-related violence. Events in 1931 foreshadowed the violence that would come in the 1940s when Yakama fishers attempted to remove the Cramers from Celilo Falls. During September of that year, Harry Issel, a white man, fired at Levi Van Pelt, a Umatilla, severing a nerve in his leg. Issel, who had formerly worked as a boxer and a Texas ranger, had been hired by Walter Downes, also white, to protect his fishing site, Downes Channel, from those he considered Indian interlopers. The site had been contested for many years and would remain so into the 1940s. A judge awarded Van Pelt $10,000 in damages a year later.[84]

Accidental deaths in and around Celilo were much more routine than criminal violence. Fishing could be a dangerous activity, and the safety ropes that dip netters wrapped around their waist did not guarantee protection from drowning and did not protect fishers as they moved to their fishing stations. One of the worst drowning accidents of Native fishers occurred when a boat occupied by four Warm Springs fishers overturned in Fivemile rapids in 1952. The fishers were using a rowboat equipped with an engine to reach fishing stations on the north side of the river when the boat overturned early in the morning.[85] Shortly before the falls were inundated, two fishers fell from a slippery bridge they attempted to traverse to reach their fishing sites. The deaths occurred a week apart, underscoring the danger associated with the swift river and its rugged bedrock.[86] And, in what seems almost an apocryphal incident, the *Chronicle* reported in 1952 that a fisher dip-netted a young Indian boy from the water when he fell into the river from a fishing platform.[87] Although it was a dramatic rescue, it was not without precedent. In 1935 Vern Craft tried to save Jack Conners when Conners slipped from a footbridge with a full load of salmon on his back. Conners was able to grab hold of Craft's dip net before he was "swept away by the on rush of water." Identified as both an Indian fisher from Montana and "generally . . . accepted as white," Conners represents the pressure on the Celilo fishery exerted by out-of-area Indians. Moreover, he slipped after having fished all night, disregarding the rules imposed by the Celilo Fish Committee.[88]

Although the work of many at Celilo was dangerous, the way in which roads and railroad lines bisected Celilo Village also proved risky to those who lived there. Felix Paul was hit by a train in May 1952 and died the next day from massive head injuries.[89] Fall fishing seasons in the 1930s and '40s saw men killed by trains. Alcohol consumption played a role in at least two of these accidents, but another occurred at five in the morning as the victim was likely walking to the river to begin a day of fishing.[90] Car accidents were also brought on by alcohol consumption, but in one instance a car hit a ten-year-old boy as he tried to cross the highway to retrieve some fishing equipment.[91] Alcohol simply heightened the risk in a community whose residents had to contend with rail lines and a highway to reach the river.

Alcohol sales to Indians was highlighted in a two-article series in the *Chronicle* in 1950.[92] A claim by Oregon Governor Douglas McKay (later appointed Secretary of the Interior in 1952) that Indians should fall under the same laws regarding alcohol as non-Indian citizens prompted an investigation on how Indians procured alcoholic beverages in The Dalles area. McKay's comments opposed an 1892 federal law that made it illegal to sell alcohol to Indian people.[93] As a supporter of termination policy, McKay believed that Indians should not receive any consideration from the federal government apart from what they would as U.S. citizens. His position was also in opposition to state and city liquor laws that replicated the federal act and the treaties that protected Indian fishing rights. Although it did not take a stance on the governor's position, the *Chronicle* complained that white "bootleggers" made their own drinking money by illicitly selling alcohol to Indians:

> How does an Indian get his wine? For Indians, it's fairly easy. He comes into town after a few days of fishing with, perhaps, $20 in his pocket. He loiters around the east end of Second street for awhile, or perhaps goes directly to the "jungles" of the willows on the waterfront. . . . Before long he meets a white man with whom he may or may not be acquainted. He gives the white man, say, a $5 bill and asks him to buy a bottle of wine.[94]

The second *Chronicle* article highlighted the use of welfare funds to buy alcohol. Although the piece focused on Indian alcohol use, it acknowledged that non-Indians also used welfare money to purchase alcohol. The paper warned that "it must be emphasized that the Indian is in the minority in the misuse of welfare money." Nonetheless, it emphasized Native abuses by citing Indian arrest statistics without citing corresponding numbers for non-Indians.[95]

Like many newspapers of its time, The Dalles *Chronicle* reported about Indian people in ways that played off and incorporated racist stereotypes. Celilo Village residents and its visitors were described as heavy drinkers, prone to violence, and in need of federal, state, county, or municipal guidance—as if they were children. Headlines capitalized on common clichés describing Indians who fought for their fishing rights and opposed construction of The Dalles Dam as being on the "warpath."

Although most Celilo news focused on tragedy, there were a few notable exceptions. The newspaper reported in 1935 that "there are some 'bad Injuns' but there are good ones, too," after an Indian "whose name the [police] officers did not take the time to learn" stopped by the precinct to warn them that there were some suspicious-looking men loitering outside a tavern that was closed for the night. Because of the warning, police were able to halt a robbery in progress.[96] The paper also printed the comments of federal district Judge Fred Wilson, who sentenced an Indian for assault and robbery. Wilson stated in 1943 that "there are many good Indians at Celilo who never get into trouble and who at all times want to see the law observed."[97] In 1944 the paper ran a very short article on Harold Culpus, a Celilo resident who had earned the Purple Heart after being partially paralyzed in battle in Europe.[98]

The *Chronicle* did more than just report local events; it constructed an image of the Celilo Village community for the consumption of the paper's white readers. That constructed image, manufactured by unsympathetic outsiders, too often shaped local non-Indian responses to the Indian community. And it was a construction not easily revised by Indians or their friends who did not have a weekly newspaper or a large regional readership at their disposal. Racist stereotypes of Celilo residents abound in the coverage of the community in The Dalles *Chronicle*, and they are reflected in the positions that town leaders took toward their neighbors. Chapter Five examines more fully the ways in which organizations such as The Dalles Chamber of Commerce and the Wasco County government interacted with Celilo Indians.

5

RELOCATION AND THE
PERSISTENCE OF CELILO VILLAGE

"We Don't 'Come From' Anywhere"

Gerald Foster wrote to Indian agent Clarence Davis in 1946 to find out whether enough people flocked to Celilo Village during the annual spring First Salmon ceremony to justify bringing in a small carnival with two rides and ten concessions. Newspaper articles suggested smaller crowds, but Davis consulted Chief Tommy Thompson and then replied that about 600 people might attend the three-day festival and that the Indian community would be happy to host the carnival, provided the community received 10 percent of the gross earnings. Nothing in the records indicates whether Foster brought his carnival to Celilo.[1] If he had, he would have found himself in the midst of one of the region's oldest continuously practiced Indian ceremonial rituals and social gatherings.

Every spring, Indians from around the region gathered at Celilo in a ceremony open to the wider public to celebrate the return of the salmon with a feast of eel, roots, vegetables, huckleberries, and, of course, salmon. The feast was accompanied by music, dance, and gambling in a festive atmosphere that would have delighted in Foster's carnival. In 1952 the atmosphere was likely subdued because construction of The Dalles Dam would necessitate the relocation of some of the Indians who lived at Celilo Village. As if to signal the change, that year's First Salmon ceremony was

First blast in the building of The Dalles Dam, 1953.
U.S. Army Corps of Engineers.

accompanied by the noise of the largest dynamite blast to be det-
onated at The Dalles Dam site up to that date. As Native people
and their guests gave thanks for the river's salmon, sturgeon killed
by the underwater blast floated to the water's surface.[2]

Crowds of white onlookers who came for both spectacles
were welcomed into the Celilo longhouse by their Indian hosts.
The longhouse was one of the largest structures at Celilo Village.
It was also the southernmost building, farthest from the rocky
outcroppings of the falls. If the river was a daily destination for
Celilo residents, the longhouse was the heart of the community,
a place for religious ceremony and community meetings. Looking toward the river from the longhouse, the way in which the
Columbia River provided a transportation corridor to the non-
Indian communities of the region was obvious. Housing and drying sheds surrounded the longhouse, which was bordered on the

north by the Oregon Trunk Railroad and the Oregon Trail Highway 30; beyond that was the housing of "old" Celilo Village. To reach the south bank of the Columbia River, it was necessary to traverse the Union Pacific Railroad and The Dalles–Celilo Canal. The village long predated the railroads and roads, which came at a cost for those who lived there. Many residents carried personal memories or family stories of relocation. As the Army Corps of Engineers held its first public meetings regarding The Dalles Dam in the mid-1940s, Wyam Chief Tommy Thompson described the precariousness of life at Celilo Village:

> When the canal was built by the white man—by the Government—our shacks were all done away with; we were made to move. Then some of us tried to go back and actually built a few shacks, but in about three years after the Canal was built we were forced to move away again. The Railroad also disturbed our shacks and we were restricted just the same as was the case with the Canal; then the highway came along and chased us out again. We have been moved here and there, always farther away from our fishing sites until we now live on some land claimed by a white man [the Seufert family], where my house stands and where our longhouse stands. And I am continually afraid that I will be chased out entirely.[3]

Although Celilo residents had frequently experienced relocation over the years, relocation would take on new meaning in the mid-1950s. Moving thirty-six families as a result of inundation of land by The Dalles Dam represented a further and more significant relocation than previous ones, with the noted exception of the relocation to reservations in the mid-1850s. In addition, simultaneous to and informing the relocation of Celilo Village was the federal policy of relocation that accompanied termination. In the midst of fluctuating populations, Indian agency personnel turnover, federal policy shifts, a decline in salmon populations,

Celilo Village, prior to 1940. Note (from the foreground toward the river) the Oregon Trail Highway 30, railroad, and Celilo Canal. National Archives— Pacific Northwest Region.

and the predominance of relocation policies, some events at Celilo, such as the annual First Salmon ceremony, provided the community with stability.

The small Celilo Indian community housed year-round residents who followed the seasonal cycles of fishing, hunting, and gathering. Its population swelled with the arrival of the salmon runs, when fishers from regional reservations joined unenrolled Wyams in a seasonal tradition of fishing, gambling, and socializing that dated from centuries before. It must have seemed impossible to them that an ancient cycle in which the return of salmon drew the return of people could be stopped by a handful of engineers and their concrete. Nonetheless, the completion of Bonneville Dam in 1938 gave proof that newcomers with little more than a century of occupation could transform a riverscape that had sustained Native culture for thousands of years.[4]

JURISDICTION

Salvage archaeology conducted during construction of The Dalles Dam confirmed that Celilo Village was an ancient fishing community that had been continually inhabited for thousands of years.[5] The successful historic community, which developed around the fisheries and trade, had since become impoverished and encumbered by the Bureau of Indian Affairs, a federal agency that frequently neglected the needs of the community. Celilo Village consisted of about thirty permanent households built on sand-covered basalt that presented few natural resources apart from access to fish runs in the Columbia River. Residents enjoyed neither electricity nor indoor plumbing (an aboveground pipe carried water from a well to homes), and there was no proper garbage disposal or way to dispose of fish remains. The average Celilo family had an annual income of $700, half that of the average white Wasco County household. Indians picked pears, apples, and hops; worked as section hands on railroads that bisected the village; or hired out to local lumber mills to supplement their salmon sales. Some Indian women made beaded crafts for the tourist trade. Most adults at Celilo Village had no more than a fifth-grade education, and many could not read or write, further limiting their ability to earn income in what was essentially a new economy. As on many larger reservations, the village lacked essential services. The closest health facilities were in The Dalles.[6]

Celilo Village in the mid–twentieth century was a mix of federally and privately owned property adjacent to the off-reservation treaty-protected fishing site—which was itself a place of ambiguous legal status. In a 1944 report, a BIA Yakima Agency official claimed that "it is very doubtful whether or not Celilo . . . would constitute a 'reservation' in every term of the word."[7] Celilo Village was not a federally recognized reservation, although it held a kind of quasifederal status because of government-acquired land holdings in the area. The Bureau of Indian Affairs tried to purchase land that Indians already used, in order to protect the off-reservation fishery in the mid-1920s. When the War Department transferred seven acres to the Department of the Interior in 1929 for the "benefit of certain Indians now using and occupying the land as a fish and game site," the area became BIA property.[8] The BIA dramatically expanded Celilo Village in 1946 by purchasing an additional thirty-four and a half acres from the Francis Seufert family, land upon which Indians had resided for decades and where Tommy Thompson's home stood.

Further complicating government oversight was the fact that many Celilo residents were enrolled on area reservations, where they were granted services. Residents at Celilo fluctuated so widely that BIA subagent C. G. Davis complained that "these people 'up and leave' so often, others come in for awhile and 'up and leave' that an enumerator is given a bad headache."[9] What Davis and other BIA officials regarded as troublesome transience reflected the seasonal cycle of ancient times. The federal government was loath to simply duplicate already available services to migratory Indians; however, there was also a small group of "unenrolled" Indians at Celilo who did not benefit from formal enrolled status on any reservation.

Apart from a brief period when a subagency under the jurisdiction of the Yakima Agency was created at The Dalles (1939–54), the Yakama, Umatilla, and Warm Springs Agencies oversaw the community from a distance and with little intervention or support. The Bureau of Indian Affairs viewed the community as an extension of the Yakama, Umatilla, and Warm Springs Reservations. The three reservations reallocated funds to Celilo Village

C. G. Davis, Bureau of Indian Affairs field agent at The Dalles; Andrew Barnhart, Celilo Fish Committee chairman; and Tommy Thompson, chief of the Wyam; all standing in front of Thompson's fish drying shed at Celilo Village, 1940. National Archives—Pacific Northwest Region.

to cover minimal maintenance expenses as part of a management program that put the Celilo residents in direct "competition [for] money allocated to their respective reservations."[10] Reservation governments were notoriously underfunded. Two decades after construction of The Dalles Dam, Francis Briscoe, director of the BIA's Portland Area Office, pointed out that "none of the tribes that get money is whole-heartedly enthused about having some of it drained out down there."[11] The historic consequence was a jurisdiction with no clear line of authority and officials who quibbled over which agency held responsibility for village residents.

Two of the men most responsible for governing the community in the 1940s and 1950s were Chief Tommy Thompson and Bureau of Indian Affairs subagent C. G. Davis. Tommy Thompson had been elected salmon chief of the Wyams when he was about twenty years old. He aided in governing Celilo, provided spiritual guidance to the community, and oversaw the fishing activities at the falls. According to Thompson, "Every year during fishing season I am always giving lectures" regarding restrictions and accident prevention. Illness prevented him from speaking to fishers directly in 1940, but from his bed he decreed that only five men were to fish at any given time, that fishing would stop for the day at 6:30 P.M., and that those who indulged in drink would not be permitted to fish.[12] In a later interview, Russell Jim recalled how Thompson insured escapement of some of the salmon run:

> One day, usually on a Sunday, he'd go down there and put two, three locks on somebody's cable cars.... He'd shut that down at least three to five days to let fish go by. You know, without going out there and writing a note or declaring war or yelling or anything—a little symbol of a lock here and there, and the word would get around, 'Hey, he shut us down.' No dispute. It would stop until they went down and the lock is gone, and they say, 'Okay, now we can go back to fishing again.'[13]

Federal, state, and county officials understood that without Thompson's approval, the community would not accept proposed projects, relocations, or regulations.

The qualities that made Thompson highly regarded by Indians at Celilo Village were the qualities that often caused BIA officials to complain. Thompson persistently fought for his treaty rights, which he interpreted broadly in the favor of Indian people. Thompson had some important white allies: Marshall Dana, with the U.S. National Bank of Portland and eventually editor of the Oregon *Journal,* and Martha McKeown, a prominent resident of Hood River and author of children's books.[14] Thompson was adept at drawing publicity to issues significant to Celilo residents and exerting outside influence on those who officially oversaw the community. Because of his skills, white officials perceived Thompson as a difficult person.

BIA subagent Davis frequently characterized Thompson as someone who attempted to "work the system," using his ethnicity and position to demand special treatment. When Thompson's wife, Ellen Andrews, died, Davis complained that Thompson burned her mattress, a traditional practice, and then expected the agency to replace it. He also became exasperated at Thompson's numerous requests that the BIA or the Wasco County welfare office offset the cost of feeding "Indians who come and stay . . . on account of old Indian custom."[15] To Davis it seemed apparent that if Thompson could not afford to feed guests, he should not invite them to stay.

Through a series of letters in the 1940s and early 1950s, Thompson and Davis exchanged accusations as to whether Thompson qualified for county welfare. Davis did not believe Thompson's claims of desperate poverty and became increasingly frustrated as the Indian leader attempted to gain redress from the county, thereby subverting the authority of the BIA subagent. Davis was concerned that "Tommy has a habit of getting into print and has many friends who get into print about him" and that "one not acquainted with the facts may immediately jump to the conclusion that Chief Tommy Thompson has been neglected."[16]

Thompson received aid from the county, which was reduced when he married Flora Cushinway because she earned income from an allotment at the Warm Springs Reservation. Davis wrote to his superior in Portland, "Although I have diligently explained this matter to him, and he has indicated that he understands the matter, nobody knows when he is going to come back again, saying that he hasn't been treated right in the matter. He is that way."[17] Flora Cushinway Thompson, writing on behalf of her illiterate husband, warned Davis, "We . . . should be respected in every way and be treated right."[18] Davis and Thompson interacted across a significant cultural divide, and it is likely that they viewed one another as rivals because they both worked to govern the fishing village. As might be expected, historical records provide a forum for Davis's complaints without affording Thompson the opportunity to defend himself.

C. G. Davis held the position of BIA subagent at The Dalles from 1939 until 1954, when Celilo residents were faced with relocation and began negotiating compensation with the Army Corps of Engineers. Davis's files indicate that he often struggled to keep up with his workload, which included solving just about every problem imaginable at Celilo. In 1942 Davis wrote in desperation to M. A. Johnson, BIA agent at the Yakima Reservation, that he was "swamped with minute writing. . . . I will soon be in the hole so badly that I cannot get out unless I receive some help from a typist." Written in pencil at the bottom of the request is "help refused."[19] Roberta Ulrich, a journalist who interviewed mid–Columbia River Indians, claimed that "most Indians who remember [Davis] considered him arrogant and opposed to their interests."[20] If accurate, they were not the only ones to bristle at Davis.

With his support of Indian fishing rights, the subagent also managed to offend numerous members of the white community. He frequently recounted to his superiors encounters such as one he had with Malcolm Wilkinson, the Wasco County attorney, in 1948. The telephone conversation was in regards to the Yakama fishers' removal of Cramer fishing equipment. Wilkinson was convinced that Davis had personally participated in the removal of equipment and became "very insulting to [Davis] at that point, saying that while he had not previously sided in with the sheriff and 'other officers' against [Davis] that he was now inclined to believe them." Although Davis denied participating in extralegal activities directly, he defended Indians and their fishing rights at Celilo throughout his career. In the Cramer case, Davis wrote to his superior, "I am taking the brunt of this fight again and if I get out of it without a nervous collapse, I am indeed lucky."[21]

Davis also defended Native fishing practices to state agencies, particularly when they published what Davis considered erroneous information about the mid-Columbia fishery. For example, he took offense at Clifford Presnall when the latter reported that Indians practiced "chicanery and waste" at Celilo Falls. Davis thought the report racist in its assessment of Indian fishers: "The Indians who fish at the Falls are severely criticized in his report, and in my opinion they have been taken to task for simply being human. I do not believe that men of any other race would do differently under like circumstances."[22] Davis followed up by disproving some of the claims made by Presnall, such as one that Indians caught salmon before the commercial season opened and iced them to sell once they could legally. It is likely that Clarence Davis felt himself at the front line of defending Native fishing practices at Celilo Falls.

Residents who spoke on behalf of the community or the Celilo Fish Committee without authorization further complicated governing Celilo Village during the 1940s and '50s. John Whiz, a Yakama fisher and permanent resident at Celilo Village, appears in the records as an occasional interpreter for Tommy Thompson and as an intermittent member of the Celilo Fish Committee. He appears more frequently as an instigator of schemes to publicize fishing issues as well as of efforts to line his own pocket. Whiz had a knack for publicity but not for politics.

In 1940 Whiz solicited money for a trip to Washington, D.C., where he planned to request funds for the "rehabilitation" of Celilo Village on behalf of the Celilo Fish Committee. Other members of the committee passed a resolution opposing the scheme, but Whiz still managed to make the trip. When Whiz did not have the funds to return home, he cabled Roy Taylor, unsuccessful Republican candidate for county sheriff. Claiming that "John wasn't able to get relief from the great Democratic white father, or any of the sub-chiefs," but had to "turn to an old reliable Wasco county Republican," Taylor wired money to

Whiz and used the publicity in his campaign.[23] Whiz returned to Oregon and was promptly removed from the Celilo Fish Committee. The remaining committee members asked Clarence Davis to draw up a resolution stating that the committee was opposed to "solicitations and representations on matters affecting the fishermen of this region by John Whiz unless he was so authorized." Davis declined, worried that "it might appear as though I were participating in partisan conflicts."[24]

In his own way, Whiz continued to fight limitations placed on Indian fishers. In 1944 he discovered a plan by the Oregon Legislature to limit the Indian harvest, and he attempted to call a special meeting of the Celilo Fish Committee. Davis wrote to his supervisor that "[Whiz] has been seeking to make a good thing out of it for himself, and I prophesy that he will make a collection on the strength of his discovery and nobody except John will know where the money goes that he collects."[25]

Davis was not above using Whiz for his own purposes. In an effort stir up Indian interest in cooperatively marketing fish, Davis suggested to Yakama BIA superintendent M. A. Johnson that they should "egg" John Whiz to start a movement among Celilo fishers. Davis hoped the plan would have the added effect of keeping "John out of other mischief."[26] Celilo Village was like a lot of small towns in which several would-be leaders vied for clout. Yet Celilo was also remarkably dissimilar due to the level of federal, state, and county intervention.

C. G. Davis's successful attempt to replace outdated communal toilets and to install garbage pits at Celilo Village in 1940 illustrates the kind of multiagency and multigovernment cooperation necessary to improve conditions at the tiny community. After conferring with several colleagues about the design of the new installations, securing $500 from the Indian Service, and assessing the equipment that would be needed, Davis solicited help from the Army Corps of Engineers, the Yakima BIA Agency, the city of The Dalles, and Chief Tommy Thompson:

One of the garbage pits that Bureau of Indian Affairs field agent C. G. Davis spearheaded as a way to increase proper sanitation at Celilo Village, 1940. National Archives—Pacific Northwest Region.

We had no trouble obtaining cooperation from all concerned. Mr. Wheeler Rucker, head of the local Army Engineers not only allowed us to build privies and garbage pits on Government land controlled by him, but loaned us an air compressor, a jack hammer and various other necessary tools for the job. Mr. Thomas L. Carter, Forest Supervisor of the Yakima Agency, loaned us a dump truck and furnished dynamite and caps. The City of The Dalles loaned us a suitable battery with special switch for setting off dynamite charges. The Celilo Chief, Tommy Thompson, loaned us the use of the Celilo Longhouse—where privies were constructed and lumber stored—assisted us to secure shovels for digging garbage pits, old railroad ties and heavy mesh wire for placing over dynamite charges to protect from flying rocks, and intervened with other Indian residents in order to obtain their consent for demolition of old privies which our new units were replacing.[27]

The Works Progress Administration sponsored the project, which employed eight Indian men, "care being taken to equalize labor from the three Reservations . . . as much as possible." Finally, after the pits were dug and the privies built, Davis arranged for nearby families to keep them clean and stocked with toilet paper. This project was an initial step in a larger effort to heighten the sanitation at the village.

PLANNING A CLEANUP

"Many plans have been suggested
for the rehabilitation of these people
but nothing has ever been done."

ANNUAL REPORT FROM THE BIA SUPERINTENDENT
AT WARM SPRINGS, 1935[28]

The metamorphosis of Celilo Village brought on by The Dalles Dam was the culmination of decades of threats to the tiny community. Beginning in 1929, The Dalles Chamber of Commerce attempted to implement several proposals to improve Celilo Village, the most severe of which called for the condemnation of the village by the state health officer. Assimilationist strategies, those that sought to replace traditional Indian practices with those of the dominant culture, always underlay these proposals. By the 1950s, proponents relied on the rhetoric of the increasingly popular federal policy of termination. The inevitable inundation of the village seemed to solve the "problem" of Celilo once and for all.

At midcentury, problems ranging from poverty to outbreaks of tuberculosis plagued Celilo Village. The ancient fishing settlement was a community whose neighbors threatened it with obliteration for decades and whose residents were too often kept

Eastern Oregon Tuberculosis Hospital, with The Dalles in the background, 1939. Oregon Historical Society, neg. 77133.

from political involvement in their own fate. The agencies most involved with the community were charged with protecting society's most marginalized people, but they failed in their responsibility by accommodating the region's majority. The history of Celilo Village is one of endurance, adaptation, and resistance within a powerful nation set on transforming the Columbia River into a source of hydroelectric power. Yet Celilo residents carried on traditions that gave shape to their lives even while they opposed solutions they believed to be unjust. Because of this perseverance, the community persists to this day.

Much of the dispute regarding Celilo Village hinged on the appearance of the town. Residents of The Dalles complained that the village's homes were nothing more than assorted shacks that disrupted the river view, a perception some Bureau of Indian Affairs employees confirmed. H. U. Sanders listed materials

Indians used to build homes as "scrap lumber, tentage, old sacks, cast-off tin, or . . . pasteboard from ordinary pasteboard boxes picked up in town." He complained, "There is no obstacle to the entry of flies because in many instances a large bird could fly through the cracks in the walls" and "fish are often hanging from the roof in the room."[29]

Barbara Mackenzie and Martha McKeown, both of whom had close contact with Celilo residents, described the residences as clean and practical. Martha McKeown, a writer and activist who was "adopted" by Wyam Chief Tommy Thompson and his wife, Flora, described the Thompson Celilo home in 1946:

> [Flora's] home, typically Indian, reminds one of pictures of Oriental interiors. There are two large rooms. The front one, opening onto the porch, contained four neatly made beds; one in each corner. There were no bedsteads; the bedding was placed directly onto the floor. In the center of the room was a round, highly ornate, antique iron stove. There was no other furniture. . . . [T]he other room . . . contained the table, chairs, cook stove, radio, a modern sewing machine, and food supplies.[30]

McKeown claimed that "only a privileged, trusted guest can get a true insight into the home life of Oregon's oldest town," calling into question representations by other outsiders.

Missing in these descriptions is a critique of the material poverty in which Celilo Indians lived. The village looked as though poor people lived there because poor people did live there. However, poverty became a way for some residents of The Dalles—who insisted that the lack of sanitation at Celilo and the potential to spread disease could impact the broader mid-Columbia region—to discriminate against their neighbors. In a 1999 interview, Barbara Mackenzie recalled both the poverty of Celilo and the pride of the people who lived there. She remembered that "it was remarkable how clean [the homes] would be under the circumstances in which they lived."[31]

Government officials also blamed Indians for their own impoverishment. In their reports, BIA employees complained that Indians lived from fishing season to season, unable to save money for longer than a few months. They described Indians as unable to plan for the future and criticized them for squandering extra money on "luxuries and impractical articles," including "celebrations" that consisted of feasting and gambling with friends. Furthermore, they claimed that a "lack of dependability" (rather than the more likely lack of marketable skills or education) prevented Indians "from getting jobs." These reports also criticize Celilo Indians for being "clannish" and "anti-social" because they did not interact much with local whites. Bureau of Indian Affairs employees found Indians suspicious of the agency's motives and commented on the lack of acceptance of outsiders.[32] One contemporary newspaper article blamed this distrust on the memories that Indian elders had of past broken promises.[33] The discrimination Indians encountered from whites who deemed them inferior was as significant, though left unmentioned in BIA reports.

Barbara Mackenzie began to understand the attitudes of The Dalles residents toward Indians when she accepted a position as Wasco County's first juvenile officer in the mid-1950s. She investigated why school-aged children from Celilo did not attend schools in The Dalles. After the county school superintendent ignored her questions, she went to the local principal, who told her that "Indians can't learn after the fourth grade and it's just not worth the effort to try to bring them into school." Mackenzie went to the village to ask parents why they were not sending their children to school:

> They said, "Well, the weather is so cold and we take them down and the school bus maybe doesn't come and we take the children

back up to the houses." So I went back [to the school] about the school bus. And the driver said, well, he didn't see how it was worth his time going out there because half the time the kids weren't there and anyhow there wasn't very much of them. I pursued that further and I said, "What happens to the rural children? Where do they wait for the school bus above the valley, above The Dalles?" And he said, "Oh, we have shelters." And I said, "Why not at Celilo?" So I went after shelters.[34]

Years earlier, H. U. Sanders, a BIA employee, had noted that local whites bused their children to schools at The Dalles "at considerable expense" to avoid their mixing with Indian children. According to Sanders, "Discrimination by whites against Indians is not so much on account of color as it is on account of personal hygiene and conduct." Indians would face far fewer difficulties and secure a stable future, he implied, if they would simply assimilate.[35]

The Dalles residents complained bitterly about Celilo Village for decades, contending that the community was unorganized, dirty, and a liability to attracting tourists and their money. According to the weekly Dalles Chronicle, The Dalles Chamber of Commerce complained that:

> The ramshackle Indian dwellings at Celilo are not only unsightly, but present conditions at the settlement are so unsanitary as to excite comment from the tourists who pass through The Dalles and stop to see the falls. . . . During the summer months odors caused by unsanitary methods of drying fish, and lack of ways to dispose of waste, become so strong that automobile travelers wishing to stop and view Celilo falls—one of the greatest scenic attractions of the Columbia river—are forced to drive on without stopping.[36]

The chamber had negotiated with the Bureau of Indian Affairs in the 1930s to replace permanent housing at Celilo with "modern camping facilities," but found that it was "impossible to obtain federal funds" to implement the plans.[37] Revisions followed, none of which came to fruition (partially due to Indian opposition), which disappointed and frustrated white residents. Members of The Dalles Chamber of Commerce forced the hand of the sluggish Bureau of Indian Affairs in 1936 when it requested that the Oregon state health department condemn the village. The BIA once again drew up a proposal, but Celilo opposition eventually grounded it as well. When the BIA's H. U. Sanders visited the village in 1940 with plans for new improvements, a state health officer told him "kindly but firmly that people from the Indian Service had been telling him that for twenty years but had done nothing."[38]

Most people at Celilo resented the plans for modernization that were developed in The Dalles. Bureau of Indian Affairs employee William Zimmerman Jr. warned The Dalles that initial BIA plans were dropped because of Indian opposition. Indians disliked proposals that nearly always called for relocating the village away from the banks of the Columbia River south of the Oregon Trail Highway 30. Such a move would have required Indians to walk across the highway and the Oregon Trunk Railroad to reach their fishing sites.

Celilo residents opposed the plans for other reasons as well. Angered by their exclusion from the decision-making process, Chief Tommy Thompson and Andrew Barnhart wrote to the state health officer in 1936. Thompson criticized The Dalles Chamber of Commerce, suggesting that "it would be very profitable that a satisfactory arrangement could be arrived at were these self-constituted custodians so disposed to have consulted with me and my people." As for the concerns of tourists about the village, Thompson said, "We do not invite them." Thompson warned that Celilo residents refused "to be ejected from our present location." He concluded by addressing the issue of sanitation and odor, claiming that the stench was notable for only about two weeks, during the fishing season, a period in which Indians faced "difficulty in disposing of refuse matter." Thompson pointed out that an incinerator could easily remedy the problem, but "of course funds are not available to us for this purpose." Furthermore, he notes that during most of the season, "The catch is immediately disposed of to the canneries, and therefore no cause exists for the complaint as alleged by meddlesome people."[39]

Non-Indians argued that resistance to modernization was rooted in a disregard among Wyams for the amenities of civilization. For their part, Indians objected to being excluded from the planning stages. They resented the assimilationist undertones of modernization and the changes in their lifeways that would have to come with new homes in new locations. Two issues were at hand: (1) control over the decision-making processes, and (2) whether plans would benefit the integrity of the community or dismantle it.

After The Dalles Chamber of Commerce intervened at Celilo with scant results, BIA Indian agents from Washington, Oregon, California, Idaho, and Nevada voted unanimously in 1946 to request federal funds for a museum, school, arts and crafts plant, and housing for Celilo Indians. The new plan, which would cost an estimated $500,000, was the most ambitious adopted for Celilo Village up to that time.[40] The BIA quickly pared it down when the agency purchased thirty used plywood and aluminum buildings from the Army in 1947.[41] Once the BIA secured congressional funding, BIA area director E. Morgan Pryse planned to locate these buildings on land south of the Oregon Trail Highway 30, the thirty-four and a half acres purchased from the Seuferts. The buildings, described by Martha McKeown as "simply shells . . . shipped to the Pacific and back again, then warped further out of shape while lying in the weeds by a railway siding,"[42] would replace houses north of the highway and necessitate crossing the highway and railroad to reach the river.

Shortly after Congress approved funds for New Celilo in June

1948, residents protested the plans, beginning an extended contest of nerves between the Indians and their federal guardians. Newspaper accounts of this period indicate that the Celilos were not happy with the removal plans; accounts also indicate that the BIA was not going to back down this time. Portland architect Charles Popkin assured residents in a July 1948 meeting that he would help build a village that would benefit "both Indians and whites" and that "Celilo is going to have nothing more than the kind of village the Indians desire." He promised attendees that no one would be forced to move to the new site, but he also warned them that "if the present shacks are not torn down . . . the tribesmen and the bureau alike will be 'accused of breaking faith'" with the Congress that appropriated funding.[43]

Three months later, The Dalles *Chronicle* proclaimed that Celilo residents would not be "forced to move from their present shacks." Instead, officials hoped that "when the present Celilo residents see the new houses they will want to occupy them."[44] The Bureau of Indian Affairs and other groups viewed the relocation and cleanup as a way to attract visitors to what one official called the "top tourist attraction in this section of the state." The plans called for the removal of Indian dwellings to "improve the view of Celilo falls, where Indians dipnet for salmon."[45]

Indians opposed both the location of the new homes and the design of the planned fish-drying sheds. The proposed site required a dangerous walk to reach the river, and it lay adjacent to the cliffs of the Columbia Gorge rather than along the riverbank. The plan called for three large fish-drying sheds to replace the individual ones Celilo families had built adjacent to their homes. Women, who were responsible for preserving harvested salmon, claimed air circulation would not be sufficient to properly dry fish. As soon as Indian leaders were aware of the proposed layout for the drying sheds, they objected. Indians wanted the plans to be redrawn with individual sheds. In an April 1949 Oregon *Journal* article, Celilo resident Andrew Barnhart claimed that the "Indian service has treated us rotten."[46] The BIA contended that Celilo Indians had approved the agency's relocation plans through the Celilo Fish Committee. The BIA based its argument on the Celilo Fish Committee decision years earlier to spend $15,000 on development at the new site from congressional allocations for improvements at Celilo Village. Because of the committee's approval of this expenditure, the BIA maintained that Celilo Indians were active in the plans.

The brief statement from Barnhart raises the question whether the Celilo Fish Committee understood that by approving the BIA plan, they were also accepting relocation. Barnhart acknowledged, "We want water and a sewer system. And we want to put new roofs on our drying shacks." But he said Indians did not see why they had to move in order to make some improvements to the village. Barnhart claimed that Indians had not made improvements to their homes earlier because workmen hired by The Dalles Chamber of Commerce had "set fire to our places" in the past as a method of cleanup: "Now you can understand why we won't spend money on this property where we don't know how soon somebody will come along and tear it down."[47]

BIA officials defended relocation, telling newspaper reporters that the move was essential because the rocky soil at Celilo Village prevented the construction of underground sewage systems or water lines. The cost of blasting through basalt made water pipes prohibitive. However, one journalist reported that highway expansion was an additional reason the government wanted to move the Indians. This claim is supported by an earlier report in which BIA agent H. U. Sanders suggested that highway expansion could justify razing the old village and replacing it with a newer, modern village somewhere else.

Despite all the arguments for relocation, many Celilos simply did not want to move. The conflict resulted in the development of a New Celilo Village adjacent to the surviving Old Celilo Village. The BIA finished New Celilo in 1949. A budget of

$125,000 covered the cost of ten modern homes, plumbing, a septic tank, four communal toilets, and four large communal drying sheds. The highway divided the old village's "shacks" from the new prefabricated buildings. Despite their ongoing struggle to redesign the new village, Celilo residents remained unsuccessful in their bid for individual drying sheds.

Resentment lingered, and many residents refused to move south of the highway. The local press ignored the legitimate concerns of Celilos and reiterated negative stereotypes, claiming that "what appears to be a shack to a white man might be suitable to the Indian. He might actually prefer to crowd closer to the river bank, even with better and more suitable quarters offered him a few hundred feet away."[48] BIA officers agreed that "the rumpus has all the earmarks of a typical dealing with the independent-minded redman." For a time, this compromise stood—a village divided into old and new, traditional versus modern homes. In less than a decade, the integrity of Celilo Village was threatened again, this time because the old village lay in the proposed flood pool of The Dalles Dam. Instead of relocating Indians to the new village, Wasco County, the BIA, and the Army Corps produced a plan that would entirely dismantle most of the community.

THE FLOODING OF OLD CELILO VILLAGE

The Bureau of Indian Affairs negotiated with the U.S. Army Corps of Engineers for funds to relocate displaced Celilo residents in the 1950s. Under the direction of Barbara Mackenzie, the BIA and Wasco County commenced the Celilo Relocation Project, the removal of thirty-six families from Old Celilo Village. Families moved to The Dalles, onto reservations where they were enrolled, and even to Gresham, Oregon, eighty miles to the west. A few stayed at Celilo Village in newly constructed homes.

Although dam-related relocation was perhaps the most intense period of direct governmental intervention in the history of Celilo

Barbara Mackenzie handing over the keys to the Georges' new home as part of the Celilo Relocation. From left to right: Charles Quitoken, Mr. and Mrs. Jimmie George, Barbara Mackenzie, and George Cloud. Celilo Relocation Project files, Oregon Historical Society, neg. 104340.

Village, it was also characterized by the usual neglect the community suffered at the hands of local, state, and federal agencies. Wasco County had heretofore been able to judge most Celilos ineligible for welfare because many were enrolled members of reservations. County officials who were engaged in relocation were motivated by their determination to keep Indians off the welfare rolls in the face of what would be an economic catastrophe for the village. The Bureau of Indian Affairs was also caught in the midst of a congressional struggle at the time of relocation. During bureaucratic restructuring, the BIA lost its subagent at The Dalles, Clarence Davis, who oversaw Celilo Village. But the agency continued to fend off efforts by congressional Republicans to dismantle the BIA in the push for termination policy. Finally, Army Corps of Engineer officials dragged their feet when it came to negotiating compensation with the four treaty tribes affected by the dam and relocation, doing so only when Congress withheld appropriations.

The Army Corps of Engineers planned to purchase Indian homes that would be flooded by the dam, but by 1954 it had no intention of relocating displaced residents. The Wasco County Welfare Commission responded to this news with alarm. County officials worried that Indians would simply move their homes to higher ground, "creating an unsightly and unsanitary condition" at a new site, and that the out-of-work fishermen posed a "serious welfare problem."[49] The Corps was legally responsible only for providing Indians with the appraised value of their homes and drying sheds, an often meager amount that would not cover the cost of a minimally acceptable replacement. The Corps had no responsibility for relocating Indians. The Corps's inaction mobilized Wasco County Judge Ward Webber, who asked Barbara Mackenzie to propose a plan for relocating displaced families. The BIA, in turn, did its best to compel the Corps to respond to the cost of the move.[50]

Part of The Dalles Dam project consisted of moving the Union Pacific Railroad to higher ground where it passed Celilo Village. The Corps needed an easement through the village from the Department of the Interior. This provided the BIA with adequate leverage to exact cooperation from the Corps. In February 1955, the BIA "urged that no right-of-way be granted" by the Interior Department to the Corps until given the chance to strike a deal,[51] a compromise that was reached in a meeting between the BIA, the Army Corps, and Wasco County. In a trade, the Corps agreed to transfer $210,000 to the Interior Department and the BIA agreed to transfer five and a half acres to the Corps for the relocation of the railroad. The Interior Department would then transfer funds to Wasco County, which would administer the relocation of the Indians. Congressional appropriations in 1955 made the swap and plans for relocation possible.[52]

Barbara Mackenzie wrote the original relocation proposal. At this early stage, Mackenzie made important decisions that affected the outcome of relocation. She insisted that the Bureau of Indian Affairs allow her great independence in her dealings with the Indians at Celilo. She recognized that, because most Celilos distrusted the BIA, "nothing would succeed" unless she could appear to act autonomously. Second, and even more important, Mackenzie organized an advisory committee that included Indians and non-Indians to handle the difficult issues that relocation was bound to raise. This group recommended families for relocation and determined which were qualified. Years later, Mackenzie recalled that she rented a trailer so that she could live at Celilo.[53] She moved to the outskirts of the village and opened her curtains, the conventional invitation in the community for visitors. For weeks she waited to be approached, until Flora Cushinway Thompson, wife of Chief Thompson, made her way to the white social worker's trailer. Thompson's visit signaled acceptance and instigated a partnership between the two women.

To prepare for relocation, Wasco County interviewed Indians who might need new homes. The survey and subsequent interviews with Indians indicated that most wanted to remain in the Celilo area, but the relocation committee, citing problems with sanitation, the availability of utilities, and access to area schools, proposed $500 bonuses for families who relocated at least ten miles from the village. The committee's plan allowed each eligible family about $7,500 apiece to put toward an existing home or to pay for building a new home. All of the houses required approval by the BIA, and in the kind of paternalism common at the time, the program would not allow Indians to sell or mortgage their new homes without a cosigner. Eligible Indians had to document residency in the village from 17 May 1950, the day Congress approved The Dalles Dam. In all, fifty families applied for aid, and the committee deemed thirty-six qualified.[54]

The biracial advisory committee (which included Marshall

Dana, J. P Elliott, Charlie Quitoken, Edward Edmo, Mathew Gowdy, Farwell Booth, Kennedy Kahclamat, and George Cloud) met nine times between January and August 1956, convening in Judge Fred Mauser's office, to decide which families to recommend to the Bureau of Indians Affairs for relocation. Barbara Mackenzie's tasks included notifying families that were approved, arranging relocation plans with individual families, determining costs of the new homes, reporting back to the advisory committee, and acting as secretary. Bert Keith initially appraised homes selected by Indian families but relinquished his duties after two weeks; Mackenzie then took on this role as well.[55]

In March 1956, the BIA awarded a contract to construct new homes at New Celilo to B & W Construction of The Dalles. Abe Showaway, an interpreter who lived at Old Celilo, and his wife, Minnie, were the recipients of one of the four new homes at New Celilo. The couple's journey through the relocation bureaucracy was rapid. By the committee's first meeting on 12 January 1956, the Corps had already relocated the Showaways into temporary quarters to make way for dam construction, which made their eligibility a moot question. Abe Showaway wanted to build at New Celilo, and in May he collected the keys to a new home, along with three other families who stayed in the community. By mid-April, seventeen families had negotiated the process of identifying and buying homes, twelve were embroiled in the details of finding suitable houses, three were contemplating where to relocate, and one family was waiting word on its eligibility. At the committee's final meeting in August 1956, only two families were still looking for homes.[56]

Although Mackenzie's advisory committee hoped to provide stability for the families it aided, relocation ultimately fragmented the Indian community at Old Celilo. The committee focused on the strength of nuclear families—by insisting that couples marry and that families with children move away from Celilo—rather than on the effects that dispersal would have on the larger Indian community. Ultimately, only five of thirty-six families moved to New Celilo, while the rest moved to Gresham, The Dalles, Washington State, or their respective reservations. The five that stayed were families without children.[57] With the fishing sites gone, men and women left to find work. Martha McKeown called the post-relocation village a town of "old people or widows with school age children."[58]

The final report on relocation insisted that the project was a success, claiming that "little discrimination was encountered" and that "probably the worst place for an Indian is on a reservation." The report described Indians as having "found a ready acceptance by white neighbors in schools, in churches, and in employment, . . . most appear quite happy in the new surroundings." But relocation was a painful process that tore at the very fabric of community at Celilo. The relocation plan moved residents who had lived within an Indian-centered community into the surrounding white community. Mackenzie was discouraged when potential neighbors of the relocated families complained about the possible devaluation of their property if Indians moved into their neighborhoods. Moreover, the relocation project evolved out of a governmental culture that largely ignored the people of Celilo Village. Except to residents and a few sympathizers, relocation was a backburner issue tended only when conflict threatened to boil over.[59]

DEATH

On a rainy Sunday in 1957, Celilo residents watched the river's current slow as the new reservoir inundated the islands, fishing sites, shores, and surrounding landmarks that had inscribed their lives. Chief Tommy Thompson spent the day at Hood River, Oregon, in a rest home. By then more than 100 years old, the chief had succumbed months earlier to an illness that left him an invalid. He visited Celilo Falls one last time after the flood, for a New Year's celebration at the village longhouse.[60]

The chief died on a Sunday evening in 1959, two years after the completion of The Dalles Dam. On Chief Thompson's final journey to Celilo, a newspaper reporter described him as "taken in darkness past the gleaming, whirring massiveness of The Dalles Dam which he bitterly opposed and which in life he had declined to look at."[61] More than 1,000 people, Native and non-Native, gathered at the Celilo longhouse to pay their respects to a leader known for his humor and the ferocity with which he defended Native fishing rights and opposed The Dalles Dam. Flora Thompson wrapped her husband's body in white buckskin and ten Pendleton blankets and placed him in a hand-hewn cedar coffin. A single eagle feather in his clasped hands denoted his rank. Friends carried his body from the village to an Indian cemetery a few hundred feet above the river for a televised funeral. The chief was a fighter to the end. He refused to accept the $3,750 due him to compensate for lost fishing sites at Celilo Falls, saying that he would never "signature away" his salmon.

Chief Thompson's death marked a significant turning point, the end of leadership that had lasted more than eighty years. His death mirrored the death of Celilo Falls. Yet Tommy Thompson and his generation left a legacy of struggle, as evidenced in his fight against the many plans for relocation and his opposition to damming the Columbia River. The Dalles Dam transformed the river environment and destroyed the economic basis of the Indians living there—and the very reason for the village. For the first time, salmon fishing was no longer the center of economic activity at the old site.

Despite this, Celilo Village remains to this day. If you travel Interstate 84 twelve miles east of the city of The Dalles to what is now Celilo Lake in the spring or fall, you may very well find Indians fishing a placid Columbia River. They are fewer in number and their catches smaller, but they continue to enact their treaty-reserved rights to fish "usual and accustomed" places. Across the freeway, Celilo Village still stands. The problems of the 1930s—poverty, confused jurisdiction over an Indian town not on a reservation, sanitation, lack of services—still trouble the tiny community. At the same time, residents continued their struggle to remain. Arita Davis, a Celilo Village resident in 1985, told yet another Celilo task force, "I hope you can understand. We don't 'come from' anywhere; this is where we were born, this is where we lived all our lives and we don't want to leave."[62]

6

NEGOTIATING VALUES

Settlement and Final Compensation

The relocation of Celilo Village residents was only one issue regarding a Native geography that the Army Corps had to negotiate. The inundation of the fishing sites at the falls also required compensation. The Celilo settlement was complicated by intertribal conflict that the Army Corps negotiators often exploited. The Umatilla and Warm Springs tribes quickly settled with the federal government with relatively little discord, perhaps because the Yakamas threatened their claims to Celilo. The Yakamas presented the most serious challenge to the federal negotiators, but ultimately they also settled for monetary compensation. Initially, the Corps decided that it would not negotiate with the Nez Perce, which it considered to have a weak claim to Celilo Falls. Congressional intervention brought the Corps to those negotiations too, however. Final compensation led to myriad other problems and mirrored federal termination policies. Fallout would stretch into the 1960s.

Celilo Falls was historically a trade crossroads that attracted Indians from many bands in what would become the states of Oregon, Washington, and Idaho. Remnants of an economically and socially vibrant past remained on the mid–Columbia River of the 1950s, and Celilo Falls still marked a place where people came together to socialize, camp, and fish. The very characteristics that made the area so culturally and economically rich would also complicate the negotiations between tribes and the Army Corps of Engineers. The falls were contested terrain, making them an ideal place to chart historic shifts in tribal power in the Pacific Northwest. Moreover, the Umatilla, Nez Perce, Yakama, and Warm Springs tribes had a long memory of the place and the shifts that had occurred there.

Federal representatives approached negotiations without this knowledge of the history of the falls, which provided a vivid context for tribal members. To ascertain appropriate compensation, the practical-minded Corps wanted simply to determine *who* fished at Celilo and *how much* they caught. Indians asked which point in time the estimates would represent: The present? Some point in the past? In determining the share of the catch for each tribe, *when* was important to Indians, though it was a question that the Corps may have thought merely lengthened already protracted meetings. Ultimately, negotiations centered on fishery estimates made by the U.S. Fish and Wildlife Service and the fisheries commissions of Oregon and Washington for the U.S. Army Corps of Engineers—numbers that represented the industry only partially and imperfectly.

To complicate matters, the Yakamas claimed to be the only treaty-protected fishers at the falls. The Yakama tribal council proclaimed that the Umatillas were guests, as were the Nez Perce, and the Warm Springs had abdicated their rights in an 1865 agreement commonly known as the Huntington Treaty. Although the Warm Springs claimed the Huntington Treaty was fraudulent, it presented a sufficient threat to the Warm Springs' treaty rights that their representatives wanted to avoid a court-determined Celilo settlement.[1] This issue tied the hands of the Warm Springs delegation, a fact that the Corps used to its advantage.

Between March 1945 and 1953 (when the first Indians—the Umatillas—signed an agreement with the federal government regarding the lost fishing sites at Celilo), Indians waged a strug-

Louis McFarland, chairman of the board of trustees of the Confederated Tribes of the Umatilla Reservation, and Colonel Thomas Lipscomb of the U.S. Army Corps of Engineers at the signing of the Umatilla Celilo settlement. Oregon Historical Society, neg. 69606.

gle against the development of the Columbia River at The Dalles. The Yakamas, Umatillas, Warm Springs, Nez Perce, and unaffiliated river Indians all passed resolutions in the first months of 1945 that allowed them to "go on record" in opposition to the proposed dam. In addition, much of the limited correspondence between local Indians and the Bureau of Indian Affairs or the Army Corps—regardless of topic—often included a note about The Dalles Dam. Both Henry Thompson and his father, Tommy Thompson, wrote letters to various people, reminding government officials that "the local Indians want to go on record as against the building of the Dalles Dam."[2] And "expressions of determination . . . to stop construction, if possible," of the dam overwhelmed Celilo Fish Committee meetings.[3] Resolutions and committee meeting minutes are important because they remain the principal evidence of dissent. However, the negotiating meetings between the Army Corps and representatives from individual tribes were even more important to Indians of the period; it was within these meetings, as the terms of compensation were negotiated, that Indians acquired a captive audience of Army Corps staff with whom to voice their opposition.

The Army Corps of Engineers began its preparations for negotiations in earnest in about 1951, following six years of resistance to the dam by Indian tribes and by the Bureau of Indian Affairs. The Army Corps came to the negotiating table after learning important lessons during its experience with Bonneville Dam. The agency wanted to avoid providing "in-lieu" fishing sites to compensate for flooded sites. Instead, the Corps focused on monetary compensation to "buy off" the Indian interest. There were several reasons for this. By the 1950s, it was increasingly hard to provide adequate in-lieu sites on a river that the Army Corps was transforming into a series of lakes. Just as important, representatives of the Army Corps entered the negotiations influenced by termination policy, perhaps hoping that negotiations would end the mid-Columbia Indian fishery. However, the early lack of progress in settling claims with the Indians eventually led the U.S. House of Representatives in 1952 to deny allocation of funds for The Dalles Dam until the Army Corps began negotiations with the Indians. This was the push that had been needed; shortly afterward, the Army Corps met with representatives from the Umatilla and the Warm Springs Reservations.[4]

To prepare for negotiations, the Corps needed to determine the worth of the Indian fishery by answering questions such as: Which Indians were fishing at Celilo? Did they have a treaty-supported right to the sites? How many fish did Indians catch to sell commercially? How many for subsistence use? What did fish buyers and tourists pay for their fish? Answers to these and other questions would allow the agency to devise an average annual value that they could parlay into a lump-sum value for the Indian fishery. The Army Corps contracted with the U.S. Fish and

Wildlife Service to conduct a four-year census of the fishery that, along with an earlier report compiled by the fish agencies of the states of Oregon and Washington, became the basis for compensating the Indians.[5] What the Army Corps did not consider in this process was the cultural significance of Celilo Falls as an intertribal gathering, trading, and fishing site. This human history literally comprised the soils of Celilo, as archaeological investigations of the area's middens would prove, and the men and women who fished the banks of the Columbia and dried their fish in the open air in the 1950s reenacted that history daily. However, within the Army Corps's procedure for measuring compensatory value, Celilo Falls had no value culturally.

The Fish and Wildlife Service collected information on the Celilo fishery by interviewing fishermen and the fish buyers who purchased Indian catches during the primary fishing periods in the spring and fall. In the fall of 1951, the agency hired nine employees to count fish and to observe fishermen, often from afar because many sites were difficult to reach and "coverage achieved was possible only by engaging the staff in much overtime."[6] The four annual reports that the agency produced also noted the incomplete coverage of sites, particularly after the second year, when the department employed fewer surveyors. According to reports, "Census takers exercised extreme caution and took no liberty in reporting . . . estimates,"[7] but the agency calculated the official numbers to be about 10 percent lower than the actual Indian take.[8]

In the last year of the study (1954), the Fish and Wildlife Service depended on just two fish buyers for its data, even though it knew Indian fishermen sold their catches to at least six different buyers. Fish and Wildlife officials also complained that Indians were not cooperating with the survey (possibly in a show of resistance). All of this, along with an unusually poor fishing season in 1954, suggests that the reports underestimated the annual value of the Indian fishery. In addition, although state and federal fish-and-wildlife agencies did not support the development of dams on the Columbia River, these agencies also believed that the "curtailing of Indian fishery will benefit the country as a whole."[9] Ironically, the agencies so often at the center of the debate over regulating the Indian fishery helped to determine its value to local Indians.[10] The U.S. Fish and Wildlife Service estimated the annual value of the Indian fishery at Celilo at $700,000 (in 1952 dollars), with a total worth of $23 million. The estimated annual take was decided from data spanning the years 1938 to 1951, though the report by the Army Corps of Engineers does not explain why these years were chosen.[11] However, the Bonneville Dam was completed in 1938, which refocused Indian interest in the Celilo area; also, 1938 was the first year in which the Corps felt that data was complete and reliable. Many Indians claimed that the salmon runs were immediately affected by the closing of the fishery at Bonneville and that their takes at Celilo were smaller, by as much as 15 percent. And because 1952 was the best year for pounds of fish caught in all the years for which there is data, some Indians felt that there was a strategic reason for not including those numbers. However, the Corps also did not include 1954, one of the worst years for mid-Columbia fishing up to that point.

But by adopting this figure, the Corps had determined the size of the compensation pie. What it did next was to ask Indians themselves to determine the size of each reservation's share, a strategy that exacerbated the ongoing conflicts among Indians over the salmon resource at Celilo.

THE WARM SPRINGS AND UMATILLA SETTLEMENT

Just a few months before the Army Corps scheduled meetings with the Oregon tribes, the agency compiled a "special report" on the "Indian fishery problem." In this document—under a section titled "Desire of the Indians"—the Army Corps listed six items: (1) the tribes did not want the dam to be built; (2) they wanted full compensation for their losses if they could not stop the dam; (3) they preferred in-lieu sites to monetary compensation; (4) none of the tribes wanted the settlement to be determined by the court system; (5) all preferred a settlement before construction of the dam was started; and (6) none of the tribes was "generally inclined" to give up their fishing rights as part of the compensation package for the lost sites.[12] Of the six "desires," Indians realized only two. They came to a settlement without entering court, and they did not relinquish their treaty fishing rights, only the fishing sites themselves. Whether Indians realized full compensation for their losses depends on whom one asks.

In separate but similarly structured settlements, the Umatilla and Warm Spring Indians did not vocalize their opposition to the dam to the extent that the Yakamas did. However, it would be a mistake to suggest that the Umatillas and Warm Springs passively supported construction of the dam. Although both confederated groups protested the dam in 1945, Warm Springs lawyer T. Leland Brown assured a newspaper reporter in 1952 that the Indians he represented were not opposed to the dam as long as they received "just compensation." They were "as patriotic as any group of Americans," Brown argued, and "willing to accept the view that The Dalles dam . . . is needed for national defense."[13] Brown's comments indicate that the cold-war justification for the dam laid out by the Army Corps in congressional hearings framed the negotiations.

More important, the Umatilla and Warm Springs tribes may very well have felt increasingly pushed to the periphery of the Celilo fishery by the 1950s, both by the more numerous Yakama fishermen and by Native fishermen from outside the Pacific Northwest. When the Yakama tribal council declared in a 1951 resolution that they were the only group to have a treaty right to Celilo Falls,[14] that move was only the most recent Yakama strategy in an ongoing dispute over who would have access to the rich resources of the mid–Columbia River. (The Yakamas did not address Nez Perce claims at this point, probably because the Army Corps did not believe the Idaho Indians had legitimate claims to Celilo, a controversy discussed later in this chapter. In addition, many people assumed that most unaffiliated Indians would enroll with the Yakamas and therefore would not compete with them for compensation but could actually enhance Yakama claims.) The Umatilla and Warm Springs tribes cooperated with each other in July 1950, protesting what they felt was the domination of the Celilo Fish Committee by the Yakama Indians. The Umatilla and Warm Springs Indians left the CFC and asked the Bureau of Indian Affairs to take over the regulation of the Indian fishery, because "in all disputes coming before the committee for action, the Yakama Indians would decide in favor of the Indians belonging to their tribe and against the Warm Springs and Umatilla Indians."[15] Warm Springs superintendent Jasper Elliott warned E. Morgan Pryse, BIA area director, that this action by the Oregon tribes "demonstrated the fact that there is a very wide breach between the three tribes concerning fishing interest at Celilo Falls."[16] It is not surprising, therefore, that the Umatillas and Warm Springs entered into negotiations with the notion that the Yakamas threatened their interests in the mid-Columbia fishery.

For its part, the Army Corps assumed that the Oregon tribes had a right to compensation, although negotiators were not above using the conflict between the Oregon tribes and the Yakamas to their advantage. On several occasions, Corps negotiator Percy Othus referred to the fact that the agency was compensating the Umatilla and Warm Springs tribes despite their shaky legal claims to Celilo.[17] One might infer that Othus used this as a strategy to limit negotiations and compensation.

In a letter he sent to the tribes on 22 February 1952,[18] Othus set the limits of what Corps representatives would negotiate. Most important, the Corps wanted to limit negotiations to the sites at hand and did not want to enter into a discussion regarding the overall depletion of the Columbia River salmon by dam construction.[19] In addition, the Army Corps would consider separate payments for Indian-owned buildings lost in the flooding. The Army Corps eventually condemned homes and drying sheds submerged under Celilo Lake. The agency estimated a monetary value for these buildings and then paid individual Indians for them, provided the agency could determine ownership. Finally, the Army Corps wanted to negotiate with individual tribes for a lump-sum settlement. The agency did not consider offering in-lieu sites as part of a settlement package, although many Indians preferred them to the money the Army Corps offered.

The Army Corps asked each tribe to appoint two or three representatives to attend these negotiations. By approaching tribes individually, the Corps was able to avoid some of the intertribal conflicts over the fishery as well as an intertribal effort to undermine the negotiations. The Army Corps protected the smaller tribes from the more aggressive Yakamas *and* then strategically reminded tribes with weaker claims of the agency's accommodation. Nonetheless, when negotiations slowed, Percy Othus strategically suggested bringing the tribes together to make a single settlement that the tribes themselves would decide how to distribute.[20]

In negotiations with the Umatillas and the Warm Springs, Percy Othus dominated the meetings, speaking primarily to the tribal attorneys. Only after the meetings were drawing to a close were the Indians themselves asked to respond to what had occurred in their mostly silent presence. In December 1952, the Umatillas and the Warm Springs accepted a settlement drafted by the Corps ("only under protest," according to a 1984 Warm Springs tribal history).[21] Both tribes relinquished rights to sue the federal government for any further compensation by accepting a package totaling $8.245 million for 2,200 tribal members, the equivalent of about $3,700 for every enrolled tribal member. In an interview with an *Oregonian* reporter, Colonel Thomas Lipscomb warned the Yakamas that "if the power needs of the Pacific

Northwest are to be met, the example of these two Indian tribes will have to be followed by other patriotic citizens of the region and of their country."[22]

THE YAKAMA SETTLEMENT

The negotiating committee for the confederated Yakama tribes was clearly upset by the Umatilla and Warm Springs settlements. Moreover, the Yakamas asserted that they were the only treaty-protected fishers at Celilo. In a pamphlet marking the centennial of the 1855 treaty, the Yakamas depicted themselves as "hosts to the visiting Indians" who "shared their tribal fishing location with them." The Yakamas described this generosity as a pretreaty tradition in which "at no time . . . did the visiting Indians ever assume any property rights in the fisheries." The Yakamas considered that the only other Indians who shared a right to the Celilo fishery were the Warm Springs Indians but argued that the 1865 Huntington Treaty had made those rights void. Even though the Corps had set aside what nearly everybody considered an unjust treaty, the Yakamas insisted that the Warm Springs be made to stand by that early treaty. The Yakamas also considered the Umatillas simply guest fishers with no claim to the fishery apart from the generosity shown by the Yakamas.[23]

The Yakama pamphlet also asserted that the tribe comprised 63 percent of the fishers at Celilo and that Yakama fishers caught 78 percent of the salmon sold commercially.[24] Figure 1 illustrates data that the U.S. Fish and Wildlife Service compiled in 1952, the only year in which surveyors noted the tribal affiliation of Indian fishers. It is clear that the surveyors often did not know the tribal affiliation of the fishermen. However, it is equally clear that an overwhelming majority of those whose affiliation could be determined were Yakama fishers. In addition, the federal agency estimated that the Yakama tribe owned approximately 68 percent of the fishing sites at Celilo (see fig. 2). These figures confirm the

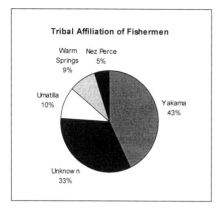

Tribal Affiliation of Fishermen

Warm Springs 9%
Nez Perce 5%
Umatilla 10%
Yakama 43%
Unknown 33%

Tribal Ownership of Fishing Sites

Unknown 8%
Other 1%
Warm Springs 10%
Nez Perce 2%
Umatilla 9%
Celilo 2%
Yakama 68%

FIG. 1. Tribal affiliation of fishermen. U.S. Fish and Wildlife Service, 1952

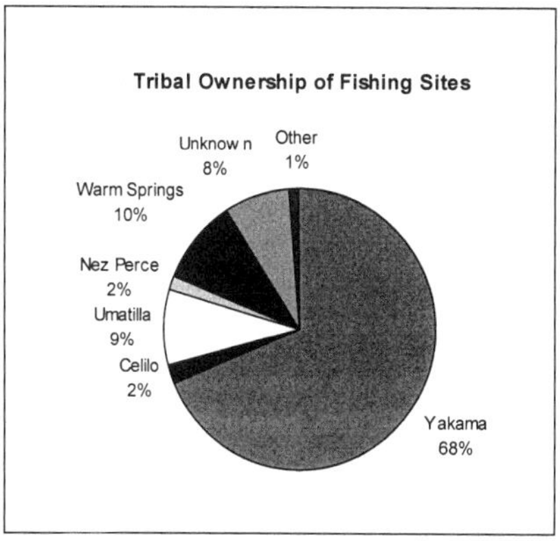

FIG. 2. Tribal ownership of fishing sites. U.S. Fish and Wildlife Service, 1952

assertion made by the Yakamas that they were the most numerous fishers at the falls.

The Warm Springs–Umatilla settlement was based on the equal division of the Celilo fishery among the reservation Indians. In other words, the Corps determined a set value for the fishery and then divided it equally among all enrolled tribal members. The Yakamas argued that they had a superior right to the fishery because their estimates and those of the U.S. Fish and Wildlife Service suggested that they were the most active fishers. Therefore the Yakamas resented being placed on the same level as the Umatilla and Warm Spring Indians and complained that the Corps had a predetermined settlement in mind for the Yakamas, one modeled on the settlement with the Oregon tribes. If that was the case, they suggested, negotiations were simply a meaningless exercise. Paul Niebell, the attorney for the Yakamas, complained that "it appears to be true . . . that we were not going to get into any negotiated settlement but that the terms of any settlement that we must accept were to be dictated by the Army Engineers."[25]

The Yakamas also objected to the way in which the early settlement undermined their ability to protest the dam. In its internal report, the Corps described the Yakamas as "doing everything in their power to prevent or forestall construction of The Dalles Dam." Kiutus Jim, a member of the tribal council, accused the Army Corps of bribing the Oregon tribes, arguing that "the legal owners [the Yakama] were not consulted and never have agreed to any dam built. We fought it to the last ditch." Jim claimed that he did "not blame the Umatillas and the Warm Springs Indians for grabbing off what they have got for they have nothing to lose but everything to gain."[26] In 1998 Johnson Meninick, the cultural resources program manager at the Yakama Nation, described the strategy of the Army Corps as knocking off two of the tribes with one (the Yakamas) to go: in other words, momentum shifted against continued efforts by the Yakamas to stop the dam when the Umatillas and Warm Springs reached a settlement.[27]

Even if one does not accept their claims to a superior right to the fishery, the Yakama negotiating committee worked differently from the Umatilla and the Warm Springs negotiating committees. At one meeting with the Corps, the Yakama negotiating committee brought with it eleven Indians and tribal employees, including a fish biologist and a court recorder, presumably to take notes for the tribal record; at this meeting, the federal agency had just six representatives, including its own note taker. Only in meetings with the Yakamas were the Army Corps representatives outnumbered. The Yakamas made their presence felt immediately: members of their negotiating team led the meeting, in cooperation with Percy Othus. The Yakamas skillfully alternated between accusing Othus of being unfair by not accepting reasonable offers made by the Yakama negotiating committee and assuring Othus that they knew he wanted to do what was honorable for the Indians even when his superiors would be happy with a minimum settlement.

Eagle Saluskin, a member of the tribal council, reminded the negotiating committee that "the Yakama nation of Indians have in the past given up their rights and are still giving up their rights today. . . . We are up here to just claim what we realize the government owes us. On the other hand, the Government is beating us down continuously." Saluskin opened his remarks by saying, "All the history that is recorded in the Department of Archives shows... that the Indians were taken for a ride. They were beaten in every deal that had been transacted by white people."[28]

At one meeting, the Yakamas even asked the Army Corps members to leave the room so that the tribe's negotiating team could speak with their attorney privately for a few minutes. This was markedly different from the meetings held between the Army Corps and the Oregon tribes. Unlike the Warm Springs and the Umatillas, the Yakama tribe negotiated the terms of their settlement from a relative position of power. It would be too easy to overstate just how effective that position was, but it would also be a mistake to underestimate the Yakamas' strength. The Yakamas were skillful at strategically protecting their fishing rights, a practice that reached back to the 1880s when they first began to use the courts to do so. They also had the strongest claim to the Celilo fishery, supported by their figures and by the official figures of the U.S. Fish and Wildlife Service surveys. Finally, the Yakamas held off negotiations longer than the Oregon tribes, knowing that the Army Corps was legally obligated to come to a settlement with them.

Yet ultimately, the Yakamas still did not negotiate a settlement completely in their favor. The Yakamas successfully raised their population (to 4,007 enrollees), which brought their share to more than $15 million (approximately 59 percent of the total dollars spent by the federal government to compensate the Indians). But the Corps refused to deliberate in-lieu sites, and the Yakamas' efforts did not halt construction of the dam.[29]

THE NEZ PERCE SETTLEMENT

Although the Army Corps of Engineers never had serious doubts about Oregon or Washington tribal claims to Celilo Falls, they did have misgivings about Nez Perce claims. Idaho Indians made up only 5 percent of the Indians fishing at Celilo in 1952. Moreover, they were not represented on the Celilo Fish Committee, and the CFC had tried to keep them from fishing at the falls. The intertribal conflict over treaty-protected rights at Celilo Falls provided the backdrop to the more serious challenge to the Nez Perce claim made by the Corps in the 1950s. In 1949 the Celilo Fish Committee asked Edward Swindell Jr., a Bureau of Indian Affairs attorney, whether it could legally prevent Nez Perce fishermen from fishing at Celilo.[30] Furthermore, the Army Corps suggested that when local Indians formed the CFC in 1935, part of their purpose was to prevent Idaho Indians from fishing traditional sites in Oregon and Washington.[31] Although there was serious conflict between the Warm Springs, Umatillas, and Yakamas, all three tribes agreed that the Nez Perce did not have a rightful claim.

In 1954 the Corps assigned Jasper Elliott, a former Warm Springs BIA superintendent who was then working for the Army Corps, to collect affidavits from river Indians about the Nez Perce who fished at the falls. In addition, the Army Corps hired Carling Molouf, an anthropologist based in Montana, to prepare a report on the Nez Perce claims "from an anthropologist's view point." By the summer of 1955, the Corps had compiled evidence ranging from exploration accounts, expert witness statements, court cases, and Bureau of Indian Affairs records to challenge the Nez Perce claim that the falls were among their usual and accustomed fishing sites. The Army Corps published this evidence in 1955 in a 211-page document, determining that the Nez Perce had no legal claim to the sites.[32] In effect, the Army Corps invested an impressive amount of labor and money to avoid compensating the Nez Perce for their claims to the Celilo fishery.

At a negotiating meeting with Nez Perce representatives, the Army Corps suggested a settlement of $1 million while still contending that the Nez Perce did not have a legal claim to Celilo. The sum was considerably less than the approximately $6 million the Nez Perce could have received if they negotiated the same per capita settlement that other Indians did. The Nez Perce wanted compensation at the same rate as the other tribes, an amount of $3,754.91 per person enrolled in the tribe, or a total sum of $6,435,905. Anything less, they argued, was an invalidation of their equitable right in the Celilo fishery. Even though government data indicated that the Nez Perce represented only 5 percent of those Indians fishing at Celilo, Angus Wilson of the Nez Perce tribal executive committee argued that their rights were "equal to those of the Yakimas and Umatillas and superior to the Warm Springs." Furthermore, "As our rights are indistinguishable from those of the Yakimas and the Umatillas, we expect settlement to be made on the same basis as those of the other tribes."[33] The Army Corps asserted that a sum of $1 million was fairer because the Nez Perce could not claim a right equal in stature to the other tribes.

After three formal meetings over three years and more than two years of research, the Nez Perce had not convinced the Army Corps's Portland District that the tribe had a right to compensation. Senator Henry Dworshak of Idaho intervened on behalf of the Nez Perce; Charles McDaniel of the Army Corps noted that Dworshak called Marvin Sonosky, the new attorney for the Nez Perce, three times during the proceedings to monitor the negotiations.[34] In June 1955, the Army Corps met with Nez Perce representatives over two days to discuss their claim; in August 1955, the Corps recommended an end to the negotiations, citing Nez Perce intransigence.

When the Army Corps proposed to end the negotiations, McDaniel reported that "it triggered a discussion among the Indian representatives themselves and it was quite apparent that a majority (not including all of counsel) were willing to make substantial compromises." At this point, Roy Sceufele, representative for the Portland District office "on a somewhat of an arbitrary basis," offered to compensate the Nez Perce to the tune of $2.8 million. This was the highest offer made by the Army

Corps to that point, although McDaniel suggested in private notes that the Army Corps was willing to go even higher. Senator Dworshak called the offer "outrageous." The Nez Perce and their attorney left the meeting after declining the proposal.[35] Although the Yakamas always seemed ready to leave negotiations when they were not going well, the negotiations between the Corps and the Nez Perce were fraught with even greater conflict.

Instead of those negotiations being cut off in 1955, a month later, the negotiations were on again and resulted in a basic agreement: that the Corps would compensate the Nez Perce for the Celilo fishery. The two groups still had to agree on the contours of the contract. The negotiations continued into 1956, but this time they took place in front of the Senate Appropriations Committee. Charles McDaniel described the negotiations as "tedious and rather lengthy," in which the amount of compensation seemed to be the only point left open.[36] Marvin Sonosky and Senators Herman Welker and Henry Dworshak of Idaho argued that in their negotiations the Corps showed a "lack of equity . . . toward the Nez Perce." Nez Perce supporters asked the Army Corps to compensate the Indians to the sum of $3.2 million, equivalent to half what it would have gotten by the terms of the compensation agreements reached with the other tribes. When General Istchner, acting for the Army Corps, refused to negotiate Senator Welker's terms, the senator ended the hearings. After the hearings, Attorney Sonosky approached Istchner, willing to settle for the offered $2.8 million, but the general was not willing to speak with him.[37] The animosity between the two groups must have eased, because the Army Corps finally settled with the Nez Perce for compensation of $2.8 million.[38]

SETTLEMENT FOR THE UNENROLLED

Unenrolled Celilo Village residents found themselves embroiled in vigorous negotiations with the Army Corps of Engineers for their fishing sites at Celilo Falls, without the united front of tribal representatives and lawyers enjoyed by reservation Indians. When Clarence Davis's post as BIA subagent at The Dalles was eliminated in July 1950, a critical link was severed between the Celilo Indians and local and federal bureaucracies. Davis's absence, and the fact that the Corps decided to contact individual Indian tribes, left the unenrolled group in a weakened position to negotiate with the Corps.

Initially, the Army Corps attempted to enroll Celilos at the region's Indian reservations, where they would be compensated through agreements reached with those tribes. Other Celilos hired a local legal firm, Easley and Whipple, to oversee the contracts the Army Corps asked them to sign. How the Corps and Celilo Indians came to an agreement about compensation remains shrouded in unrecorded individual meetings. Evidence suggests that Army Corps employees cornered individual Indians alone in this stage of negotiations.

In a "daily log" of the negotiations between the agency and Celilo Chief Tommy Thompson, Percy Othus described how he and an employee of the Real Estate Division of the Army Corps avoided discussing compensation with groups of Celilos. During one of their attempts to contact Thompson, the two Army Corps employees were met by a large number of Indians. Deciding that it "would not be possible to intelligently discuss the problem" with Thompson under those circumstances, they arranged a second meeting at the Project Engineer's office, on what could be considered agency territory. At this meeting, Thompson was unwilling to make a decision but asked for another meeting to be held at his home; neither he nor his wife, Flora, showed up for this second appointment. Finally, Thompson told Othus that he would not sign the agreement.[39] Thompson continued to refuse to sign the papers that would have provided compensation for his fishing site, until his health failed and he was simply unable to negotiate further. (After Thompson's death in 1959,

Flora Thompson signed the agreement for the $3,754.91, using the funds to defer the costs of Tommy Thompson's elaborate funeral.[40])

Irene Brunoe's description of the negotiations between herself and the Army Corps (filed as a complaint against the Army Corps and its tactics) illustrates how the Army Corps persuaded some Celilo Indians to sign contracts. Brunoe complained that when Percy Othus and Jasper Elliott came to her home and asked her to sign some papers, she told them she would have to show them to her husband because she could not read. They returned over the next two days, staying each time for several hours. Brunoe attested that although she wanted to negotiate with the men while someone else was present, Othus wanted to speak only with her alone. Finally, in a last effort to get Brunoe to sign the contract, Othus promised her "the money in thirty days, then I could have a new car, new clothes for the children and steaks every day for all the family." Othus also claimed that, if Brunoe did not sign, he would use her "as a guinea pig in setting all of the cases."[41] Eventually the Corps compensated unenrolled Celilo Indians about $3,750 per person (the same amount granted to most reservation Indians).

THE WEALTH OF INDIANS

In the end, the Corps compensated the Yakama Indians $15,019,640; the Warm Springs Indians $4,451,784; the Umatilla Indians $4,616,971; and the Nez Perce Indians $2,800,000. The more than $3,000 awarded each tribal enrollee was a significant sum, equivalent to a year's salary for the average Dalles family. Yet the payments did not represent a windfall for most Indians. Instead, the money represented scant compensation for a tremendous loss. During the negotiations between the Yakamas and the Army Corps, Alex Saluskin reminded Percy Othus that for some Indians, no amount of money would adequately compensate them for the loss of the falls. One Yakama suggested to Saluskin that the fisheries were worth more than $100 million, but even that sum seemed inadequate for "when [the Falls are] all covered by water, the history and legendary value will be lost to our people."[42] It is one thing to claim that no money could compensate for the loss of the falls, the wild river, and the salmon that sustained generations of Indians who fished from the rocky shores of the Columbia. The gravity of that statement, made by so many tribal and unenrolled leaders, becomes apparent as one examines what compensation really meant.

The year 1959 looked to be promising for Yakama enrollee Jacob Mann and his daughter Martha. In the fall, seventeen-year-old Martha Mann would begin her third and final year at Midway Junior College, in Midway, Kentucky, where she would complete her high school education on a full scholastic scholarship. In addition, the Manns were due thousands of dollars from The Dalles Dam settlement. That summer Jacob Mann wrote from White Swan, Washington, to the commissioner of the Bureau of Indian Affairs to request that his daughter be allowed to withdraw funds from The Dalles Dam settlement to offset some of the expenses of going to school out of state.[43] Commissioner Glenn Emmons referred the letter to his assistant, Selene Gifford, who replied in late November that the tribes were in the process of securing minors' trust funds and that Mann would receive full information once they were established. Gifford wrote, "We are hopeful that this will occur in the near future, and you will then be in a position to determine whether you wish to draw upon your daughter's funds for her high school education or conserve her funds for her post high school training."[44] By the time Gifford's letter reached the Manns, Martha had already begun her final year of high school and would see no benefit from The Dalles settlement that academic year.

Lavina Williams, a Nez Perce, hoped to use her lump-sum settlement of $600 to pay for dental work for her two sons. She wrote with some alarm to Idaho Representative Gracie Pfost for help when it became clear to her that the Idaho state welfare agency wanted to garnish $570 of her $600 settlement for welfare assistance that she had accepted previously when apparently she was not qualified for welfare. She hoped Pfost could tell her about her rights regarding the money and whether the state had "any right" to her Celilo payment. She complained that the welfare agency "treated me rather odd at times, they keep the check and hold out on me, and mail it whenever they get good and ready." Williams evidently had been told that if she accepted the $600 Celilo payment, she would no longer qualify for welfare. She wrote, "I will just be dropped from the welfare for the rest of my life, that I could never get help again. I would work if there was jobs here, but its [sic] such a small town, no one has work."[45] The Nez Perce General Council discussed the removal of Nez Perce from state welfare rolls during a meeting in February 1957, indicating that the onetime payment threatened the long-term qualifications of many welfare-dependent Indians.[46]

Representative Pfost asked BIA Commissioner Emmons to investigate the Williams case, expressing concern that "if the welfare payments are reduced the amount indicated in the letter, it would be most difficult for her to provide adequate medical and dental care for her children."[47] Within a matter of days, Emmons responded that Williams's assistance grants were "only supplementations [sic] when income and resources fall short of needs." He suggested that the issue should be taken up with the county director of public assistance in Grangeville, Idaho, because "the Bureau of Indian Affairs has no authority in the matter."[48] Emmons sent the exchange to the BIA Portland Area Office, which contacted BIA superintendent William Ensor at Lapwai, Idaho. Superintendent Ensor reported that Lavina Williams had "visited this office several times to discuss her welfare problems" and had been advised to "prepare a program" for the use of her Dalles funds. Ensor complained that the office was thwarted by a lack of cooperation on the part of Williams, who had not prepared a plan in consultation with the welfare office, a place at which she evidently felt mistreated.[49] Williams may have written to Pfost hoping to avoid discussing her plans for spending her portion of The Dalles Dam settlement with a social worker. Unfortunately she, like many others, would find that state and county welfare offices were eager to shape how Indians used their settlement funds.

For many Indian families, the settlement represented potential: education for their children, better homes, additional land, a reliable vehicle that would take a breadwinner to work, dental work, or new eyeglasses. It is easy to imagine an individual spending the funds many times over in her head as she waited for them to be disbursed. And it is likely that at least some thought about spending a portion of the money on luxuries that mostly eluded them. But most found themselves in situations similar to those encountered by Jacob Mann or Lavina Williams. They faced delays in the disbursement of funds, which could be used for only identified expenditures. Furthermore, Indians risked losing state and county welfare benefits as a result of their "windfall." If the settlement represented promise in the face of tremendous loss, the promise was delayed—and in some cases, denied.

DISBURSING THE SETTLEMENT: TRIBAL PLANS

Once the Umatillas, Warm Springs, Yakamas, and Nez Perce negotiated agreements in 1953 and 1954 with the Army Corps of Engineers for their losses, money was earmarked in the U.S. Treasury for disbursement to the tribes. The Bureau of Indian Affairs—which wanted no responsibility for disbursing funds to individuals—demanded that each tribe propose a disbursement plan before the agency would disburse the funds. As far as BIA officials were concerned, the approval phase of the tribal plans was essential to the agency's ability to supervise the disbursement of tribal funds. Once the BIA approved the plans, money would be transferred from the U.S. Treasury to the tribes as "unrestricted funds" and, although tribes were restrained by the bounds of the negotiated plans, the funds came, by and large, without government restrictions. The BIA recognized tribal sovereignty in disbursing funds and at the same time moved to constrict the hands of tribal governments by putting in place the necessity of agency approval.[50]

The disbursement of settlement funds was not a straightforward proposition. Moreover, disbursement was fraught with meaning beyond what could have been the simple process of paying for usurped property. Tribal governments faced several options when it came to the settlement funds. Each tribe could have publicly denounced their treatment by the federal government and refused the funds. The Yakamas, the most vocal of the tribes, continued to skirt outright refusal after 1957 and regularly vied with the BIA for control over the funds once they were allocated. When the tribes accepted compensation, they faced other options: allocating the funds on a per capita basis, putting the funds into a trust for the enrollees, or using a combination of both these strategies. Of course, Congress distributed funds to the tribes, not to individuals. This meant that the tribes could withhold a portion of the award from individual members.

It would be common sense to view the settlement funds as replacement income for the income lost as a result of the inundation of fishing stations. Moreover, many families derived at least a portion of their annual income from the fish caught at those stations, so the money could be understood as payment for those specific stations. But although the tribes regarded those fishing stations as individually owned, the federal government defined them as tribal property. Therefore tribes, not individuals, were harmed by their inundation. Because of this, the BIA refused to approve tribal plans that called solely for a per capita payment and, in fact, connected per capita payments to termination policy. If a tribe such as the Yakama, which had hoped to carry out a plan based on an unregulated per capita payment, adopted such a process, it would also be required to accept termination.

The settlement funds that were meant to compensate Indians for the loss of real estate that provided an *income* could not simply replace that income. Rather than "in-lieu" income, the compensatory payments had to be invested tribally, individually, or, preferably, both—in land, home improvements, or education. The Bureau of Indian Affairs deemed this approach to be in the best interest of the Indians it served, though this severely limited the ways in which Indians could use the funds. For many reasons, including age and circumstances, individuals might not want to invest in education or property; and also for myriad reasons, many individuals might want the option of spending their funds to meet immediate everyday needs.

The Warm Springs planned to add The Dalles Dam settlement to earnings from their considerable timber resources to fund a "long-range program." The Warm Springs tribal council hired Oregon State College to survey human and natural resources on the reservation and to present recommendations for building future economic capacity. In the meantime, the Warm Springs asked the BIA for a "token payment" of $500 as a gesture of goodwill. Eventually, the Warm Springs would make per capita payments of $350 from The Dalles settlement to each enrolled member.[51]

The BIA used the Warm Springs plan as a model for the long-range planning it endorsed when it negotiated with the other three tribes, but the Nez Perce were the first to submit a plan. Initially, the Nez Perce tribal council requested full per capita payments, which the BIA commissioner soundly rejected. Later, Allen Slickpoo warned the tribal general council (comprised of all voting enrolled members of the tribe) that "100 percent per capita would harm the Nez Perce" because "the Bureau would release the Nez Perce as wards" if they insisted on the payment. Martin

Holm, who represented the BIA at this meeting, did not refute Slickpoo's understanding of the risks of per capita payments.[52] If the Warm Springs represented what would be approved, the Nez Perce experience represented the limits the BIA placed on the funds, even while the agency purported that there would be few governmental restrictions.

Navigating the termination threat, the Umatilla carefully prepared for closely monitored per capita payments of $3,300. The tribe's leadership recognized that half their membership lived off-reservation and would not benefit from an investment in reservation infrastructure.

Yakima Tribal Celilo Program Committee members met with representatives of the BIA in February 1957 to hammer out an agreement to disburse the Celilo settlement. They came to an agreement in February, but disbursement was slowed into the 1960s by numerous conflicts between the federal agency and the Yakama Nation. Eagle Saluskin made it clear in the February 1957 meeting that "the Yakama Tribal Council didn't want The Dalles money to begin with," setting the tone for a contentious meeting. The root of the difficulties between the governmental representatives—tribal and federal—was also summed up by a sentiment attributed to Saluskin in the official minutes: "Mr. Saluskin did not feel that the Yakimas were worse than other people. He also said that the Yakima Tribal Council did not want to interfere in the private lives of the Yakima members."[53] However, the BIA required tribal meddling into the lives of its membership if the tribe was to receive the settlement. Nonetheless, the council resisted overseeing its members' use of the funds.

Two years later, the Yakamas were still embroiled in negotiations with the BIA, this time regarding the disbursement of minors' portion of the funds, which were to be placed in trust until a minor reached the age of majority. Problems continued, and by March 1959 Washington Representative Thor Tollefson introduced House Resolution 5134, which threatened to nullify the plans approved by the BIA by circumventing the agency altogether. The bill would have allowed for a onetime per capita payment to every Yakama Nation member; the funds would not be regulated by the BIA or by the tribe and would be distributed to all adults. The bill did not make it out of committee and was never passed.[54]

All of the tribal plans ended up looking remarkably alike, with the exception of the Warm Springs, who accepted smaller per capita payments and invested the balance in reservation resources. At the insistence of the BIA, all of the tribes placed minors' money in trust funds that would be available when individuals turned majority age. Tribal plans included provisions to have individuals submit plans for how they would use their individual settlements, and in that way, they continued the pattern of agency paternalism. Tribes established committees to evaluate the competency of enrollees, to provide assistance to members, and to ultimately determine who qualified for the funds. Once the tribal committee approved a plan, individuals could claim funds ranging from a few hundred to a few thousand dollars.

THE DALLES DAM SETTLEMENT
AND PUBLIC ASSISTANCE

Complicating the settlement-plan negotiations between the tribes and the BIA were state welfare agencies, which initially viewed this compensation as income that could replace public assistance funds. Welfare officials saw the potential to lessen their rolls and threatened to remove anyone who accepted settlement. Some welfare agencies began removing qualified tribal members as soon as the federal government announced that it had concluded negotiations with the tribes—months, even years, before individual tribal members would benefit from the funds.[55]

Conflict between the BIA and the welfare offices of Washington, Oregon, and Idaho centered around differing interpretations of the settlement funds: the BIA considered the funds to be capital assets, whereas the welfare offices considered them replacement income. Considering the funds replacement income would have certainly freed individuals to use the money in any way that they saw fit. What the welfare offices did not take into account, however, was that the settlement was a onetime replacement of income that would have been earned over several years of fishing. As replacement income spread out over time, the funds would not alter the need for assistance among individual Indians. In 1958 the BIA and Washington's state welfare office agreed that tribal members would be eligible for state assistance at least until the settlement was disbursed, which halted the removal of qualified Indians from the welfare rolls before they received their settlement.[56]

Less than a year later, the state agency in Olympia, Washington, was again complaining to the BIA Portland Area Office, this time about the payments held in trust for minors. Claiming that the agency was "very much in sympathy with the need to see that per capita payments to Indian children are used in their best interests," field services supervisor Maurice Powers questioned placing funds in trust when "the paramount need of the child is for money for his current maintenance." Powers argued that assisting Indian children with state aid when they had funds "withheld for some future need which may never materialize" resulted in "discrimination against non-Indian children."[57]

Oregon also worried that Indians on welfare who received Celilo settlement funds without any curtailment of their state aid represented prejudice against non-Indian applicants. This prompted the agency to coin the term "*alleged* financially needy child" to describe an Indian child who drew welfare despite a trust fund. J. E. Harness, director of the Umatilla County Juvenile Department, pointed out to David Hall of the BIA Umatilla Agency that the county had long provided emergency clothing and housing for Indian children without "reimbursement from the particular families involved." Harness asked that the funds set aside for children once they reached adulthood be made available to local agencies.[58]

The BIA responded to state welfare agencies by urging Indian recipients of The Dalles settlement to contact the agencies to discuss an arrangement for spending the funds that would not imperil their eligibility for welfare aid. While the BIA instigated disbursement plans at the tribal level, welfare agencies and their desire to remove enrollees drove the need for disbursement plans at the individual level. The BIA and state welfare agencies throughout the region agreed that if individuals used their funds in designated ways, the agencies would not remove individuals from the welfare rolls, even after they received their share of the settlement. The designated ways in which people could use their funds, not surprisingly, were based on the categories already approved by the BIA: education, property purchase, or property improvement.

In Nez Perce County, Idaho, thirty recipients of the Celilo settlement received welfare. More than half were dropped from the rolls shortly after receiving their payments. According to the Nez Perce County welfare department records, twelve recipients requested that their welfare cases be closed. The county dropped four other cases because they did not submit plans for the use of their funds. Those who continued to receive assistance spent their funds on roofing, water heaters, stoves, refrigerators, furniture, and home repairs.[59]

One of the myths of the Pacific Northwest, undoubtedly reflected in the history of Indian-white relations in other regions, is that the federal government fairly compensated Indian people for the inundation of fishing sites along the Columbia River and that Indians frittered the money away, buying alcohol, fancy clothes, or cars that were soon wrecked. Perhaps there is some truth to these tales, but it is difficult to blame some people for indulging in luxuries. More important, this myth diverts attention from the more typical, devastating, and horribly predictable stories such as those of Jacob Mann or Lavina Williams, who found that they were not really compensated for the loss of Celilo Falls.

In the final settlement involving the construction of The Dalles Dam, annual income was transformed into capital investment, and these expenditures were carefully monitored by the Bureau of Indian Affairs and state welfare agencies. Moreover, in many cases, settlement funds threatened welfare claims, and individuals opted to remove themselves from aid rolls or were removed by the state of Washington, Oregon, or Idaho. For people who lost their welfare eligibility, the settlement did not compensate for the loss of Celilo Falls; it merely replaced aid they already had been receiving.

Moreover, The Dalles settlement negotiations exacerbated pre-existing intertribal conflicts over fishing sites that had long been contested. Prior to contact with whites, whichever Indian group controlled the Long Narrows controlled passage and trade on the Columbia River. When contact with whites came, Native ability to control the river slowly passed into the hands of new settlers. Indians long remained on the river, but they witnessed their power over the riverscape diminish, which mirrored diminished salmon runs. By the mid–twentieth century, Celilo fishing sites were crowded with Indians who held long-standing rights, outsider Indians, and even white fishers. It was contested terrain, a fact exploited by federal agencies intent on turning a wild river into a series of navigable lakes behind enormous hydroelectric turbines. Many Pacific Northwesterners recognize the tragedy that the inundation of Celilo Falls now represents; fewer recognize the tragedy of how the tribes were compensated for their loss.

CONCLUSION

Losses

Many of the Indians who fished at Celilo prayed at a large stone they called Skuch-pa. They filled a naturally occurring hole in this rock with mud, small rocks, and grasses to assure good weather before they ventured out to their scaffolds. One spring morning in 1953, Tommy Thompson was dismayed to find the stone—four feet across and six feet tall—missing. The disappearance became a mystery of sorts, and it represents a larger story of Indian removal at Celilo. The *Oregonian* initially reported that Army Corps engineers moved the stone to the Seufert cannery, where professional archaeologists stored materials before the Corps dynamited the area where the stone had been located. Later, the newspaper revealed that William Seufert (brother of Arthur Seufert, the president of the cannery) had moved it to the Seufert property several months earlier. Defending his actions, William Seufert claimed that "it was partially buried under soil for some 17 years. . . . at no time were the Indians interested enough to dig it out."[1]

Because the stone was on his property, Arthur Seufert may have decided to care for the stone himself rather than return it to the river Indians for whom it had religious significance. The Seufert brothers had assured Indians that they would not prevent them from praying at the stone as it sat in front of the cannery and that, eventually, they would ensure that the stone was housed properly in "some museum." According to Arthur Seufert, "we wanted to take care of it. They [the Indians who claimed the stone] haven't been there for eight or so years, and now they started howling about it was so holy."[2] According to Chief Tommy Thompson, however, river Indians cared for the stone, which had been significant for those who fished and lived along the river for as long any of them could remember.

The rock was sacred cultural property, and its story represents just one of a series of removals that accompanied dam building at The Dalles. The removal of the prayer rock mirrors the removal of scaffolds from the falls, of residents from Old Celilo Village, of petroglyphs from the river's edge, of rapids and even salmon from the Columbia River.[3] The removals of the 1950s fit into a larger pattern of Native loss, a pattern that began with reservation policies 100 years earlier, the allotment policies at the turn of the twentieth century, and the termination policy of the 1950s. Indeed, the story of the inundation of Celilo Falls and the dislocation of fishers who worked there is shockingly unremarkable and predictable.

The removal of the prayer rock epitomizes the larger story of the region during the 1950s in yet another way. Tommy Thompson and William Seufert struggled over the custody of the prayer rock, reflecting a larger battle over Pacific Northwest resources. Just as the rock could not be kept in its original location and also be housed in a museum, the Columbia River could not be transformed into a series of lakes and still support significant numbers of Indian salmon fishers. Seufert displayed the same kind of arrogance as the city of The Dalles and the federal government toward Indian-utilized resources when he claimed the rock as his, though it held no spiritual significance for him, because he did not think Indians cared for the stone properly. The stone might be honored in a museum, but the people who used it just a few months prior would not receive similar honor. Again, there is nothing surprising in William Seufert's statements; he borrowed from arguments about Indians and their use of resources that hearken back to the earliest stages of American imperialism. Historians have not emphasized enough the effects of river development on Native and disenfranchised people around the world, but a good number have turned their attention to this issue. That record clearly shows that the removal of Indians from the mid–Columbia River follows similar activity in other places.[4]

Although many non-Native residents of the mid–Columbia River celebrated what The Dalles Dam would bring to the region—economic opportunity, flood control, increased navigability of the river, lower energy costs—Indians foresaw a multitude of losses. But the farther one moves from the period of dam construction, the more complicated is the story of loss because non-Indian people in the Pacific Northwest have come to feel the destruction of Celilo Falls profoundly. The white photographers who flocked to the falls just prior to the closing of the dam and the inundation of the mid-Columbia intentionally documented a riverscape and scenes of traditional fishing they knew would soon be gone. Their photographs, which have come to symbolize the region, hang in the homes of many Northwest residents. Celilo Falls is commemorated in murals on downtown streets in The Dalles, in hotel lobbies, and in a local resort. When recently asked about the legacy of Celilo Falls, photographer Laffie Foster responded with gruff emotion that he was "deeply sorry that Celilo is gone." Foster is of a generation of folks who remember not just the images of Celilo Falls but the roar of the falls themselves. It will not be long before the memory of living rapids is replaced completely by that of a cold, imposing stone structure.

The loss is made more acute when measured against the long-term lack of economic gains in The Dalles and the surrounding area. Since the 1980s, The Dalles has been faced with a faltering timber industry and a declining aluminum industry. Today developers in The Dalles put on a cheerful face despite high unemployment, empty downtown buildings, and diminishing federal dollars for improvements. The optimism of the 1950s is a thing of the past. What is left are unfulfilled promises of progress and prosperity.

Where the prayer stone was finally located is unknown. Initially, people such as William Seufert hoped that Congress would allocate funds for a museum that would celebrate the human history along the Columbia River and the progress made in taming it.[5] Congress did not allocate funds for such an interpretive center until decades later, when the celebration of progress was tempered by the awareness of environmental damage that dams came to represent. When it was completed in 1997,[6] the Columbia Gorge Discovery Center overlooked a river that embodied contentious struggles over the region's resources among people divided by race, class, environmental proclivities, length of residency in the region, occupation, recreational uses of the river, and proximity to Portland. It is somewhat ironic that the museum, which looks out over a river once crowded with fish and fishers near one of Native America's wealthiest trading communities, interprets progress and the inevitable loss that accompanies it.

NOTES

INTRODUCTION: DAM DECISIONS

1. Description of the gym comes from a photograph and caption on page 1 of The Dalles *Chronicle*, 15 March 1957. See also "Celebration Set at Dam," The Dalles *Chronicle*, 12 March 1957; and "Reservoir Starts New Rise Today," The Dalles *Chronicle*, 15 March 1957. All articles from The Dalles *Chronicle* appear on page 1 unless otherwise noted.

2. "Reservoir Starts New Rise Today," The Dalles *Chronicle*, 15 March 1957.

3. "Spillway Takes Columbia," The Dalles *Chronicle*, 11 March 1957.

4. "Hydroelectric Power, Soviet Race," The Dalles *Chronicle*, 10 October 1959.

5. Jeanie Senior, "Indians Mark 25th Year of Loss of Celilo Falls," *Oregonian*, 21 March 1982, sec. B, Metro/Northwest, 7.

6. Jay Minthorne, interview by Clark Hansen, 16 August 2000, tape recording, OHS inv. #2784, Oregon Historical Society Research Library, Portland.

7. Elizabeth Woody, *Seven Hands, Seven Hearts* (Portland, Ore.: Eighth Mountain Press, 1994), 67.

8. Richard White, *The Organic Machine: The Remaking of the Columbia River* (New York: Hill and Wang, 1995).

9. Donald Worster's *Rivers of Empire: Water, Aridity, and the Growth of the American West* (New York: Oxford University Press, 1985) is a history of the hydraulic West; this history is dramatized and personalized

in treatments such as William Kittredge's *Hole in the Sky* (New York: Vintage Books, 1992), a memoir of irrigated agriculture in Oregon's Warner Valley. For more on the importance of water in the region, see also Mark Fiege, *Irrigated Eden: The Making of an Agricultural Landscape in the American West* (Seattle: University of Washington Press, 1999); Donald Pisani's numerous works on water policy in the West; Marc Reisner, *Cadillac Desert: The American West and Its Disappearing Water* (New York: Viking, 1986); John Walton, *Western Times and Water Wars: State, Culture, and Rebellion in California* (Berkeley: University of California Press, 1992); and Charles Wilkinson, *Crossing the Next Meridian: Land, Water, and the Future of the West* (Washington, D.C.: Island Press, 1992).

10. Even Worster diverges from his primary argument—which links hydro-engineering to centralized governmental and economic structures—to take note, when he discusses the writings of Mary Austin and John Van Dyke, of desert dwellers who found an inherent beauty in arid lands.

11. The 1990s brought a number of important works related to the history of the Columbia River, such as White, *The Organic Machine*; William Dietrich, *Northwest Passage: The Great Columbia River* (Seattle: University of Washington Press, 1996); Robin Cody, *Voyage of a Summer Sun: Canoeing the Columbia River* (Seattle: Sasquatch Books, 1995); Robert Clark, *River of the West: Stories from the Columbia* (San Francisco: HarperCollins West, 1995); Blaine Harden, *A River Lost: The Life and Death of the Columbia* (New York: W. W. Norton, 1996); William Lang and Robert Carriker, eds., *Great River of the West: Essays on the Columbia River* (Seattle: University of Washington Press, 1999); and Carlos Schwantes, *Columbia River: Gateway to the West* (Moscow, Idaho: University of Idaho Press, 2000). Apart from contributing several significant essays to the area of Columbia Basin history, Lang and Carriker also provide a comprehensive overview of the literature of the field in their introduction to *Great River of the West*. Many of these works were informed by earlier treatments of the river, such as Stewart Holbrook, *The Columbia* (New York: Rinehart, 1956), and Anthony Netboy, *The Columbia River Salmon and Steelhead Trout: Their Fight for Survival* (Seattle: University of Washington Press, 1980).

12. Journalist Dietrich's *Northwest Passage* traces the transformation

of the river through to its current iteration as a "developed" river. Paul Pitzer, in *Grand Coulee: Harnessing a Dream* (Pullman: Washington University Press, 1994), focuses on a single Columbia River dam, the Grand Coulee, to record the Byzantine process whereby an enormous, expensive dam was sited. White's *The Organic Machine* provides a compelling model for thinking about the complexities of a harnessed and managed river. Nature, in this brief but illuminating treatise, has become Frankensteinian, at once both a reflection of human technology and a defiance of the perfection of technology. Moreover, the river is both a natural space and a contested social space defined by human labor and recreation.

13. Books regarding the contemporary salmon crisis in the Pacific Northwest include Joseph Cone, *A Common Fate: Endangered Salmon and the People of the Pacific Northwest* (Corvallis: Oregon State University Press, 1995); Joseph Cone and Sandy Ridlington, eds., *The Northwest Salmon Crisis: A Documentary History* (Corvallis: Oregon State University Press, 1996); and Jim Lichatowich, *Salmon Without Rivers: A History of the Pacific Salmon Crisis* (Washington, D.C.: Island Press, 1999). See also Joseph Taylor's *Making Salmon: An Environmental History of the Northwest Fisheries Crisis* (Seattle: University of Washington Press, 1999).

14. Ulrich, *Empty Nets*. My investigation has benefited from not only Ulrich's book, but also works that put at their center questions of Native access to resources in areas outside of the Columbia River Basin, such as James Waldram's *As Long as the Rivers Run: Hydroelectric Development and Native Communities in Western Canada* (Winnipeg: University of Manitoba Press, 1988); Michael Lawson's *Dammed Indians: The Pick-Sloan Plan and the Missouri River Sioux, 1944–1980* (Norman: University of Oklahoma Press, 1982); and Valerie Kuletz, *The Tainted Desert: Environmental and Social Ruin in the American West* (New York: Routledge, 1998).

15. Donald Fixico examines "a struggle between two different [and mutually incomprehensible] cultural worlds. . . . incongruent in philosophies, goals, values, and cultures" in *The Invasion of Indian Country in the Twentieth Century: American Capitalism and Tribal Natural Resources* (Niwot: University Press of Colorado, 1998), xv.

1 / VILLAGE AND TOWN

1. The Bureau of Indian Affairs was divided into a dozen regional area offices, each of which was headed by a regional director. The Portland Area Office implemented federal policies at the regional level and supervised agents at the Yakama, Umatilla, Warm Springs, and Nez Perce reservations and the sub- or field agent at The Dalles, when there was one.

2. The Yakama Indian Nation officially changed the spelling of Yakima to Yakama, the original spelling, in 1992. This book uses "Yakama" throughout, except when referring to the BIA's Yakima agency of the period before 1992. The spelling "Yakima" is also kept intact in quotations.

3. The removal of Indians from the river parallels a shift in salmon production over the last century and a half. Cain Allen, in "Replacing Salmon: Columbia River Indian Fishing Rights and the Geography of Fisheries Mitigation" (*Oregon Historical Quarterly* 104, summer 2003, 196–227), shows how federal and state fisheries policies have literally moved concentrations of salmon populations from the mid- and upper river (both areas dominated by Indian fishers) to the lower Columbia (dominated by a non-Indian fishery).

4. William G. Loy, et al., "Precipitation Regimes," in *Atlas of Oregon*, 2nd ed. (Eugene: University of Oregon Press, 2001), 157.

5. Robin Cody, *Ricochet River* (Hillsboro, Oregon: Blue Heron Publishing, 1992), 34.

6. Works Progress Administration, "Wasco County Historical Sketch," Extract from Inventory of County Archives of Oregon, No. 33, Wasco County (The Dalles), Project 65-194-25, February 1941, in Oregon Historical Society, vertical file Wasco County—Oregon Counties, Oregon Historical Society Research Library, Portland. See also Ira A. Williams, *Geologic History of the Columbia River Gorge, as Interpreted from the Historic Columbia River Scenic Highway* (Portland: Oregon Historical Society Press, 1991).

7. *The Journals of the Lewis and Clark Expedition,* Volume Five, *July 28–November 1, 1805*, ed. Gary E. Moulton (Lincoln: University of Nebraska Press, 1996), 328–29.

8. Alexander Ross, *Adventures of the First Settlers on the Oregon or*

Columbia River, 1810–1813 (Corvallis: Oregon State University Press, 2000), 130.

9. See both Cone, *A Common Fate*, and White, *The Organic Machine*.

10. B. Robert Butler, "The Physical Stratigraphy of Wakemap Mound: A New Interpretation" (MA thesis, University of Washington, 1960), citing U.S. Department of the Interior, unpublished report for the National Park Service, *Cultural Sequences at The Dalles, Oregon* (1958), by Luther S. Cressman.

11. David French and Katherine French, "Wasco, Wishram, and Cascades," in vol. 12 of *Handbook of North American Indians*, ed. Deward Walker Jr. (Washington, D.C.: Smithsonian Institution, 1998), 374.

12. Moulton, ed., *Journals of Lewis and Clark, Volume 5*, 329. William Clark, journal entry 27 October 1805, quoted in Henry Biddle, "Wishram," *Oregon Historical Quarterly* 27 (1926), 123.

13. For more information on these two groups, see French and French, "Wasco, Wishram, and Cascades," and Eugene Hunn and David French, "Western Columbia River Sahaptins," in vol. 12 of *Handbook of North American Indians*, ed. Deward Walker Jr. (Washington, D.C.: Smithsonian Institution, 1998), 379.

14. U.S. Army Corps of Engineers, *Special Report on Indian Fishery Problem, The Dalles Dam, Columbia River, Washington-Oregon*, 10 March 1952, 8.

15. French and French, "Wasco, Wishram, and Cascades," 368.

16. Theodore Stern, *Chiefs and Change in the Oregon Country Indian Relations at Fort Nez Percés, 1818–1855* (Corvallis: Oregon State University Press, 1996), 20.

17. Kathryn Anne Toepel reports that most of the actual trading activity occurred from about August through October, after fishing slowed (U.S. Department of Agriculture, U.S. Forest Service, *Prehistory and History of the Columbia River Gorge National Scenic Area, Oregon and Washington*, 15 July 1988, by Stephen Dow Beckham, Rick Minor, Kathryn Anne Toepel, and Jo Reese, 124).

18. Coastal cultures practiced slavery and at The Dalles traded women and children captured in battle (Robert Boyd, *People of The Dalles, The Indians of Wascopam Mission: A Historical Ethnography Based*

on the *Papers of Methodist Missionaries* [Lincoln: University of Nebraska Press, 1996], 90). For more about slavery at The Dalles, see Eugene Hunn, *Nch'I-Wána, "The Big River": Mid-Columbia Indians and Their Land* (Seattle: University of Washington Press, 1991).

19. This list comes from Hunn, *Nch'i-Wána*, 224.

20. In contrast, Lewis and Clark estimated that when they passed through in October 1805, approximately 600 Indians lived near Celilo Falls (Boyd, *People of The Dalles*, 50).

21. Ross, *Adventures of First Settlers*, 129. Although Alexander Ross observed the elaborate and extensive trade activity that took place at Celilo Falls, he erroneously demoted it to "chiefly . . . gambling and speculation." Historian Elizabeth Vibert, in *Trader's Tales: Narratives of Cultural Encounters in the Columbia Plateau, 1807–1846* (Norman: University of Oklahoma Press, 1997, 123), warns that early descriptions of the trade activity at The Dalles must be analyzed carefully because the area was "notorious from the early days of the [fur] trade as a place where business was difficult, and the people who gathered there were at best indifferent, at worst violently hostile, to fur traders." Although non-Native observers righteously disparaged Native gambling, the practice was a method of economic exchange integral to the social and economic life around Celilo Falls.

22. Anthropologist Erna Gunther has done considerable work on the significance of the First Salmon ceremony in her two articles, "An Analysis of the First Salmon Ceremony," *American Anthropologist* 28 (1926), 605–17, and "A Further Analysis of the First Salmon Ceremony," *University of Washington Publications in Anthropology* 2 (1928), 129–73.

23. U.S. Army Corps of Engineers, *Special Report on the Indian Fishery Problem*, 11.

24. Author Martha McKeown frequently referred to Celilo Village as Oregon's oldest town in her writings, a claim supported by contemporary archaeology research.

25. Boyd, *People of The Dalles*, 22.

26. Priscilla Knuth, *"Picturesque" Frontier: The Army's Fort Dalles* (Portland: Oregon Historical Society Press, 1967), 20.

27. The Dalles League of Women Voters, "The Dalles—A Hundred

Years and More of Our Town," 1961, Oregon Collection, Multnomah County Library, Portland, Oregon.

28. William Loy, Stuart Allan, Aileen Buckley, and James Meacham, *Atlas of Oregon*, 2nd ed. (Eugene: University of Oregon Press, 2001), 94–95.

29. Charles Hageman, "Report on City, Port and County Planning, The Dalles, Oregon and Metropolitan Area with Recommendations," unpublished report January 1940, Oregon Collection, Multnomah County Library, Portland, Oregon.

30. U.S. Department of the Interior, Bureau of Reclamation, *The Dalles Project, Oregon, Western Division* (November 1959), Boise, Idaho, 34.

31. H. U. Sanders, "Report on the Sanitary Conditions at Celilo, Oregon," 10 October 1940, in Bureau of Indian Affairs, Portland Area Office, Property and Plant Management, Celilo Relocation Records, 1947–1957, Box 1934, Record Group 75, National Archives—Pacific Northwest Region, Seattle, Washington.

32. Ed Edmo, interview by Kelly Carpenter, 5 April 1999, OHS inv. #1936, Oregon Historical Society Research Library, Portland.

33. Barbara Mackenzie, interview by Katrine Barber, 27 August 1999, inventory #1936, Oregon Historical Society Research Library.

34. William Robbins, "The Indian Question in Western Oregon: The Making of a Colonial People," in *Experiences in a Promised Land: Essays in Pacific Northwest History*, ed. G. Thomas Edwards and Carlos A. Schwantes (Seattle: University of Washington Press, 1986), 53.

35. Frederick K. Cramer, "Recollections of a Salmon Dipnetter," *Oregon Historical Quarterly* 75 (September 1974), 225.

36. Francis Seufert, *Wheels of Fortune* (Portland: Oregon Historical Society Press, 1980), 45.

37. Ed Edmo, interview by Britta Blucher, 20 June 2003, videotape in the possession of Britta Blucher. Incidentally, Ed Edmo spent several seasons as the mascot for The Dalles Indians, the high school football and basketball teams, when he was in elementary and middle school.

38. This advertisement appears in The Dalles *Chronicle*, 11 October 1956.

39. Philip Deloria, *Playing Indian* (New Haven: Yale University Press, 1999).

40. Incidentally, Marshall Dana was also the chairman of the Pacific Northwest Regional Planning Commission in the 1930s, a body that advocated economic development of the region's rivers (Richard Lowitt, *The New Deal and the West* [Norman: University of Oklahoma Press, 1993], 139).

41. U.S. Army Corps of Engineers, *Army Engineers and the Development of Oregon: A History of the Portland District and U.S. Army Corps of Engineers,* by William F. Willingham (Washington, D.C.: U.S. Government Printing Office, 1992), 94.

42. Charles McKinley, *Uncle Sam in the Pacific Northwest* (Berkeley: University of California Press, 1952), 66.

43. Dietrich, *Northwest Passage,* 263.

44. By 1950 the two states would comprise nearly 2.6 percent of the total population of the United States (U.S. Department of Commerce, Bureau of the Census, *Historical Statistics of the United States: Colonial Times to the Present, Part I;* Washington, D.C., 1975).

45. White, *Organic Machine,* 55.

46. Dietrich, *Northwest Passage,* 250–51. For an in-depth analysis of the promise of electricity during this period see chapter 11, "The Electric Revolution."

47. Both Richard White and William Robbins refer to Lewis Mumford as one of the most articulate advocates of the transformation of society by its adoption of alternative energy sources. Lewis Mumford visited the Columbia River in 1938 and described Oregon as a place "not yet . . . fully mastered" in William Robbins, *Landscapes of Promise: The Oregon Story, 1800–1940* (Seattle: University of Washington Press, 1997), 283.

48. U.S. Congress, House Committee on Appropriations, *Civil Functions, Department of the Army, Appropriations for 1952 Hearings, Part 1,* 82nd Cong., 1st and 2nd sess., 10 May 1951, report prepared by William E. Warne, Assistant Secretary, U.S. Department of the Interior (Washington, D.C.: Government Printing Office, 1951).

49. Robbins, *Landscape of Promise,* 239.

50. McKinley, *Uncle Sam in Pacific Northwest,* 7.

51. Carlos Schwantes, *The Pacific Northwest: An Interpretive History*, rev. ed. (Lincoln: University of Nebraska Press, 1996), 413.

52. McKinley, *Uncle Sam in Pacific Northwest*, 19.

53. For more information on the transformation of the Pacific Northwest during World War II, see Gerald Nash, *The American West Transformed: The Impact of the Second World War* (Bloomington: Indiana University Press, 1985), especially chapter 5, "Western Cities in Wartime: The Pacific Northwest, Mountain States, and the Southwest."

54. McKinley, *Uncle Sam in Pacific Northwest*, 20.

2 / A RIVERSCAPE AS CONTESTED SPACE

1. Russell Jim, interview by Michael O'Rourke, 16 October 1999, OHS inventory #2627, tape 4, side 1, Oregon Historical Society Research Library, Portland.

2. Oregon Fish Commission, "The Indian Dip Net Fishery at Celilo Falls on the Columbia River" (November 1951), by R. W. Schoning, T. R. Merrell Jr., and D. R. Johnson, 11. Not all fishing sites were accessible during all periods. Typically, Indians fished Celilo Falls proper after the heavy spring runoff and downstream from the falls and along the Washington shore during the spring flow. In *Wheels of Fortune*, Francis Seufert claims that the Bureau of Indian Affairs made Indians rope themselves to their scaffolds in the 1930s. But Indians were using safety ropes as early as 1905, according to Louis Simpson and Leslie Spier, *Wishram Ethnography* (Seattle: University of Washington Press, 1930).

3. Statement made by Edward G. Swindell Jr., Regional Counsel, to the Celilo Fish Committee, the Nez Perce Delegation, and Members of the Yakama, Umatilla, Warm Springs, and Mid-Columbia Indians at a meeting at The Dalles, Oregon, 15 September 1949, in U.S. Bureau of Indian Affairs, Portland Area Office, file of Edward G. Swindell, Counsel, 1947–53, re: Celilo Matters, Box 1933, Record Group 75, National Archives—Pacific Northwest Region.

4. U.S. Army Corps of Engineers, *Special Report on Indian Fishery Problem*. U.S. Army Corps of Engineers, *The Dalles Dam Indian Fishery: Minutes of the Meeting with Nez Perce Negotiating Committee* (1–2 June 1955).

5. Cramer, "Recollections of a Salmon Dipnetter," 227. Oregon Fish Commission, *Indian Dip Net Fishery*, 8. U.S. Army Corps of Engineers, *Special Report on Indian Fishery Problem*, 9. U.S. Department of the Interior, U.S. Fish and Wildlife Service, *Summary Report on Indian Fishery Census, Celilo Falls and Vicinity* (1947–1954), 3. In addition, in the 1920s and 1930s Oregon and Washington voters outlawed a fishing method utilized heavily by canners on the mid–Columbia River: fish wheels. Fish wheels looked like wooden Ferris wheels whose buckets, instead of cupping fairgoers, dipped into the Columbia and scooped out fish. They were highly efficient equipment, able to operate continuously day and night with very little human oversight. At their most successful, the Seuferts operated twenty-seven fish wheels along the Long Narrows. When fish wheels were outlawed, the Seuferts began to rely more heavily on Native dip-net fishers and non-Native set-net fishers.

6. Flora Cushinway Thompson, interview by unknown, n.d., Oregon Historical Society Research Library, Portland. There is evidence that some Indians did fish at night by the 1950s, reflecting the diminished control Tommy Thompson had over the fishery (Oregon Fish Commission, "Indian Dip Net Fishery," 10, 28).

7. Charles Hopkins to Carl Donaugh, 9 September 1938, in U.S. Burea of Indian Affairs, Portland Area Office, Celilo Falls files, Record Group 75, National Archives—Pacific Northwest Region.

8. U.S. Army Corps of Engineers, Portland District, *Summary of Evidence Relating to the Nez Perce Fishery at Celilo Falls, Oregon* (15 August 1955), 88–89.

9. Swindell Jr. to Celilo Fish Committee, 15 September 1949, in U.S. Army Corps of Engineers, Portland District, files of Edward G. Swindell, Counsel, 1947–1953.

10. Handwritten note in "Records of C. G. Davis, Field Aide at The Dalles, OR, 1939–50," in U.S. Bureau of Indian Affairs, Portland Area Office, files of C. G. Davis, Box 1940, Record Group 75, National Archives—Pacific Northwest Region.

11. H. U. Sanders, "Report on the Sanitary Conditions at Celilo, Oregon," 10 October 1940, in U.S. Bureau of Indian Affairs, Portland Area Office, Property and Plant Management, Celilo Relocation Records,

1947–1957, Box 1934, RG 75, National Archives—Pacific Northwest Region, 5–6.

12. Fixico, *Termination and Relocation*, 29.

13. T. Leland Brown to Pryse, 28 September 1950, in U.S. Army Corps of Engineers, Portland District, files of Edward G. Swindell, Counsel, 1947–1953, re: Celilo Matters, Box 1933, RG 77, National Archives—Pacific Northwest Region.

14. The Army Corps of Engineers decided, in line with the BIA, that the treaty signed by the Warm Springs in 1865 was procured fraudulently. In addition, the Corps did not question the Umatilla claim to the fishery. In contrast, the Corps would challenge the Nez Perce in their claim to the Celilo fishery (U.S. Army Corps of Engineers, Portland District, *Summary of Evidence Relating to the Nez Perce Fishery at Celilo Falls, Oregon*, 15 August 1955).

15. Seufert, *Wheels of Fortune*, 29. Francis Seufert claims that the scope of the modern Indian fishery of the 1950s was made possible by the cannery's cable lines, which allowed for hundreds more to fish from hard-to-reach spots. According to Seufert, "In less than ten years [after the Seuferts placed the first cableway] Celilo had developed from a few Indian fishermen to an estimated 1,000 Indians coming to fish in the fall fishing season" (40). However, due to the archaeological evidence that points to the importance of fishing at Celilo for more than 11,000 years, it is likely that Indians found other means, including canoes, to cross the river to access their fishing sites. For a description of cable cars, see Oregon Fish Commission, "Indian Dip Net Fishery," 12.

16. Seufert, *Wheels of Fortune*, 76.

17. Ibid., 102.

18. Chris Friday, *Organizing Asian American Labor: The Pacific Coast Canned-Salmon Industry, 1870–1942* (Philadelphia: Temple University Press, 1994), 2.

19. Courtland Smith, *Salmon Fishers of the Columbia* (Corvallis: Oregon State University Press, 1979), 23–24; and Friday, *Organizing Asian American Labor*, 78.

20. The San Francisco *Chronicle* is quoted in Smith, *Salmon Fishers of the Columbia*, 25.

21. Seufert, *Wheels of Fortune*, 100.

)r more information on the dual labor system in the West, see White, *"It's Your Misfortune and None of My Own": A New f the American West* (Norman: University of Oklahoma Press, ‑85.

23. Seufert, *Wheels of Fortune*, 65.

24. Minutes of a meeting called by Carl Donaugh to discuss "Indian fishing matters," 1938, in U.S. Bureau of Indian Affairs, Portland Area Office, Celilo Falls files, RG 75, National Archives—Pacific Northwest Region; and Seufert, *Wheels of Fortune*, 66–67.

25. *Seufert Brothers Company v. United States*, No. 187, 188, Supreme Court of the United States, 249 U.S. 194 (1919); 39 S. Ct. 203 (1919); 63 L. Ed. 555 (1919); 1919 U.S. Lexis 2245.

26. Minutes of Celilo Fish Committee meeting, August 27, 1945, "115 Fish Committee Minutes—Extra Copies 1951–61," in U.S. Bureau of Indian Affairs, Portland Area Office, Celilo Fish Committee files, Box 122, RG 75, National Archives—Pacific Northwest Region. In the 1887 case *United States v. Taylor*, the United States sued for access to traditional fishing sites after Frank Taylor curtailed access by fencing his property; the Supreme Court of Washington Territory ruled in favor of the United States and the Yakama Indians (Felix Cohen, *Handbook of Federal Indian Law* [Albuquerque: University of New Mexico Press, 1982], 54–55). See also Mark Allen Suagee, "The Creation of an 'Indian Problem': Nisqually and Puyallup Off-Reservation Fishing" (MA thesis, University of Washington, 1973), 22.

27. Minutes of a meeting of the board of directors of The Dalles Chamber of Commerce, 21 August 1945, in U.S. Army Corps of Engineers, Portland District, Civil Works Project files, 1910–1983, Box 209, Record Group 77, National Archives—Pacific Northwest Region.

28. Seufert, *Wheels of Fortune*, 6.

29. Meeting notes by O. C. Hartman, 15–16 May 1951, in U.S. Army Corps of Engineers, Portland District, Civil Works Project files, 1910–1983, File 28, NPP 800.15, The Dalles Dam, Box 356, RG 77, National Archives—Pacific Northwest Region. One interesting aspect regarding the closing of Seufert cannery was that Colonel T. H. Lipscomb asked the Army Corps liaison to Native fishers, Percy Othus, to "ascertain if the Indians would have any objection to our closing out this cannery."

He stated that "if the Indians do not object, it appears that the best thing to do from a real estate viewpoint may be to simply purchase the entire holdings this fall" (T. H. Lipscomb to Engineering Division, 11 March 1954, in U.S. Army Corps of Engineers, Portland District, Civil Works Project Files, 1910–1983, File 19, NPP 631, The Dalles Dam, RG 77, National Archives—Pacific Northwest Region). Although the practical needs of dam construction often overrode attention to the way in which the transformation of the landscape led to a transformation of lives, there is also evidence that occasionally engineers paused to mitigate the degree and pace of that transformation.

30. Wilkinson, *Crossing the Next Meridian*, 178. Roberta Conner, director of the Tamastslikt Cultural Institute on the Umatilla Indian Reservation, points out ("The Umatilla and the Lewis and Clark Expedition," 22 July 2003, paper presented at "History of the American West: The Legacy of Exploration and Encounter," National History Day summer institute, 19–26 July 2003), as other Native commentators have, that the significance of the Lewis and Clark Expedition among Indians is easy to overstate. In her presentation, Conner reminded participants that Lewis and Clark represented simply two weeks of visits to the mid-Columbia region.

31. From the 1855 treaty with the Yakima, quoted in Click Relander, *Treaty Centennial, 1855–1955: The Yakimas* (Yakima, Wash.: The Republic Press, 1955), 22, 27.

32. Kent Richards, *Isaac I. Stevens: Young Man in a Hurry* (Pullman: Washington State University Press, 1993), 198.

33. Fay Cohen, *Treaties on Trial: The Continuing Controversy over Northwest Indian Fishing Rights* (Seattle: University of Washington Press, 1986), 37–39.

34. There is some disagreement among historians about which interpretation is more accurate. See, for example, William Robbins, comments to keynote speaker John Findlay at Pacific Northwest History Conference, April 1997, Tacoma, Washington; and John Findlay, "A Fishy Proposition: Regional Identity in the Pacific Northwest," in *Many Wests: Place, Culture and Regional Identity*, ed. Michael C. Steiner and David M. Wrobel (Lawrence: University Press of Kansas, 1998).

35. Eugene Hunn, in his essay "Whatever Happened to the First

Peoples of the Columbia?" (in Lang and Carriker, *Great River of the West*), examines the negotiations of mid-Columbia treaties and their lasting ambiguity. Although treaties confined (and controlled) Indians to a land base, they also provided for that land base as well as off-reservation rights. Hunn reveals the extent of Native resistance to the treaties during negotiations, stating, "From the Indian perspective, this contract was not negotiated in good faith." This experience would be repeated during the negotiations for The Dalles Dam compensation.

36. Donald Parman, "Inconsistent Advocacy: The Erosion of Indian Fishing Rights in the Pacific Northwest, 1933–1956," *Pacific Historical Review* 53 (1983), 166. The decision in the Cramer case seems to undermine the argument made by Parman that Indian fishing rights were eroded between the 1930s and 1950s. But *U.S. v. Earnest F. Cramer and E. R. Cramer* was just a small step forward as the nation was fully embroiled in plans for the dams that would devastate Indian fishers.

37. Felix Cohen, *Handbook of Federal Indian Law*, 442.

38. These cases, which each have a history of their own, are too numerous and complex to cover here; I am referring to cases such as *U.S. v. Taylor* (1887), *U.S. v. Winans* (1905), and *Seufert Brothers v. the U.S.* (1919). For more information, see Felix Cohen, *Handbook of Indian Law*.

39. James H. McCool, "Tribes Defy Joint Pact on Fishing; Redskins, Whites Swap Punches in Celilo Falls Scuffle," *Oregonian*, 27 August 1946, 1.

40. "The Indian Experience," section four in Cone and Ridlington, *The Northwest Salmon Crisis*, provides an overview of Indian fishing rights in the Pacific Northwest through primary documents and commentary.

41. Cramer, "Recollections of a Salmon Dipnetter," 221.

42. Indians continued to barter fish for farm goods into the 1950s, and this practice eventually played a part in the valuation of the Indian fishery at Celilo Falls.

43. Cramer, "Recollections of a Salmon Dipnetter," 227.

44. W. R. Sheldon to O. L. Babcock, 20 August 1938, in U.S. Bureau of Indian Affairs, Portland Area Office, Property and Plant Management, Celilo Relocation Records, 1947–1957, Box 1934, RG 75, National Archives—Pacific Northwest Region.

45. Ibid.

46. Minutes from a meeting on "Indian Fishing Matters," October

1938, in U.S. Bureau of Indian Affairs, Portland Area Office, Property and Plant Management, Celilo Relocation Records, 1947–1957, Box 1934, RG 75, National Archives—Pacific Northwest Region.

47. Ibid. Chuck James, BIA archaeologist, made specific Portland Area Office files available to me during July 1997. James indicated that these particular records, which came out of metal filing cabinets on the ninth floor of the Federal Building in Portland, Oregon, would be transferred in the near future to the National Archives, Pacific Northwest Region, Seattle, Washington. I requested records pertinent to Celilo Village covering the years 1930 to 1960. Material examined included records dealing with real estate, field agent correspondence, fishing rights, and the U.S. Army Corps of Engineers.

48. Wilerton C. Curtis to Senator Thomas Hennings, 21 February 1952, in U.S. Bureau of Indian Affairs, Portland Area Office, File 155, Spearfish Committee, 1939–1940, Box 1942, RG 75, National Archives—Pacific Northwest Region.

49. Charles Hopkins to Carl Donaugh, 9 September 1938, in U.S. Bureau of Indian Affairs, Portland Area Office, Celilo Falls files, RG 75, National Archives—Pacific Northwest Region.

50. Although there appears to have been general support at the local level for either of these solutions, neither occurred for a number of reasons. Nationwide, after World War II there was a growing trend to eliminate reservations; therefore, a new reservation site would have garnered critics on the federal level as well as those already mobilized locally among non-Native fishers and residents of The Dalles. In addition, because of growing federal support for a termination policy, the BIA operated with decreasing funds by the end of the 1940s, which may have prohibited the purchase of property at the falls.

51. Carl Donaugh to the U.S. Attorney General, 20 October 1938, in U.S. Bureau of Indian Affairs, Portland Area Office, Celilo Falls files, RG 75, National Archives—Pacific Northwest Region.

52. C. G. Davis to Pryse, 15 April 1946, in U.S. Bureau of Indian Affairs, Portland Area Office, Celilo Falls files, 1938, RG 75, National Archives—Pacific Northwest Region.

53. *United States v. Earnest Cramer and E. R. Cramer,* in U.S. District Court of Oregon at Portland, Civil and Criminal Case files, 1922–1943,

77, Case 3557, Box 928, Record Group 21, National Archives—Pacific Northwest Region.

54. Minutes of a meeting on "Indian Fishing Matters," October 1938, in U.S. Bureau of Indian Affairs, Portland Area Office, Celilo Relocation Records, 1947–1957, RG 75, National Archives—Pacific Northwest Region.

55. *United States v. Earnest Cramer and E. R. Cramer,* in U.S. District Court of Oregon at Portland, Civil and Criminal Case files, 1922–1943, 8, RG 21, National Archives—Pacific Northwest Region.

56. Vinton H. Hall, "Motor Cruise of 1939: Celilo Falls Tour," *Oregonian,* 30 April 1939, Magazine sec., 3.

57. C. G. Davis to Kenneth Simmons, 6 May 1948, in U.S. Bureau of Indian Affairs, Portland Area Office, Celilo Fishing Commission, RG 75, National Archives—Pacific Northwest Region; and C. G. Davis to L. W. Shotwell, 3 May 1948, re: relations including fish controversies with non-Indian, private individuals, etc., in U.S. Bureau of Indian Affairs, Portland Area Office, Celilo Fishing Commission, Box 1946, RG 75, National Archives—Pacific Northwest Region.

58. This study was the second of its kind. In 1887, G. W. Gordon conducted an investigation of traditional fishing sites at the behest of BIA commissioner John Atkins. This study was initiated "in view of the great difficulties between whites and Indians over the fishery," in U.S. Army Corps of Engineers, *Summary of Evidence Relating to the Nez Perce Fishery at Celilo Falls, Oregon,* 45.

59. Parman, "Inconsistent Advocacy," 177–78. This oversight is indicative of the lack of care extended to protecting fishing rights in the Pacific Northwest during a period of dam building favored by the Franklin Roosevelt administration. It also illustrates the ways in which New Dealers often worked at cross-purposes.

60. Katrine Barber, notes from "Environmental Education and Native American Tribes in the Pacific Northwest," 9–10 April 1998, a meeting held at Washington State University, Pullman, Washington.

3 / DEBATING THE DAM

1. U.S. Representative Louis Rabaut, Michigan, in House U.S. Congress, Subcommittee of the House Committee on Appropriations,

Civil Functions, Department of the Army, Appropriations for 1953 Hearings, Part 2, 19 February 1952, 82nd Cong., 1st and 2nd sess., 1952 (Washington, D.C.: Government Printing Office, 1952).

2. Sam Hunters to Senator Guy Gillette, 16 March 1954, U.S. in U.S. Bureau of Indian Affairs, Portland Area Office, File 920, Conservation of Fish and Wildlife, Celilo Fisheries, 1953–1954, Record Group 75, National Archives—Pacific Northwest Region, Seattle Washington.

3. Summary of Petition and Supporting Statement for Authorization and Construction of The Dalles Dam, 22 September 1945, in U.S. Bureau of Indian Affairs, Portland Area Office, File 920, Conservation of Fish and Wildlife, Celilo Fisheries, 1953–54, "PO 800.92 The Dalles Dam," RG 75, National Archives—Pacific Northwest Region. The meeting described was held shortly after the Corps of Engineers sponsored a meeting in April 1945 for Indians affected by the proposed Dalles Dam.

4. Katrine Barber and Janice Dilg, "'I Didn't Do Anything Anyone Else Couldn't Have Done': A View of Oregon History Through the Ordinary Life of Barbara Mackenzie," *Oregon Historical Quarterly* 103 (winter 2002), 480–509.

5. Summary of Petition and Supporting Statement for Authorization and Construction of The Dalles Dam, 22 September 1945, in U.S. Bureau of Indian Affairs, Portland Area Office, File 920, Conservation of Fish and Wildlife, Celilo Fisheries, 1953–54, "PO 800.92 The Dalles Dam," RG 75, National Archives—Pacific Northwest Region.

6. "Fishing Industry Against Dam," *Oregonian*, 24 September 1945, sec. 2, 3. "Civil Works Project Files, 1910–1983," in U.S. Army Corps of Engineers, Portland District files, Box 209, Record Group 77, National Archives—Pacific Northwest Region.

7. As historian Jeff Crane points out in "Protesting Monuments to Progress: A Comparative Study of Protests Against Four Dams, 1838–1955" (*Oregon Historical Quarterly* 103, fall 2002, 295–319), protests by Americans to dam building is a 300–year tradition, with most early opponents resisting the structures for economic reasons, until environmental concerns became prominent in the 1950s. Most protestors of The Dalles Dam were not what one would consider environmentalists. Instead, they viewed the dams as a shift in the economic order away

from commercial fishing and treaty-protected fishing activities and toward an emphasis on hydropower, irrigation, and recreation.

8. Robert Gottlieb, *A Life of Its Own: The Politics and Power of Water* (San Diego: Harcourt Brace Jovanovich, 1988), 46–47.

9. Daniel A. Mazmanian and Jeanne Nienaber, *Can Organizations Change?: Environmental Protection, Citizens Participation, and the Corps of Engineers* (Washington, D.C.: The Brookings Institution, 1979), 13, 18.

10. Wayne Morse to Herbert West, 26 September 1945, in U.S. Army Corps of Engineers, Portland District, Civil Works Project files, 1910–1983, Box 209, RG 77, National Archives—Pacific Northwest Region.

11. On 17 May 1954, Mrs. Ward Webber appeared before The Dalles City Council on behalf of the county's Red Cross chapter and described it as "strictly a volunteer organization" (The Dalles City Council, meeting minutes 1940–1960, City Clerk's Office, City Hall, The Dalles, Oregon).

12. For more information, see Barber and Dilg, "A View of Oregon History."

13. U.S. Army Corps of Engineers, Portland District, *Summary of Evidence Relating to the Nez Perce Fishery at Celilo Falls, Oregon* (15 August 1955), Portland, Oregon, 1955, 142–57.

14. Mazmanian and Nienaber, *Can Organizations Change?*, 17.

15. Thomas Yallup, 19 February 1952, in U.S. Congress, House Committee on Appropriations, *Civil Functions, Department of the Army, Appropriations for 1952 Hearings, Part 2,* 82nd Cong., 1st and 2nd sess., 1951, 158.

16. Quoted in Mazmanian and Nienaber, *Can Organizations Change?*, 19.

17. Dr. Lloyd Meehan (26 April 1951, in U.S. Congress, House Committee on Appropriations, *Civil Functions, Department of the Army, Appropriations for 1952 Hearings, Part 1,* 82nd Cong., 1st and 2nd sess., 1951) explained to the House Appropriations Committee that "hatcheries are being rebuilt and new ones constructed to aid in the development of maximum fish populations in these [lower Columbia] streams. By this means, it is expected that the maximum increase of populations

in the lower river streams will compensate in part for the anticipated loss of the valuable middle and upper river populations." See also Allen, "Replacing Salmon," 196–227.

18. Columbia Basin Fisheries Development Association, "Wealth of the River: A Presentation of Fact Concerning the Salmon Industry at and Near Celilo Falls on the Upper Columbia River and a Petition for the Conservation of This Industry," 22 September 1945, in Oregon Historical Society, files of Columbia Basin Fisheries Development Association, 2, Oregon Historical Society Research Library, Portland, Oregon.

19. For more information regarding Bonneville Dam in-lieu sites, see Roberta Ulrich, "Justice Delayed: A Sixty Year Battle for Indian Fishing Sites" (MA thesis, Portland State University, 1996), or Ulrich, *Empty Nets.*

20. In Martin Medhurst, Robert Ivie, Philip Wander, and Robert Scott, *Cold War Rhetoric: Strategy, Metaphor, and Ideology* (East Lansing: Michigan State University Press, 1997), a collection of essays about cold-war rhetoric, Robert Scott points out two significant factors that resonate with the way Indian supporters and the Army Corps of Engineers used cold-war rhetoric during these debates, in "Cold War and Rhetoric: Conceptually and Critically," 1–16. First, according to Scott, cold-war rhetoric "has often been a touchstone in domestic affairs that seem, at least at first glance, quite remote from the zones of tension between the super powers." Second, Scott's example of how civil rights activists used cold-war rhetoric parallels how supporters of Indian rights called on the federal government to protect the Native minority as part of the cold-war struggle. Conversely, the Army Corps used the cold war to justify requesting funds for a domestic project only peripherally connected to defense.

21. I lump white fishermen together as if they were united as a group because, in large part, they did unite against nonwhite fishers. However, white sports fishermen and white commercial fishers often warred over the division of the Columbia River fishery in a struggle over river resources, a history that extends beyond the scope of this project.

22. Columbia Basin Fisheries Development Association, "Wealth of the River," in Oregon Historical Society, files of Columbia Basin Fisheries Development Association. Because the Army Corps did not

collect fish counts before 1938 (the same year the agency completed Bonneville Dam), it is impossible to use its records as a check against the association's claim, although it is certainly an exaggeration.

23. "Dam Labeled Threat to Fish," *Oregonian*, 12 June 1946, 7.

24. "Will Dalles Dam Finish Fishing? It's Possibility," *Oregon Journal*, 21 October 1951, 4A.

25. "Fishing Industry Against the Dam," *Oregonian*, 24 September 1945, sec. 2, 3.

26. Columbia Basin Fisheries Development Association, "Wealth of the River," 28, in Oregon Historical Society, files of Columbia Basin Fisheries Development Association (emphasis added).

27. James Blackeagle, Secretary, Nez Perce Tribal Executive Committee, 10 May 1951, in U.S. Congress, House Committee on Appropriations, *Civil Functions, Department of the Army, Appropriations for 1952 Hearings, Part 1*, 82nd Cong., 1st and 2nd sess., 1951.

28. It is likely that Seufert overstated opposition to the dam among Dalles businesspeople. The Dalles Chamber of Commerce voted to support the development, save a single vote—that of C of C President Francis Seufert (Minutes of Meeting, Dalles Chamber of Commerce, 21 August 1945, in U.S. Army Corps of Engineers, Portland, District, Civil Works Projects files, 1910–1983, Box 209, RG 77, National Archives—Pacific Northwest Region).

29. Francis Seufert to Senator Wayne Morse, 28 September 1945, in U.S. Bureau of Indian Affairs, Portland Area Office, File 920, Conservation of Fish and Wildlife, Celilo Fisheries, 1953–54, "PO 800.92 The Dalles Dam," Folder 1, RG 75, National Archives—Pacific Northwest Region.

30. Richard Grace to E. W. Barnes, 1 August 1945, in U.S. Army Corps of Engineers, Portland District, Civil Works Project files, 1910–1980, "Correspondence," Box 209, RG 77, National Archives—Pacific Northwest Region.

31. Francis Seufert to J. W. Elliott, 1 February 1946, in U.S. Bureau of Indian Affairs, Portland Area Office, Celilo Falls files, RG 75, National Archives—Pacific Northwest Region.

32. Seufert, *Wheels of Fortune*, 43.

33. Herbert West, executive vice president, Inland Empire Waterways

Association, 7 May 1951, in U.S. Congress, House Appropriations Committee, *Civil Functions, Department of the Army, Appropriations for 1952 Hearings, Part 1,* 82nd Cong., 1st and 2nd sess., 1951, 298–301.

34. U.S. Representative Louis Rabaut, Michigan, ibid.

35. Colonel W. H. Potter, U.S. Army Corps of Engineers, 11 April 1951, ibid., 193.

36 General Chorpening, U.S. Army Corps of Engineers, 21 January 1952, ibid., 150.

37. As various sources during these appropriations hearings show, Indian witnesses frequently noted that they wanted to avoid the pitfalls of the Bonneville Dam negotiations, in which the Army Corps promised $50,000 for the improvement of "in-lieu" or replacement fishing sites, which had yet to be expended.

38. Herbert G. West, vice president, Inland Empire Waterways Association, 7 May 1951, in U.S. Congress, House Appropriations Committee, *Civil Functions, Department of the Army, Appropriations for 1952 Hearings, Part 1,* 82nd Cong., 1st and 2nd sess., 1951, 298.

39. Mazmanian and Nienaber, *Can Organizations Change?,* 13.

40. Herbert G. West, vice president, Inland Empire Waterways Association, 7 May 1951, in U.S. Congress, House Appropriations Committee, *Civil Functions, Department of the Army, Appropriations for 1952 Hearings, Part 1,* 82nd Cong., 1st and 2nd sess., 1951, 298.

41. U.S. Army Corps of Engineers, "Projects in Pacific Northwest, Need for Power," 5 April 1951, ibid., 178.

42. Representative Lowell Stockman, Oregon, 3 March 1952, ibid., 802.

43. Charles Baker, president, Inland Empire Waterways Association, 7 May 1951, ibid., 310.

44. Colonel W. H. Potter, 11 April 1951, ibid., 206.

45. Dr. Lloyd Meehan, U.S. Fish and Wildlife Service, 26 April 1951, ibid., 690, 700.

46. Colonel W. H. Potter, 11 April 1951, ibid., 206.

47. Representative Christopher C. McGrath, New York, 10 May 1951, ibid., 747.

48. William Warne, assistant secretary, Department of the Interior, ibid., 741.

49. U.S. Representative Louis Rabaut, Michigan, ibid., 742.

50. U.S. Representative Glenn Davis, Wisconsin, ibid., 749.

51. William Warne, assistant secretary, Department of the Interior, U.S. Congress, House Committee on Appropriations, *Civil Functions, Department of the Army, Appropriations for 1952 Hearings,* 82nd Cong., 1st and 2nd sess., 1951, 741.

52. Written statement submitted by the Yakama tribal delegation, 7 May 1951, in U.S. Congress, House Committee on Appropriations, *Civil Functions, Department of the Army, Appropriations for 1952 Hearings,* 82nd Cong., 1st and 2nd sess., 1951, 319.

53. Nez Perce tribal delegation, 10 May 1951, ibid., 682.

54. Louis Pitt, interview by Clark Hansen, 23 February 2001, OHS inv. #2791, tape 1, side 1, Oregon Historical Society Research Library, Portland.

55. Kenneth William Townsend, *World War II and the American Indian* (Albuquerque: University of New Mexico Press, 2000), 72.

56. Yakama tribal delegation, 7 May 1951, ibid., 319.

57. "Resolution of Kah-Milt-Pah, Also Known as Rock Creek Indians," ibid., 317.

58. Exchange between Thomas Yallup, member of Kah-Milt-Pah Tribe, and U.S. Representative Louis Rabaut, 7 May 1951, ibid., 317–18.

59. Thomas Yallup, member of Kah-Milt-Pah Tribe, 7 May 1951, ibid., 317–18.

60. William Minthorne, 8 May 1951, ibid., 374. Ironically, according to Fixico, *Termination and Relocation,* 14–20, it was the successful participation in the military and the war industries during World War II that fueled arguments in Congress for the termination of reservations and treaty rights in the 1950s.

61. Ed Forest Jr., 8 May 1951, in U.S. Congress, House Committee on Appropriations, *Civil Functions, Department of the Army, Appropriations for 1952 Hearings, Part 2,* 82nd Cong., 1st and 2nd sess., 1951, 377.

62. T. Leland Brown, attorney for Tribal Council, Confederated Tribes of Warm Springs Indians of Oregon, ibid., 382.

63. Exchange between William Minthorne and committee members, ibid., 376–77.

64. T. Leland Brown, attorney for Tribal Council, Confederated Tribes of Warm Springs Indians of Oregon, ibid., 378.

65. Watson Totus, member of Yakama Tribe, 7 May 1951, ibid., 321.

66. Former Yakama attorney Kenneth Simmons was also tribal attorney for the Nez Perce; his relationship with the Yakama was probably ended to avoid any conflict of interest.

67. Dr. F. A. Davidson, fish biologist, 19 February 1952, in U.S. Congress, House Committee on Appropriations, *Civil Functions, Department of the Army, Appropriations for 1952 Hearings, Part 2,* 82nd Cong., 1st and 2nd sess., 1951, 161.

68. That Celilo Falls be set aside as part of a protected corridor was also suggested by Gertrude Jensen, a member of the Portland Women's Forum and head of its Save the Columbia Gorge Committee. Jensen met with congressional representatives in February 1953 (Charles Castner, "Help Save Celilo Falls," letter to the editor, 7 February 1953, in U.S. Bureau of Indian Affairs, Portland Area Office, File 920, Conservation of Fish and Wildlife, Celilo Fisheries 1953–54, RG 75, National Archives—Pacific Northwest Region).

69. William Warne, 10 May 1951, in U.S. Congress, House Committee on Appropriations, *Civil Functions, Department of the Army, Appropriations for 1952 Hearings, Part 2,* 82nd Cong., 1st and 2nd sess., 1951, 745.

70. Colonel W. H. Potter, 11 April 1951, ibid., 198.

71. Robert Jones, Oregon's fish commissioner, "expressed the opinion that such a dam might not possibly be as destructive to fish life as are the Indians" in "Fish Bosses Protest Dam," *Oregonian,* 12 September 1945, 9.

72. William Warne, 10 May 1951, in U.S. Congress, House Committee on Appropriations, *Civil Functions, Department of the Army, Appropriations for 1952 Hearings, Part 1,* 82nd Cong., 1st and 2nd sess., 1951, 745.

73. Ibid., 757.

74. "Indians Want It Moved but The Dalles Dam Goes Ahead," *Oregonian,* 10 May 1953, sec. 2, 26.

75. Charles Castner, "Help Save Celilo Falls," letter to the editor, 7 February 1953, in U.S. Bureau of Indian Affairs, Portland Area Office, File 920, Conservation of Fish and Wildlife, Celilo Fisheries 1953–54, RG 75, National Archives—Pacific Northwest Region.

76. Castner, ibid. I have yet to find any corroborating evidence that supports Castner's assertion regarding the widespread desire of Oregonians that the dam be relocated.

77. "Are Indian Rights Again Being Betrayed? Yakima Tribes," *Christian Century* 70 (15 April 1953), 437.

78. Angier Goodwin to Douglas McKay, 25 September 1953, in U.S. Bureau of Indian Affairs, Portland Area Office, File 920, Conservation of Fish and Wildlife, Celilo Fisheries, 1953–54, RG 75, National Archives— Pacific Northwest Region.

79. Marion C. Frenyear to Evan L. Flory, 7 October 1953, ibid.

80. Gibson Lewis to Senator Irving Ives, 18 September 1953, ibid.

81. J. N. Baldwin to director of the BIA, 19 March 1953, ibid.

82. Sam Hunters to Senator Guy Gillette, 16 March 1954, ibid. According to the U.S. Department of Health and Human Services's annual publication *Trends in Indian Health* (Washington, D.C.: Public Health Service, Indian Health Service, Office of Planning, Evaluation and Legislation, Division of Program Statistics, 1991, 56), in 1950 Indians and Alaskan Natives had an average life expectancy of sixty years.

83. "Garrison Dam: Missouri Valley Project Raises Land Prices and Indian War Whoops," *Life* 21 (8 July 1946), 30–31. This extremely short piece includes a paragraph of text and four photographs, one of Chief Thomas Spotted Wolf confronting Corps officials.

84. Lawson, *Dammed Indians*, xxi.

85. "After They Have Killed Us," *Time* 41 (19 April 1943), 26.

86. William Brophy to chairman of the Interior Coordinating Committee, 11 October 1946, in U.S. Bureau of Indian Affairs, Portland Area Office, Celilo Falls files, RG 75, National Archives—Pacific Northwest Region.

87. Clifford Trafzer, *Death Stalks the Yakama: Epidemiological Transitions and Mortality of the Yakama Indian Reservation, 1888–1964* (East Lansing: Michigan State University Press, 1997), 173.

88. Ulrich, "Justice Delayed," 21.

89. Felix Cohen, *Handbook of Federal Indian Law*, 26.

90. Ibid., 144–46.

91. Larry J. Hasse, "Termination and Assimilation: Federal Indian Policy, 1943 to 1961" (PhD diss., Washington State University, 1974), 15; and Parman, "Inconstant Advocacy," 163–89.

92. Collier is best known for sponsoring the Indian Reorganization Act (IRA), legislation passed by Congress in 1934. The IRA reversed

the Dawes General Allotment Act, provided for the acquisition of additional tribal lands, and organized a structure under which Indian tribes could develop a constitution and reservation government recognized by the federal government. Opponents of the IRA argued that it was an instrument for the spread of communism and that it was anti-Christian (an indication of the influence of Christians who supported assimilation policies rather than policies based on cultural pluralism). Terminationists called for a new federal policy to "emancipate" individual Indians from the "socialism" of the reservation system, a policy that would, incidentally, also open reservation resources once again to non-Indian interests. Termination and its attendant policy of relocating Indians from reservations to urban areas eliminated 1.37 million acres of land from Indian ownership and removed 12,000 Indians from their homes.

93. W. Barton Greenwood to Homer Ferguson, 15 October 1953, in U.S. Bureau of Indian Affairs, Portland Area Office, Celilo Falls files, RG 75, National Archives—Pacific Northwest Region.

94. Wilerton C. Curtis to Thomas C. Hennings and Morgan Moulder, 21 February 1952; and Dillon S. Myer to Morgan Moulder, 17 March 1952; both in U.S. Bureau of Indian Affairs, Portland Area Office, File 155, Spearfish Committee 1939–1940, Field Agent—The Dalles, Oregon, General Subject Correspondence, 1939–1953, Box 1947, RG 75, National Archives—Pacific Northwest Region.

95. W. Barton Greenwood to E. Morgan Pryse, 15 August 1952, in U.S. Bureau of Indian Affairs, Portland Area Office, Celilo Falls files, The Dalles—General, 1951–52, RG 75, National Archives—Pacific Northwest Region.

4 / NARRATIVES OF PROGRESS

1. "Community Due to Show Major Benefits," The Dalles *Chronicle,* 28 September 1933. All articles from The Dalles *Chronicle* are located on page 1 unless otherwise noted.

2. The description "Hiroshima-like" comes from the caption of the photo that accompanied "Sidelights at Project Celebration," The Dalles *Chronicle,* 13 March 1952. See also editorial, The Dalles *Chronicle,* 3

December 1931; and "Local Brief to Aid Portland's Representatives," The Dalles *Chronicle,* 7 January 1932.

3. The kinds of booster activities in The Dalles were not unique to that city. In his book about the U.S. Bureau of Reclamation's Grand Coulee Dam, historian Paul Pitzer traces the dam boosterism of the Spokane Chamber of Commerce and the Wenatchee *Daily World* (Pitzer, *Grand Coulee).*

4. In the development of The Dalles Dam, W. S. Nelson played a similar role to what Rufus Woods played in regards to Grand Coulee Dam, according to Robert E. Ficken in *Rufus Woods, the Columbia River and the Building of Modern Washington* (Pullman: Washington State University Press, 1995).

5. Oregon Governor John H. Hall appointed Ward Webber, a Wasco County businessman, to the position of county judge in 1948 to succeed Judge R. J. Wilson, who could no longer perform his duties. In 1950 voters elected Ward Webber to a six-year term as county judge. The judge died in office, succumbing to a heart attack while on vacation in 1955 ("Judge Webber Dies," The Dalles Library clippings, vol. 56, 51, The Dalles Library, The Dalles, Oregon).

6. "Judge Webber Dies," ibid.; and "Community Due to Show Major Benefits," The Dalles *Chronicle,* 28 September 1933.

7. The description of Nelson is in an untitled, undated article by Jack Zimmerman in the Oregon *Journal,* in Oregon Historical Society, vertical file Dams, Columbia River—The Dalles Dam, Oregon Historical Society Research Library, Portland, Oregon.

8. "Nelson, Mrs. Seufert Win City's Top Honor," The Dalles *Chronicle,* 10 February 1953; and "Long Process Ends with Funds for Dam," The Dalles *Chronicle,* 21 October 1951.

9. "Growth Forecast for Dalles, Due to Bonneville," The Dalles *Chronicle*, 30 January 1941, 2.

10. For more information on federal-state efforts at regional planning during the Depression, see Lowitt, *New Deal and the West,* especially chapter nine, "The Planned Promised Land." Gerald Nash also prefaces his discussion of wartime transformation of the West with economic changes brought on by the Great Depression, stating that dur-

ing this period, "public funds were replacing private capital in fostering development of the trans-Mississippi area" (Nash, *American West Transformed*, 5).

11. "River Project Given Support During Hearing," The Dalles *Chronicle*, 17 January 1936, 8.

12. "'Cooperation' Note Sounded," The Dalles *Chronicle*, 20 December 1951.

13. Mel Scott, *American City Planning Since 1890* (Berkeley: University of California Press, 1969).

14. "Experiments with TV Successful," The Dalles *Chronicle*, 20 April 1952.

15. These ideas—of imaginary cities, the cost effectiveness of planning, and planning as the expansion of governmental activity—are influenced by Carl Abbott's work, particularly *Portland: Planning, Politics, and Growth in a Twentieth-Century City* (Lincoln: University of Nebraska Press, 1983), 6–8. In addition, Gerald Nash emphasizes planning as one of the outcomes of World War II on the West (and, more generally, nationally as well) in the conclusion to *The American West Transformed*.

16. "Orderly Industrial Development Assured Under County Planning," The Dalles *Chronicle*, 18 December 1953. The Dalles County Planning Commission was comprised of between seven and twelve appointed members who served without compensation, the majority of whom resided outside of The Dalles city limits. This model, recommended by a University of Oregon researcher, was adopted as a direct result of concerns regarding future changes brought on by The Dalles Dam ("Petition to Court Seeks Creation of Wasco County Planning Commission," The Dalles *Chronicle*, 25 February 1951).

17. The description of unkempt housing comes from Fred Ingram, Deputy Chief, Planning Branch, Army Corps of Engineers, Notes on Meeting with the Executive Committee of The Dalles Community Council [U.S Army Corps' designation of the Problem Council], 22 July 1952, in U.S. Army Corps of Engineers, Portland District, Civil Works Project files, 1910–1983, Box 356, File 18, NPP.624—The Dalles, RG 77, National Archives—Pacific Northwest Region.

18. "Commercial, Industrial Building Proceeds at Rapid Pace in

City," The Dalles *Chronicle*, 23 April 1952. In 1951 alone, 292 new building permits were issued by The Dalles.

19. "Apartments Sign of Times," The Dalles *Chronicle*, 23 April 1952. This article highlights three apartment houses built over the preceding eighteen months that provided a total of forty-eight one-, two-, and three-bedroom units. At the writing of the article, none had vacancies.

20. Oregon State Unemployment Compensation Commission, *A Survey of Industry and Employment in Oregon Counties* (Salem, Oregon, 1957), 165. According to the Wasco County Planning Office, existing housing units rose from 2,758 in 1950 to 3,644 in 1960 (Wasco County Planning Office, *Cherry Industry: What Does it Mean for Wasco County*, by James Snyder [Oregon State University and Wasco County Planning Office, 1974], 4).

21. "Home Construction Soaring," The Dalles *Chronicle*, 23 April 1952. The total value of construction between 1946 and 1951 was more than $6 million (Oregon State Unemployment Compensation Commission, "Survey of Industry and Employment," 165–66).

22. "Trailer Homes Dot Dalles Area," The Dalles *Chronicle*, 18 December 1953.

23. "Post Office Feels Pressure as City Population Rises," The Dalles *Chronicle*, 23 April 1952.

24. "Firemen Visualize Their Second Station," The Dalles *Chronicle*, 28 September 1952.

25. "Police Services Are Spread Thin," The Dalles *Chronicle*, 14 February 1954.

26. "$250,000 Asked for Water Jobs," The Dalles *Chronicle*, 14 February 1952.

27. The Dalles City Council, meeting minutes, 6 December 1954, 290, City Clerk's Office, City Hall, The Dalles, Oregon.

28. "Council Orders Dalles Cleanup," The Dalles *Chronicle*, 14 July 1953. Although the cleanup was prompted by state attention to this local vice, Mayor Davidson prided himself on the fact that the raid was ordered by local officials and carried out by city police. He told The Dalles *Chronicle* that "it's not a good thing for the state to come in and do the job we should have done." He went on to suggest that cleanup was necessary due to the increased scrutiny of the federal government.

29. Seufert, *Wheels of Fortune*, 4.

30. Oregon Bureau of Municipal Research and Service, *Population of Oregon Cities, Counties and Metropolitan Areas, 1850 to 1957*, a compilation of census counts and estimates, Information Bulletin No. 106 (University of Oregon, April 1958), 4; and Wasco County Planning Office, *Cherry Industry*, 4.

31. Oregon Bureau of Municipal Research and Service, *Population of Oregon Cities*.

32. "Refuse Disposal Problem Mulled," The Dalles *Chronicle*, 24 January 1954.

33. "Traffic Headache Growing Worse," The Dalles *Chronicle*, 22 August 1954.

34. "Conservation Needed in Dalles Water Use," The Dalles *Chronicle*, 2 February 1953.

35. "$250,000 Asked for Water Jobs," The Dalles *Chronicle*, 14 December 1952; and "Conservation Needed in Dalles Water Use," The Dalles *Chronicle*, 2 February 1953.

36. District Twelve Superintendent Dave Bates, quoted in "Self-Help Required Before Federal Aid," The Dalles *Chronicle*, 1 March 1953.

37. "School Facilities Growing Steadily," The Dalles *Chronicle*, 18 December 1953.

38. The city of The Dalles accounted for the majority of students in Wasco County: 1,681 of 2,000 in fall 1951 ("Future Load on School System Presents Poser," The Dalles *Chronicle*, 23 April 1952). According to The Dalles *Chronicle* ("School Facilities Growing Steadily," 18 December 1953), consolidation was a result of the "desire of school patrons to have adequate-sized school districts. Elections in 1952 and 1953 reduced the number of school districts in Wasco County from forty-eight to twenty." However, voters did not always approve consolidation, which often necessitated travel by young students. Mill Creek voted not to consolidate with the county's largest district, District Twelve ("School Levy Passes," The Dalles *Chronicle*, 4 March 1953).

39. Only one school in District Twelve had not reached capacity in 1952 ("District 12 School Squeeze Increases," The Dalles *Chronicle*, 12 September 1952).

40. Oregon State Unemployment Compensation Commission,

Survey of Industry and Employment, Table I, "The Dalles Dam: Estimate of Working Population—Expedited Program."

41. Of those, 1,014 were enrolled in grade school, 316 in junior high, and 476 in high school; 370 were tuition students from outside the district ("Hope Dim for School Aid," The Dalles *Chronicle,* 10 October 1952).

42. District Twelve experienced a sharp decline in enrollment in September 1953 that it attributed to "changes to work load at Dalles dam" ("School Rolls in County Show Increase of 417," The Dalles *Chronicle,* 25 September 1953).

43. "Junior High School 'Local Obligation'," The Dalles *Chronicle,* 25 February 1953.

44. The District Twelve school board interviewed Superintendent A. O. Larive of Hermiston and Superintendent Robert Van Houte of Stanfield, who told them that funding for buildings was extremely hard to get and that the nationwide demand for federal assistance greatly outweighed the funds available, making the pool of requests quite competitive ("Self-Help Required Before Federal Aid," The Dalles *Chronicle,* 1 March 1953).

45. "Self-Help Required Before Federal Aid," The Dalles *Chronicle,* 1 March 1953; and "Hope Dim for School Aid," The Dalles *Chronicle,* 10 October 1952.

46. "Junior High School 'Local Obligation'," The Dalles *Chronicle,* 25 February 1953.

47. "Self-Help Required Before Federal Aid," The Dalles *Chronicle,* 1 March 1953.

48. City residents in January 1952 voted by a margin of three to one to pass a tax levy of $147,000. This reversed the results of an earlier vote in June 1951 in which residents voted down a special levy. The total budget for District Twelve that year was $482,000 ("Future Load on School System Presents Poser," The Dalles *Chronicle,* 23 April 1952; and "Junior High School 'Local Obligation'," The Dalles *Chronicle,* 25 February 1953). In March 1953, residents again passed a school levy, this time for $82,000 ("School Levy Passes," The Dalles *Chronicle,* 4 March 1953).

49. A. F. Moberg, acting regional representative at the Housing and Home Finance Agency, to Fred Ingram, Army Corps of Engineers, 29 December 1952, in U.S. Army Corps of Engineers, Portland District, Civil

Works Project files, 1910–1983, Box 356, File 18, NPP.624—The Dalles Dam, RG 77, National Archives—Pacific Northwest Region.

50. Loyd Brady, The Dalles City Manager, to Roger Spaulding, Housing and Home Finance Agency, 25 March 1952, in U.S. Army Corps of Engineers, Portland District, Civil Works Project files, 1910–1983, Box 356, File 18, NPP.624—The Dalles Dam, RG 77, National Archives—Pacific Northwest Region.

51. "Dalles City Resists Housing Authority," The Dalles *Chronicle*, 8 April 1952.

52. Fred Ingram, Deputy Chief, Planning Branch, Army Corps of Engineers, Notes on Meeting with the Executive Committee of The Dalles Community Council [U.S Army Corps' designation of the Problem Council], 24 July 1952, in U.S. Army Corps of Engineers, Portland District, Civil Works Project files, 1910–1983, Box 356, File 18, NPP.624—The Dalles Dam, RG 77, National Archives—Pacific Northwest Region.

53. "Junior High School 'Local Obligation'," The Dalles *Chronicle*, 25 February 1953.

54. The vote was 803 in support of the levy and 146 against. David Bates, District Twelve Superintendent, to Colonel T. H. Lipscomb, Army Corps of Engineers, 21 May 1953, in U.S. Army Corps of Engineers, Portland District, Civil Works Project files, 1910–1983, Box 412, File NPP.00.8—The Dalles Dam, RG 77, National Archives—Pacific Northwest Region.

55. "Possible Snag Seen for School Project," The Dalles *Chronicle*, 29 May 1953. See also Colonel T. H. Lipscomb to Senator Sam Coon, 2 June 1953; and Colonel T. H. Lipscomb to David Bates, 26 May 1953; both in U.S. Army Corps of Engineers, Portland District, Civil Works Project files, 1910–1983, ibid.

56. "'Problem Council' Goes into Action," The Dalles *Chronicle*, 21 January 1951; and "Civic Agency Has Key Role," The Dalles *Chronicle*, 23 April 1952.

57. "'Cooperation' Note Sounded," The Dalles *Chronicle*, 20 December 1951.

58. Congress had adopted Public Law 139, which established critical defense areas, in the summer of 1950. Fred Ingram, Deputy Chief

of the Planning Branch of the Army Corps of Engineers, recorded in Notes on Meeting with the Executive Committee of The Dalles Community Council [U.S. Army Corps' designation of the Problem Council], 24 July 1952, that, in his opinion, "very little if any temporary housing will be provided in The Dalles unless the area receives a critical defense housing designation" (U.S. Army Corps of Engineers, Portland District, Civil Works Project files, 1910–1983, Box 356, File 18, NPP.624—The Dalles Dam, RG 77, National Archives—Pacific Northwest Region); see also Colonel T. H. Lipscomb, memo for file, 7 October 1952, ibid. Marshall Nelson, mayor of The Dalles, resubmitted a request to the Housing and Home Finance Agency on 30 July 1952 (Nelson to L. R. Durkee, 30 July 1952, in The Dalles City Council, Meeting Minutes 1940–1960, City Clerk's Office, City Hall, The Dalles, Oregon).

59. The Housing and Home Finance Agency recommended the use of trailers from Chief Joseph Dam site as a way to avoid a "trailer disposal problem" there (L. R. Durkee to Colonel Itschner, 10 June 1952, in U.S. Army Corps of Engineers, Portland District, Civil Works Project files, 1910–1983, Box 356, File 18, NPP.624—The Dalles, RG 77, National Archives—Pacific Northwest Region).

60. "Critical Defense Status Certified," The Dalles *Chronicle*, 12 November 1952.

61. Monroe Sweetland, Democratic National Committee for Oregon, to Frank McKinney, Democratic National Committee, 12 February 1952, in U.S. Army Corps of Engineers, Portland District, Civil Works Project files, 1910–1983, Box 356, File 18, NPP.624—The Dalles, RG 77, National Archives—Pacific Northwest Region.

62. "Urgency Given Plans for Housing, Water," The Dalles *Chronicle*, 11 February 1953.

63. "Corps Won't Build Housing," The Dalles *Chronicle*, 30 June 1953.

64. "Noted Designer Serves County," The Dalles *Chronicle*, 18 December 1953.

65. Prior to passage of Chapter 440, only the state could issue revenue bonds for an interstate bridge ("1949 Law Aided Bridge Project," The Dalles *Chronicle*, 18 December 1953).

66. "Bridge Project Gains Speed," The Dalles *Chronicle*, 25 February 1951.

67. "Bridge Change May Be Asked," The Dalles *Chronicle*, 1 February 1951.

68. "Time Saving Cited at Agency Meet," The Dalles *Chronicle*, 24 January 1952; and "U.S. Moves to Condemn Bridge," The Dalles *Chronicle*, 19 February 1952.

69. "U.S. Moves to Condemn Bridge," The Dalles *Chronicle*, 19 February 1952.

70. "Bridge Conference Planned in Capital," The Dalles *Chronicle*, 5 March 1952.

71. "Webber Optimistic on Bridge Settlement," The Dalles *Chronicle*, 14 March 1952.

72. "Drama of Bridge and Dam Leads to Fiasco in Wasco," *Oregonian*, 21 February 1951, in Oregon Historical Society, vertical file Bridges—Columbia River—General and Misc., Oregon Historical Society Research Library, Portland.

73. The Dalles League of Women Voters, "The Dalles," 5. The Army Corps of Engineers estimated that nearly 4,000 dependents would reside in the area in 1955 but also estimated that only 3,000 people would be working on the dam that year, so actual figures of dependents could be higher (Oregon State Unemployment Compensation Commission, *Survey of Industry and Employment*, Table I, "The Dalles Dam: Estimate of Working Population—Expedited Program," 164).

74. "Strike Occurs at Dam Site," The Dalles *Chronicle*, 1 December 1952.

75. "Bridge Worker Dies After Earth Bank Collapse," The Dalles *Chronicle*, 26 December 1952.

76. "Two Killed on Project," The Dalles *Chronicle*, 16 May 1954.

77. "Cliff Hanging 'Just a Job'," The Dalles *Chronicle*, 9 March 1954.

78. "Joblessness Hits Peak Since 1947," The Dalles *Chronicle*, 4 June 1953.

79. "'Do It Now' Campaign Aimed at Unemployed," The Dalles *Chronicle*, 10 February 1954.

80. "Dalles Area Project Employment Reaches Total of 2,350 in July," The Dalles *Chronicle*, 8 August 1954.

81. The Dalles City Council, meeting minutes 17 May 1954, 244, City Clerk's Office, City Hall, The Dalles, Oregon.

82. "Indian Found Dead; Theories of Killing, Accident Get Study," The Dalles *Chronicle*, 3 July 1950; and "Experts Seeking Clues to Death," The Dalles *Chronicle*, 5 July 1950.

83. "Tribesmen Battle, Fall Through Plate Glass Store Window," The Dalles *Chronicle*, 25 July 1935.

84. "Indian Shot at Celilo Obtains $10,000 Damages," The Dalles *Chronicle*, 16 June 1932.

85. "Fishermen's Boat Found Overturned," The Dalles *Chronicle*, 25 May 1952.

86. "Indian Falls from Bridge," The Dalles *Chronicle*, 14 August 1956.

87. "Celilo Dipnetter Bags Indian Boy," The Dalles *Chronicle*, 11 September 1952.

88. "Indian Drowns at Celilo with Rescue at Hand," The Dalles *Chronicle*, 3 October 1935.

89. "Man Discovered Lying on Track Critically Injured," The Dalles *Chronicle*, 19 May 1952; and "Injury-Caused Death of Indian Held Accidental," The Dalles *Chronicle*, 20 May 1952.

90. "Indian Boy Killed by Train at Celilo," The Dalles *Chronicle*, 16 September 1937; and "Indian, 26, Dies at Celilo Under Wheels of Train," The Dalles *Chronicle*, 23 September 1948.

91. "Indian Boy Believed to be Fatally Injured," The Dalles *Chronicle*, 24 May 1928.

92. "Liquor-Indian Evil Increases," The Dalles *Chronicle*, 16 July 1950.

93. Act of July 23, 1892, 27, U.S. Statutes at Large 260, revised in 1938 as Act of June 15, 1938, 52, U.S. Statutes at Large 696, codified at U.S. Code 25, 241 (Felix Cohen, *Handbook of Federal Indian Law*).

94. "Liquor-Indian Evil Increases," The Dalles *Chronicle*, 16 July 1950.

95. "Welfare Funds Used for Wine," The Dalles *Chronicle*, 23 July 1950.

96. "Indian Gives Police Tip that Results in Arrest of Marauders," The Dalles *Chronicle*, 26 September 1935.

97. "Indian Receives 4–Year Sentence for Robbery," The Dalles *Chronicle*, 29 April 1943.

98. "Indian Veteran of Cassino Battle Home on Leave," The Dalles *Chronicle*, 4 May 1944.

5 / RELOCATION AND THE PERSISTENCE
OF CELILO VILLAGE

1. Gerald Foster to C. G. Davis, 17 February 1946; and Davis to Foster, 15 March 1946; both in U.S. Bureau of Indian Affairs, Portland Area Office, files of C. G. Davis, Field Agent—The Dalles, Oregon, General Subject Correspondence, 1939–53, 003-006, Box 1945, Folder 155-M Councils—Celilo Fish—Feasts and Ceremonials, RG 75, National Archives—Pacific Northwest Region.

2. "Blast, Tribal Rites Draw Sunday Throng," The Dalles *Chronicle,* 21 April 1952.

3. Tommy Thompson, statement to Wasco County, State of Oregon, 17 February 1945, in U.S. Bureau of Indian Affairs, Portland Area Office, files of C. G. Davis, Field Agent, The Dalles, Oregon, General Subject Correspondence, 1939–1953, Box 1945, Folder 155L—Councils Celilo Falls—Ownership of Rocks near Celilo Falls, RG 75, National Archives— Pacific Northwest Region.

4. Abundant salmon runs and easy access to resources in the Cascade Mountains drew Indians to The Dalles region about 11,000 years ago, according to archaeologist Luther S. Cressman (in U.S. Department of the Interior, National Park Service, *Cultural Sequences at The Dalles, Oregon,* 1958), an unpublished report cited in Butler, "Physical Stratigraphy of Wakemap Mound."

5. Butler, "Physical Stratigraphy of Wakemap Mound," 20.

6. H. U. Sanders, "Report on the Sanitary Conditions at Celilo, Oregon," 10 October 1940, 5, in U.S. Bureau of Indian Affairs, Portland Area Office, Property and Plant Management, Celilo Relocation Records, 1947–1957, Box 1934, RG 75, National Archives—Pacific Northwest Region. In comparison, the average family on the Yakima Reservation earned $1,250 annually (U.S. Army Corps of Engineers, Portland District, *Special Report on Indian Fishery Problem*).

7. U.S. Bureau of Indian Affairs, Yakima Agency, *Program: Celilo, Oregon, 1946–1955,* March 1944, 1–2.

8. Ibid.

9. C. G. Davis to Edward Swindell, 30 March 1942, in response to

Swindell's request for a list of Celilo Village residents, in U.S. Bureau of Indian Affairs, Portland Area Office, files of C. G. Davis, Field Agent—The Dalles, Oregon, General Subject Correspondence, 1939–53, 003-006, Box 1944, Folder 155-E, Councils—Celilo Fish—Legal Matters, RG 75, National Archives—Pacific Northwest Region.

10. Steve Erickson, "Dissension, Winds, Plastic Plumbing Plague Indian Village of Mixed Tribes," *Oregonian*, 22 February 1976, 16.

11. Ibid.

12. Chief Tommy Thompson, remarks, 28 April 1940, in U.S. Bureau of Indian Affairs, Portland Area Office, files of C. G. Davis, Field Agent—The Dalles, Oregon, General Subject Correspondence, Box 1943, 009-155 A-D, 155-A Councils—Celilo Fish Committee C41939-48, File A Misc., RG 75, National Archives—Pacific Northwest Region.

13. Jim, interview.

14. Martha McKeown and Marshall Dana eventually married.

15. Clarence Davis to Dorothy Eakin, Administrator, Wasco County Welfare Commission, 22 January 1952, in U.S. Bureau of Indian Affairs, Portland Area Office, files of C. G. Davis, Field Agent—The Dalles, Oregon, General Subject Correspondence, 1939–53, Box 1939, 006 Thompson, Tommy, Otis and Ellen Andrews—Wilbur Kunehi, RG 75, National Archives—Pacific Northwest Region.

16. Clarence Davis to Dorothy Eakin, 22 January 1952, ibid.; and Clarence Davis to L. W. Shotwell, 4 February 1946, in U.S. Bureau of Indian Affairs, Portland Area Office, files of C. G. Davis, Field Agent—The Dalles, Oregon, General Subject Correspondence, Box 1943, 009-155 A-D, 121 Indian Travels, Visiting Among Indians, RG 75, National Archives—Pacific Northwest Region.

17. Clarence Davis to L. W. Shotwell, 19 January 1949, ibid.

18. Flora Thompson to Clarence Davis, n.d., in U.S. Bureau of Indian Affairs, Portland Area Office, files of C. G. Davis, Field Agent—The Dalles, Oregon, General Subject Correspondence, 1939–53, Box 1939, 006 Thompson, Tommy, Otis and Ellen Andrews—Wilbur Kunehi, RG 75, National Archives—Pacific Northwest Region.

19. Davis had hoped to employ Isabella Lumaguip, a Yakama woman (Clarence Davis to M. A. Johnson, 30 April 1942, in U.S. Bureau of Indian Affairs, Portland Area Offic, files of C. G. Davis, Field Agent—The Dalles,

Oregon, General Subject Correspondence, 1939–53, Box 1943, 099-155 A-D, 155-A Councils—Celilo Fish Commission, C41939-48, File A Misc., RG 75, National Archives—Pacific Northwest Region).

20. Ulrich, *Empty Nets*, 35.

21. Davis to L. W. Shotwell, 3 May 1948; and Clarence Davis to L. W. Shotwell, 3 May 1949; both in U.S. Bureau of Indian Affairs, Portland Area Office, files of C. G. Davis, Field Agent—The Dalles, Oregon, General Subject Correspondence, Box 1946, File 155Y Celilo Fishing Commission 16—Relations Including Fish Controversies with Non-Indians, private individuals, etc., RG 75, National Archives—Pacific Northwest Region.

22. Clifford Presnall, extract of "Indian Salmon Fishing in Oregon and Washington," 19 December 1941; Clarence Davis to M. A. Johnson, 17 February 1942; and Clarence Davis to M. A. Johnson, 28 February 1942, all in U.S. Bureau of Indian Affairs, Portland Area Office, files of C. G. Davis, Field Agent—The Dalles, Oregon, General Subject Correspondence, Box 1943, File 155-B Councils—Celilo Fish—Salmon—Conservation and fish caught for food by the Indians, RG 75, National Archives—Pacific Northwest Region.

23. "When Financial Doldrums Beset Him in Capital J. Whizz Found Ron Taylor a Friend," The Dalles *Optimist*, 26 April 1940, 1. John Whiz's name was spelled both as Whiz and as Whizz. Although it is not clear in the newspaper article, it is likely that Taylor was running for candidacy in 1940; Harold Saxton, also a Republican, won election in 1939 and in 1941 (Glenn Harding, *Our Oregon Heritage: Almanac of Public Officials, 1931–1987* [Lake Oswego: Oregon Family Publishing, 1988], 465).

24. Columbia River Tribal Council, Rock Creek, 4 March 1940; and Clarence Davis to M. A. Johnson, 26 January 1940; both in U.S. Bureau of Indian Affairs, Portland Area Office, files of C. G. Davis, Field Agent—The Dalles, Oregon, General Subject Correspondence, Box 1943, 009-155 A-D, File 155-A Councils—Celilo Fish Committee C41939-48, File A Misc., RG 75, National Archives—Pacific Northwest Region.

25. Clarence Davis to L. W. Shotwell, 6 January 1944, in U.S. Bureau of Indian Affairs, Portland Area Office, files of C. G. Davis, Field Agent—The Dalles, Oregon, General Subject Correspondence, Box 1945, 155-K

Relations and Correspondence with States (1939–48), RG 75, National Archives—Pacific Northwest Region.

26. Clarence Davis to M. A. Johnson, 8 October 1940, in U.S. Bureau of Indian Affairs, Portland Area Office, files of C. G. Davis, Field Agent—The Dalles, Oregon, General Subject Correspondence, Box 1943, 009-155 A-D, File 155-A Councils—Celilo Fish Committee C41939-48, File A Misc., RG 75, National Archives—Pacific Northwest Region.

27. Clarence Davis to M. A. Johnson, 2 October 1940, in U.S. Bureau of Indian Affairs, Portland Area Office, files of C. G. Davis, Field Agent—The Dalles, Oregon, General Subject Correspondence, Box 1943, 009-155 A-D, File 155-C Councils, Celilo, Fish, Sanitary Health, RG 75, National Archives—Pacific Northwest Region.

28. U.S. Bureau of Indian Affairs, "Narrative Report of the Warm Springs Agency Jurisdiction, 1935," in *Superintendents Annual Narrative and Statistical Reports from Field Jurisdictions of the Bureau of Indian Affairs, 1907–1938*. National Archives Microfilm Publication M1011, Roll 196S, 27, Records of the Bureau of Indian Affairs, Record Group 75, National Archives Building—Washington, D.C.

29. H. U. Sanders, "Report on the Sanitary Conditions at Celilo, Oregon," 10 October 1940, 21, in U.S. Bureau of Indian Affairs, Portland Area Office, Property and Plant Management, Celilo Relocation Records, 1947–1957, Box 1934, RG 75, National Archives—Pacific Northwest Region.

30. Martha McKeown, "Celilo Indians: Fishing Their Way of Life," *Oregonian*, 6 October 1946, Magazine sec., 3.

31. Mackenzie, interview by Katrine Barber, 30 September 1999, tape recording, OHS inv. #1936, Oregon Historical Society Research Library, Portland.

32. U.S. Bureau of Indian Affairs, Yakima Agency, *Program: Celilo, Oregon, 1946–1955*, 9; H. U. Sanders, "Report on the Sanitary Conditions at Celilo, Oregon," 10 October 1940, 12–13, in U.S. Bureau of Indian Affairs, Portland Area Office, Property and Plant Management, Celilo Relocation Records, 1947–1957, Box 1934, RG 75, National Archives—Pacific Northwest Region.

33. Joe Stein, "Indian Colony Complains It's Getting a Bad Deal from

U.S.," Oregon *Journal*, 17 April 1947, in Oregon Historical Society vertical files, Indians—General—Fishing Rights, Oregon Historical Society Research Library, Portland.

34. Mackenzie, interview, 27 August 1999.

35. H. U. Sanders, "Report on the Sanitary Conditions at Celilo, Oregon," 10 October 1940, 13–14, in U.S. Bureau of Indian Affairs, Portland Area Office, Property and Plant Management, Celilo Relocation Records, 1947–1957, Box 1934, RG 75, National Archives—Pacific Northwest Region. According to U.S. Bureau of Indian Affairs, Yakima Agency, Program: Celilo, Oregon, 1946–1955, the Indian Service had a contract with District Fifteen in 1944 for tuition for Celilo children that covered the cost of a single full-time teacher who taught grades one through eight. Schooling had been a problem for some time. The Warm Springs superintendent complained in 1920 that "there are children at Celilo . . . who have not been in school during the past year. I do not see any remedy as the white people will not try to force them into their schools and the Indians do not care to send their children to school at all" (U.S. Bureau of Indian Affairs, "Narrative Report of the Warm Springs Agency, 1920," in *Superintendents' Annual Narrative and Statistical Reports, 1907–1938*; National Archives Microfilm Publication M1011, Roll L64, 6, Records of the Bureau of Indian Affairs, RG 75, National Archives Building—Washington, D.C.).

36. "Celilo Cleanup Delay Provokes Dalles Chamber," The Dalles *Chronicle,* 26 March 1936.

37. "Fishing Village Menaces Health," *Oregonian*, 29 March 1936, sec. 1, 17; and "Celilo Cleanup Found Legally Possible," The Dalles *Chronicle,* 7 May 1936.

38. H. U. Sanders, "Report on the Sanitary Conditions at Celilo, Oregon," 10 October 1940, 15, in U.S. Bureau of Indian Affairs, Portland Area Office, Property and Plant Management, Celilo Relocation Records, 1947–1957, Box 1934, RG 75, National Archives—Pacific Northwest Region.

39. "Celilo Indians Strike Back at Critics," The Dalles *Chronicle,* 23 April 1936.

40. "Celilo Village Plan Favored," *Oregonian*, 10 August 1946, sec. 1,

7. The plan laid out in U.S. Bureau of Indian Affairs, Yakima Agency, *Program: Celilo, Oregon, 1946–1955*, in 1944 was very likely the precursor to the plan adopted in 1946.

41. "Indians Hoping for New Village," *Oregonian*, 2 April 1947, sec. 1, 10.

42. Martha McKeown, "The Wy-ams-pums of Celilo," *Christian Century* 77 (24 August 1960), 967.

43. "Tribesmen Weigh Plans for New Village," The Dalles *Chronicle*, 11 July 1948.

44. "Celilo Fish Group O.K.'s Village Plan," The Dalles *Chronicle*, 24 October 1948.

45. "Celilo Unit Included in Interior Bill," The Dalles *Chronicle*, 20 June 1948.

46. Celilo women signed a petition in 1949 asking that replacement homes be placed in the location of the original homes. Evidently the BIA misplaced the petition. According to Indian advocate Martha McKeown, the petition was "at the bureau carefully tacked away in a closed file, unanswered and unacted on, and, for all I know, unlooked at" ("Celilo Indians' Plea Gathers Dust," Oregon *Journal*, 19 April 1949, sec. 1, 13).

47. Joe Stein, "Indian Colony Complains It's Getting a Bad Deal from U.S.," 17 April 1949, in Oregon Historical Society vertical file Indians—General—Fishing Rights.

48. Ibid.

49. "Fishing Village Menaces Health," *Oregonian*, 29 March 1936, sec. 1, 17.

50. Memo to BIA Commissioner from Portland Area Office, 17 February 1955, in U.S. Bureau of Indian Affairs, Yakima Agency, *Program: Celilo, Oregon, 1946–1955*.

51. Memo to BIA Commissioner from Portland Area Office, 17 February 1955, in U.S. Bureau of Indian Affairs, Yakima Agency, *Program: Celilo, Oregon, 1946–1955*.

52. The funds covered $7,500 for an estimated twenty-six families, plus $15,000 in administrative costs (Public Law 1963, 84th Cong., 1st sess., 15 July 1955).

53. Mackenzie, interview, 30 September 1999.

54. This survey was conducted in March 1953. In addition, the BIA completed another survey in February 1955 of Indians to be relocated. The two surveys used different residency requirements to determine which families were eligible for relocation support (Don Foster to Mr. Greenwood, 6 May 1955, in U.S. Bureau of Indian Affairs, Yakima Agency, *Program: Celilo, Oregon, 1946–1955*). Acceptable proof included letters, bills, and affidavits ("Narrative Report—Celilo Relocation Project," n.d., "Misc. Pertaining to Celilo Relocation," in U.S. Bureau of Indian Affairs, Portland Area Office, Celilo Relocation Records, 1947–1957, RG 75, National Archives—Pacific Northwest Region).

55. Oregon Historical Society, Celilo Relocation Project files, 1955–1957, MS 2678, Box 1, File 3, "Minutes of Committee Meetings," Oregon Historical Society Research Library, Portland, Oregon.

56. A fifth family relocated to a refurbished home at New Celilo. Minutes of Committee Meetings, 26 April 1956, 28 May 1956, and 22 August 1956, in Oregon Historical Society, Celilo Relocation Project files, Box 1, Folder 3, "Celilo Falls Indian Relocation Project Records, 1955–1957," MS 2678, Oregon Historical Society Research Library, Portland.

57. "Narrative Report—Celilo Relocation Project," n.d., "Misc. Pertaining to Celilo Relocation," 3, in U.S. Bureau of Indian Affairs, Portland Area Office, Celilo Relocation Records, 1947–1957, RG 75, National Archives—Pacific Northwest Region.

58. McKeown, "Wy-ams-pums of Celilo," 967.

59. "Narrative Report—Celilo Relocation Project," n.d., "Misc. Pertaining to Celilo Relocation," 4–5, in U.S. Bureau of Indian Affairs, Portland Area Office, Celilo Relocation Records, 1947–1957, RG 75, National Archives—Pacific Northwest Region.

60. Martha Ferguson McKeown, a white schoolteacher and writer whom Chief Thompson "adopted" as his daughter, arranged to have the chief placed in the Hanby Nursing Home in Hood River, the town in which she lived (Martha McKeown to Flora Thompson and Barbara Mackenzie, 26 August 1956, in Oregon Historical Society, Celilo Relocation Project files, Box 1, folder 2, "Correspondence, July 1956–1957," MS 2678, Oregon Historical Society Research Library, Portland). Barbara Mackenzie described McKeown as "a very prominent person"

who could assure the chief's good treatment (Mackenzie, interview, 30 September 1999).

61. Chief Tommy Thompson died on 12 April 1959 (Ann Sullivan, "Indian Drums, Voices Pay Homage to Chief Tommy Thompson," *Oregonian*, 15 April 1959, sec. 1, 6; Ann Sullivan, "Indians, Whites Meet at Celilo Falls to Pay Honor to Last of Great Chiefs," *Oregonian*, 16 April 1959, sec. 1, 1; and "Chief Tommy's Memory a Reproach," Oregon *Journal*, 15 April 1959, 22A).

62. Jeanie Senior, "Celilo Residents Seek Housing, Health-care Aid," *Oregonian*, 10 April 1985, 2C.

6 / NEGOTIATING VALUES

1. Because the legality of the Huntington Treaty had yet to be ruled on by a court, the Warm Springs wanted to avoid going to court for a settlement. The treaty was finally nullified in 1969 (Confederated Tribes of the Warm Springs of Oregon, *The People of Warm Springs, Profile: The Confederated Tribes of the Warm Springs Reservation of Oregon* [Warm Springs, Ore.: Confederated Tribes of the Warm Springs, 1984], 26).

2. Henry Thompson to senators and representatives, 16 March 1951, in U.S. Bureau of Indian Affairs, Portland Area Office, File 920, Conservation of Fish and Wildlife, Celilo Fisheries, 7-1-49 to 6-30-53, RG 75, National Archives—Pacific Northwest Region.

3. Minutes of Celilo Fish Committee meeting, 3 April 1952, in U.S. Bureau of Indian Affairs, Portland Area Office, Celilo Fish Committee files, Box 1947, Field Agent—The Dalles, OR, General Subject Correspondence, 1939–53, RG 75, National Archives—Pacific Northwest Region.

4. In 1964 Congress debated two proposals regarding Indian fishing rights. One was to buy out the Indian rights to various fisheries altogether, thereby ending any treaty rights Indians in the Pacific Northwest had to the Columbia River salmon and steelhead populations. This was perhaps the most radical example of how termination policy had the potential to affect the Indian fishery. When President Eisenhower recommended in his 1951 budget that $18 million be allocated for the construction of The Dalles Dam, local Indians quickly trav-

eled to the capitol to testify before the House Appropriations Committee regarding their fishery. The testimony of the Indians swayed the committee, which refused to appropriate funds to the Army Corps "on the premise that the Indian problem had not been settled." The Senate disagreed with the House, and eventually the Army Corps was able to start construction with an allocation of $4 million. Within three days of receiving funds, the Army Corps appointed Percy Othus as Special Negotiator and sent out letters to the four tribes identified as having a legal right to the fishery, to start negotiations for a settlement of the sites to be inundated (Minutes of the Conference of Warm Springs Indians, 2 May 1952, in U.S. Bureau of Indian Affairs, Portland Area Office, "Celilo–Warm Springs Dalles Damage Claims, 1951–1952," 1, in Federal Building, Portland, Oregon).

5. In 1946 Congress decided that the U.S. Fish and Wildlife Service, at that time an agency interested primarily in the collection of data, had to be consulted regarding the effects that proposed river structures such as dams would have on local fish and wildlife, in large part as a result of pressure from sports fishermen (McKinley, *Uncle Sam in the Pacific Northwest*, 109).

6. U.S. Department of the Interior, U.S. Fish and Wildlife Service, *Summary Report on Indian Fishery Census*, 11.

7. Ibid., 13–14.

8. The reports did not differentiate between tribal groups; instead, they simply lumped all Indian fishers together. This would become a sticking point in the Corps's negotiations with the Yakama Nation.

9. E. Morgan Pryse to BIA Acting Director, memo of 19 July 1951, in U.S. Bureau of Indian Affairs, Portland Area Office, files of C. G. Davis, Box 1947, Field Agent—The Dalles, General Subject Correspondence, 1939–53, RG 75, National Archives—Pacific Northwest Region.

10. U.S. Army Corps of Engineers, *Special Report on Indian Fishery Problem, The Dalles Dam, Columbia River, Washington-Oregon*, 62.

11. Ibid., 85.

12. Ibid., 19.

13. "Celilo Falls Flooding Poses Question of Compensation to Indians," Portland *Oregonian*, 18 May 1952, sec. 1, 20.

14. U.S. Army Corps of Engineers, *Special Report on Indian Fishery*

Problem, The Dalles Dam, Columbia River, Washington-Oregon (10 March 1952), Portland, Oregon, 1952, 32.

15. T. Leland Brown to E. Morgan Pryse, 28 September 1950, in U.S. Bureau of Indian Affairs, Portland Area Office, Property and Plant Management, Celilo Relocation Records, 1947–57, files of Edward G. Swindell, Counsel, 1947–53, re: Celilo Matters, Box 1933, RG 75, National Archives—Pacific Northwest Region.

16. Jasper Elliott to E. Morgan Pryse, 17 July 1950, in U.S. Bureau of Indian Affairs, Portland Area Office, Property and Plant Management, Celilo Relocation Records, 1947–57, files of Edward G. Swindell, Counsel, 1947–53, re: Celilo Matters, Box 1933, RG 75, National Archives—Pacific Northwest Region.

17. Minutes of the Conference of Warm Springs Indians, 2 May 1952; and Eugene W. Barrett, "Report on the Two Meetings of the Warm Springs and Umatilla Delegations, and their Attorneys, the Corps of Army Engineers Represented by Mr. Othus and His Staff on the Celilo Fisheries Settlement," n.d.; both in U.S. Bureau of Indian Affairs, Portland Area Office, "Celilo–Warm Springs Dalles Damage Claims, 1951–1952," in the Federal Building, Portland, Oregon.

18. Percy Othus to Celilo Fisheries Tribal Negotiating Committees, 22 February 1952, in U.S. Bureau of Indian Affairs, Portland Area Office, "Celilo–Warm Springs Dalles Damage Claims, 1951–1952," in Federal Building, Portland, Oregon.

19. Several claims regarding the depletion of the fishery were in the process of going through the Federal Indian Claims Commission, which attempted to resolve Indian-federal conflict by compensating successful claims brought by tribes. For example, the Yakamas sued the federal government to recover the costs of the decline in the fisheries of Columbia River tributaries (estimated at 20 percent) as a result of dam building. The Warm Springs Indians filed Docket No. 198 with the Indian Claims Commission to ask for compensation for the fisheries lost to Bonneville Dam. And the Confederated Tribes of the Umatilla Reservation sued the government for fisheries losses in the Umatilla River (U.S. Army Corps of Engineers, *Special Report on Indian Fishery Problem*, 30, 40, 47).

20. "Indians and the Dam," The *Oregonian*, 29 March 1952, 8.

21. Confederated Tribes of the Warm Springs, *People of the Warm Springs*, 44.

22. "Indians Sign Pact on Falls," The *Oregonian*, 9 December 1952, sec. 1, 1.

23. Relander, *Treaty Centennial, 1855–1955*, 44–48.

24. Ibid., 47. Even though the tribal affiliation of fishers was compiled, the annual catch itself was not divided along tribal affiliation. One would assume that the Yakamas caught the most fish at Celilo in 1952 because the majority of fishers were Yakama, but nothing within the Fish and Wildlife reports confirms this.

25. Minutes of Meeting with Yakima Negotiating Committee, 20 July 1954, Portland District Corps of Engineers, The Dalles Dam Indian Fishery, in U.S. Bureau of Indian Affairs, Portland Area Office, "Celilo Settlement 1953," 26, in the Federal Building, Portland, Oregon.

26. Ibid., 27, 31.

27. Johnson Meninick, conversation with the author, 30 June 1998.

28. Minutes of Meeting with Yakima Negotiating Committee, 20 July 1954, Portland District Corps of Engineers, The Dalles Dam Indian Fishery, in U.S. Bureau of Indian Affairs, Portland Area Office, "Celilo Settlement 1953," 11, 14, in the Federal Building, Portland, Oregon.

29. The records do not indicate whether the Yakamas retained the right to sue the federal government for compensation due to the loss of "intangible" factors.

30. Edward Swindell Jr. to Celilo Fish Committee, 15 September 1949, in U.S. Bureau of Indian Affairs, Portland Area Office, files of Edward G. Swindell, Counsel, 1947–53, re: Celilo Matters, Box 1933, RG 75, National Archives—Pacific Northwest Region.

31. U.S. Army Corps of Engineers, Portland District, *Summary of Evidence Relating to the Nez Perce Fishery at Celilo Falls, Oregon*, 91–92.

32. Ibid., 61.

33. Minutes of Meeting with Nez Perce Negotiating Committee, 1–2 June 1955, Portland District Corps of Engineers, The Dalles Dam Indian Fishery, in U.S. Bureau of Indian Affairs, Portland Area Office, "Celilo–Nez Perce; Dalles Dam Damage Claim," 6, in the Federal Building, Portland, Oregon.

34. Charles McDaniel, Report of Negotiations with the Nez Perce

Indian Tribe, Celilo Falls Fishery, 27 April 1956, in U.S. Army Corps of Engineers, Portland District, Civil Works Project files, 1910–1983, Box 209, RG 77, National Archives—Pacific Northwest Region.

35. Ibid.

36. Ibid.

37. Clifford Comisky, memo for file, sub: Nez Perce Claim—Celilo Falls Fishery, 29 March 1956, in U.S. Army Corps of Engineers, Portland District, Civil Works Project files, 1910–1983, Box 209, "NEP 800.217 The Dalles Dam folder 2," RG 77, National Archives—Pacific Northwest Region.

38. Instead of receiving $3,754.91 for each person enrolled in the tribe, the Nez Perce were willing to settle for $1,877.46 for 1,714 people (Oregon *Journal*, 19 July 1956).

39. Percy Othus, "Daily Log," n.d., in U.S. Army Corps of Engineers, Portland District, Real Estate Division, Box 187, Record Group 77, National Archives—Pacific Northwest Region.

40. Jimmie James to Secretary, U.S. Engineers, 11 May 1959, U.S. Army Corps of Engineers, Portland District, Real Estate Division, Box 187, RG 77, National Archives—Pacific Northwest Region. Although she had been widowed before, this time Flora Thompson did not remarry but continued to live at Old Celilo and work as a spokesperson for the river Indians. She died in 1979 when a fire engulfed her small home (Joan Arrivee Wagenblast and Jeanne Hillis, *Flora's Song: A Remembrance of Chief Tommy Kuni Thompson of the WyAms* [The Dalles, Ore.: The Optimist Printers, 1993], 22).

41. Irene Brunoe, affidavit filed in Wasco County, 28 March 1954, in U.S. Bureau of Indian Affairs, Portland Area Office, Property and Plant Management, Celilo Relocation Records, 1947–1957, Box 1933, "Preliminary Correspondence—Celilo Relocation 1954–58," RG 75, National Archives—Pacific Northwest Region. Eugene W. Barrette, who was present at some of the meetings with Irene Brunoe, wrote a letter apparently on behalf of Percy Othus regarding this complaint. Barrette wrote that "it is true that you made a diligent effort to have her sign an agreement to settle, but at no time did you act in a manner unbecoming to a gentleman" (Eugene W. Barrette to Percy Othus, 9 March 1956, ibid.).

42. U.S. Army Corps of Engineers, Portland District, *The Dalles Dam Indian Fishery: Minutes of Meeting with Yakima Negotiating Committee*, 13.

43. Jacob Mann to Commissioner of Indian Affairs, 4 August 1959, in U.S. Bureau of Indian Affairs, Portland Area Office, files of the Area Social Worker, General Subject Correspondence, 1951–68, Box 1903, Folder 051, RG 75, National Archives—Pacific Northwest Region.

44. Selene Gifford to Jacob Mann, 20 November 1959, in U.S. Bureau of Indian Affairs, Portland Area Office, files of the Area Social Worker, General Subject Correspondence, 1951–68, "Negotiations with Indians— The Dalles Dam Judgement, Yakima, 1956–65," ibid.

45. Lavina Williams to Gracie Pfost, 12 September 1957, ibid.

46. Martin Holm to Don Foster, 11 February 1957, *Report on Nez Perce General Council Meeting 9 February 1957*, in U.S. Bureau of Indian Affairs, Portland Area Office, files of Area Social Worker, General Subject Correspondence, 1951–68, Box 1903, Folder 051—Negotiations with Indians—The Dalles Dam judgement, Nez Perce—1957–61, RG 75, National Archives—Pacific Northwest Region.

47. Gracie Pfost to Glenn Emmons, 16 September 1957, in U.S. Bureau of Indian Affairs, Portland Area Office, files of Area Social Worker, General Subject Correspondence, 1951–68, Box 1903, Folder 051, RG 75, National Archives—Pacific Northwest Region.

48. Glenn Emmons to Gracie Pfost, 19 September 1957, ibid.

49. William Ensor to Don Foster, 26 September 1957, in U.S. Bureau of Indian Affairs, Portland Area Office, files of Area Social Worker, General Subject Correspondence, 1951–61, "Negotiations with Indians— The Dalles Dam Judgement; Nez Perce, 1957–61," ibid.

50. Office of the Solicitor, Portland, to Martin Holm, Assistant Area Director, 16 April 1957, in U.S. Bureau of Indian Affairs, Portland Area Office, files of Area Social Worker, General Subject Correspondence, 1951–61, "Negotiations with Indians—The Dalles Dam Judgement; Umatilla, 1954–68," ibid.

51. Martin Holm, Assistant Area Director, to Don Foster, 15 March 1957, in U.S. Bureau of Indian Affairs, Portland Area Office, files of Area Social Worker, General Subject Correspondence, 1951–61, "Negotiations with Indians—The Dalles Dam Judgement; Nez Perce, 1957–61," ibid.

52. Minutes of the Special Meeting of the Nez Perce General Council, 9 February 1957, ibid., 2.

53. Programming of Yakima Celilo Settlement Funds, Portland, Oregon, 20 February 1957, in U.S. Bureau of Indian Affairs, Portland Area Office, files of Area Social Worker, General Subject Correspondence, 1951–61, "Negotiations with Indians—The Dalles Dam Judgement; Yakima, 1956–65," ibid.

54. HR 5134, 86th Cong., 1st sess., Congressional Record, bound ed. (1959), H 3178.

55. As early as 1957, the same year that the Army Corps completed The Dalles Dam, Floyd Phillips, the BIA superintendent of the Yakama Reservation, requested that the BIA Portland Area Office investigate tribal complaints that the state welfare office had denied Yakama enrollees their benefits as a result of the settlement. Martin Holm contacted Washington, D.C., headquarters regarding the complaints and, on 8 January 1958, met with the State Department of Public Assistance in Olympia, Washington (Martin Holm to Floyd Phillips, 2 September 1959, in U.S. Bureau of Indian Affairs, Portland Area Office, files of Area Social Worker, General Subject Correspondence, 1951–68, "Negotiations with Indians—The Dalles Dam Judgement; Yakima, 1956–65," Box 1903, Folder 051, RG 75, National Archives—Pacific Northwest Region).

56. Acting Area Director to BIA Commissioner, 2 January 1957, ibid.

57. Maurice Powers, Supervisor of Field Services, Washington Department of Public Assistance, to Don Foster, 6 November 1958, in U.S. Bureau of Indian Affairs, Portland Area Office, files of Area Social Worker, General Subject Correspondence, 1951–68, "Negotiations with Indians—The Dalles Dam Judgement; Umatilla, 1954–63," ibid.

58. J. E. Harness, Director of the Umatilla County Juvenile Department, to David S. Hall, Secretary-Treasurer, Board of Trustees, Umatilla Indian Agency, 21 November 1961, ibid.

59. List of Nez Perce County Welfare Recipients—Disposition and Plan for Per Capita Money Received from Dalles Dam Settlement, in U.S. Bureau of Indian Affairs, Portland Area Office, files of Area Social Worker, General Subject Correspondence, 1951–61, "Negotiations with Indians—The Dalles Dam Judgement; Nez Perce, 1957–61," ibid.

CONCLUSION: LOSSES

1. "Indian Rock Onus Denied," *Oregonian*, 30 March 1953, 11.

2. "Indian Chief Steamed Up Over Removal of Stone," *Oregonian*, 27 March 1953, sec. 1, 19.

3. One removal not addressed in this text is that of gravesites and ancestors from Memaloose Island in the Columbia River.

4. See, for example, Katherine Weist, "For the Public Good: Native Americans, Hydroelectric Dams, and the Iron Triangle" in *Trusteeship in Change: Toward Tribal Autonomy in Resource Management*, ed. Richmond Clow and Imre Sutton (Boulder: University of Colorado Press, 2001); Joy Ann Bilharz, *The Allegany Senecas and Kinzua Dam: Forced Relocation through Two Generations* (Lincoln: University of Nebraska Press, 1998); Waldram, *As Long as the Rivers Run*; and Lawson, *Dammed Indians*.

5. The Dalles City Museum Commission, *Request for Establishment of a Museum of Natural History and for Recovery and Preservation of Petroglyphs in Conjunction with Water Resources Projects, Columbia River System* (Wasco County, 10 February 1956).

6. The Columbia River Gorge Discovery Center was partially funded through the Columbia River Gorge Scenic Act passed in 1983.

BIBLIOGRAPHY

Abbott, Carl. *Portland: Planning, Politics, and Growth in a Twentieth Century City.* Lincoln: University of Nebraska Press, 1983.

Ackerman, Lillian. *A Necessary Balance: Gender and Power Among Indians of the Columbia Plateau.* Norman: University of Oklahoma Press, 2003.

"After They Have Killed Us." *Time* 41 (19 April 1943), 26.

Allen, Cain. "Replacing Salmon: Columbia River Indian Fishing Rights and the Geography of Fisheries Mitigation." *Oregon Historical Quarterly* 104 (summer 2003), 196–227.

"Are Indian Rights Again Being Betrayed? Yakima Tribes." *Christian Century* 70 (15 April 1953), 437.

"Are the Yakima Indians Helpless?" *Christian Century* 70 (2 September 1953), 982–83.

Bailey, Barbara, and Mary Howell. *Upper Mill Creek Community: An Illustrated History.* The Dalles, Ore.: Barbara Bailey, 1973.

Barber, Katrine. Notes taken at meeting "Environmental Education and Native American Tribes in the Pacific Northwest" (9–10 April 1998). Pullman: Washington State University.

Barber, Katrine, and Janice Dilg. "'I Didn't Do Anything Anyone Else Couldn't Have Done': A View of Oregon History Through the Ordinary Life of Barbara Mackenzie." *Oregon Historical Quarterly* 103 (winter 2002), 480–509.

Beckham, Stephen Dow. Ethnohistorical Context of Reserved Indian

Fishing Rights, Pacific Northwest Treaties, 1851–1855. Portland, Ore.: Lewis and Clark College, 1984.

Biddle, Henry. "Wishram." *Oregon Historical Quarterly* 27 (1926), 113–30.

Bilharz, Joy Ann. *The Allegany Senecas and Kinzua Dam: Forced Relocation through Two Generations.* Lincoln: University of Nebraska Press, 1998.

Bloch, Ivan. "The Dalles Dam Area, Oregon-Washington, Industrial Location Facts: Population, Transportation, Electric Power, Water Supply, Fuels, Taxation, Plant Sites, Climate." 1952. Oregon Collection, Multnomah County Library, Portland, Oregon.

Boyd, Robert. *People of The Dalles, The Indians of Wascopam Mission: A Historical Ethnography Based on the Papers of Methodist Missionaries.* Lincoln: University of Nebraska Press, 1996.

Butler, B. Robert. "Art of the Lower Columbia Valley." *Archaeology* 10 (autumn 1957), 158–65.

————. "The Physical Stratigraphy of Wakemap Mound: A New Interpretation." MA diss., University of Washington, 1960.

Caldwell, Warren Wendell. "The Archaeology of Wakemap: A Stratified Site Near The Dalles of the Columbia." PhD diss., University of Washington, 1956.

Clark, Robert. *River of the West: Stories from the Columbia.* San Francisco: HarperCollins West, 1995.

Clarkin, Thomas. *Federal Indian Policy in the Kennedy and Johnson Administrations, 1961–1969.* Albuquerque: University of New Mexico Press, 2001.

Cody, Robin. *Ricochet River.* Hillsboro, Oregon: Blue Heron Publishing, 1992.

————. *Voyage of a Summer Sun: Canoeing the Columbia River.* Seattle: Sasquatch Books, 1995.

Cohen, Fay G. *Treaties on Trial: The Continuing Controversy over Northwest Indian Fishing Rights.* Seattle: University of Washington Press, 1986.

Cohen, Felix. *Handbook of Federal Indian Law.* Albuquerque: University of New Mexico Press, 1982.

Collier, John. "Back to Dishonor?" *Christian Century* 71 (12 May 1954), 578–80.

Cone, Joseph. *A Common Fate: Endangered Salmon and the People of the Pacific Northwest.* Corvallis: Oregon State University Press, 1995.

Cone, Joseph, and Sandy Ridlington, eds. *The Northwest Salmon Crisis: A Documentary History.* Corvallis: Oregon State University Press, 1996.

Confederated Tribes of the Warm Springs of Oregon. *The People of Warm Springs, Profile: The Confederated Tribes of the Warm Springs Reservation of Oregon.* Warm Springs, Ore.: Confederated Tribes of the Warm Springs, 1984.

Conner, Roberta. "The Umatilla and the Lewis and Clark Expedition." Paper presented at "History of the American West: The Legacy of Exploration and Encounter," National History Day summer institute, Portland, Oregon, 19–26 July 2003.

Crane, Jeff. "Protesting Monuments to Progress: A Comparative Study of Protests Against Four Dams, 1838–1955." *Oregon Historical Quarterly* 103 (fall 2002), 295–319.

Cramer, Frederick K. "Recollections of a Salmon Dipnetter." *Oregon Historical Quarterly* 75 (September 1974), 221–31.

The Dalles City Council. Meeting minutes, 1940–1960. City Clerk's Office, City Hall, The Dalles, Oregon.

The Dalles City Museum Commission. *Request for Establishment of a Museum of Natural History and for Recovery and Preservation of Petroglyphs in Conjunction with Water Resources Projects, Columbia River System* (10 February 1956). Wasco County, 1956.

The Dalles League of Women Voters. "The Dalles—A Hundred Years and More of Our Town." 1961. Oregon Collection, Multnomah County Library, Portland, Oregon.

The Dalles Library clippings. The Dalles Library, The Dalles, Oregon.

Delloff, Linda-Marie, Martin E. Marty, Dean Peerman, and James M. Wall. *A Century of the Century.* Grand Rapids, Mich.: William B. Eerdmans Publishing Co., 1984.

Deloria, Philip. *Playing Indian.* New Haven: Yale University Press, 1998.

Dietrich, William. *Northwest Passage: The Great Columbia River.* Seattle: University of Washington Press, 1995.

Due, John Fitzgerald, and Giles French. *Rails to the Mid-Columbia*

Wheatlands: The Columbia Southern and Great Southern Railroads and the Development of Sherman and Wasco Counties, Oregon. Washington, D.C.: University Press of America, 1979.

Edmo, Ed. "After Celilo." In *Talking Leaves: Contemporary Native American Short Stories,* ed. Craig Lesley. New York: Dell, 1991.

———. Interview by Britta Blucher, 20 June 2003. Videotape in the possession of Britta Blucher.

———. Interview by Kelly Carpenter, 5 April 1999, OHS inv. #1936. Oregon Historical Society Research Library, Portland, Oregon.

Fey, Harold E. "Indian Winter." *Christian Century* 72 (2 March 1955), 267.

———. "Most Indians Are Poor." *Christian Century* 72 (18 May 1955), 592–94.

Ficken, Robert E. *Rufus Woods, the Columbia River and the Building of Modern Washington.* Pullman: Washington State University Press, 1995.

Fiege, Mark. *Irrigated Eden: The Making of an Agricultural Landscape in the American West.* Seattle: University of Washington Press, 1999.

Findlay, John. "A Fishy Proposition: Regional Identity in the Pacific Northwest." In *Many Wests: Place, Culture and Regional Identity,* ed. Michael C. Steiner and David M. Wrobel. Lawrence: University Press of Kansas, 1998.

Fisher, Andrew H. "People of the River: A History of the Columbia River Indians, 1855–1945." PhD diss., Arizona State University, 2003.

Fixico, Donald L. *The Invasion of Indian Country in the Twentieth Century: American Capitalism and Tribal Natural Resources.* Niwot: University Press of Colorado, 1998.

———. *Termination and Relocation: Federal Indian Policy, 1945–1969.* Albuquerque: University of New Mexico Press, 1986.

French, David, and Katherine French. "Consultation or Consent?" *Christian Century* 73 (25 January 1956), 103–104.

———. "Wasco, Wishram, and Cascades." In vol. 12, *Handbook of North American Indians,* ed. Deward Walker Jr. Washington, D.C.: Smithsonian Institution, 1998.

Friday, Chris. *Organizing Asian American Labor: The Pacific Coast Canned-Salmon Industry, 1870–1942.* Philadelphia, Penn.: Temple University Press, 1994.

"Garrison Dam: Missouri Valley Project Raises Land Prices and Indian War Whoops." *Life* 21 (8 July 1946), 30–31.

Gottlieb, Robert. *A Life of Its Own: The Politics and Power of Water.* San Diego: Harcourt Brace Jovanovich, 1988.

Gunther, Erna. "An Analysis of the First Salmon Ceremony." *American Anthropologist* 28 (1926), 605–17.

———. "A Further Analysis of the First Salmon Ceremony." *University of Washington Publications in Anthropology* 2 (1928), 129–73.

Hageman, Charles. "Report on City, Port and County Planning, The Dalles, Oregon and Metropolitan Area with Recommendations." Unpublished report, January 1940. Oregon Collection, Multnomah County Library, Portland, Oregon.

Harden, Blaine. *A River Lost: The Life and Death of the Columbia.* New York: W. W. Norton, 1996.

Harding, Glenn. *Our Oregon Heritage: Almanac of Public Officials, 1931–1987.* Lake Oswego: Oregon Family Publishing, 1988.

Harris, Bruce. *The Wasco County History Book.* The Dalles, Ore.: Bruce Harris, 1983.

Hasse, Larry J. "Termination and Assimilation: Federal Indian Policy, 1943 to 1961." PhD diss., Washington State University, 1974.

Holbrook, Stewart. *The Columbia.* New York: Rinehart, 1956.

Hunn, Eugene. *Nch'i-Wána, "The Big River": Mid-Columbia Indians and Their Land.* Seattle: University of Washington Press, 1991.

Hunn, Eugene, and David French. "Western Columbia River Sahaptins." In vol. 12, *Handbook of North American Indians,* ed. Deward Walker Jr. Washington, D.C.: Smithsonian Institution, 1998.

Jim, Russell. Interview by Michael O'Rourke, 16 October 1999. OHS inv. #2627, tape recording, Oregon Historical Society Research Library, Portland, Oregon.

Kittredge, William, *Hole in the Sky.* New York: Vintage Books, 1992.

Knuth, Priscilla. *"Picturesque" Frontier: The Army's Fort Dalles.* Portland: Oregon Historical Society Press, 1967.

Kuletz, Valerie. *The Tainted Desert: Environmental and Social Ruin in the American West.* New York: Routledge, 1998.

Landeen, Dan, and Allen Pinkham. *Salmon and His People: Fish and Fishing in Nez Perce Culture.* Lewiston, Idaho: Confluence Press, 1999.

Lang, William, and Robert Carriker, eds. *Great River of the West: Essays on the Columbia River*. Seattle: University of Washington Press, 1999.

Lawson, Michael. *Dammed Indians: The Pick-Sloan Plan and the Missouri River Sioux, 1944–1980*. Norman: University of Oklahoma Press, 1982.

Lichatowich, Jim. *Salmon Without Rivers: A History of the Pacific Salmon Crisis*. Washington, D.C.: Island Press, 1999.

Lowitt, Richard. *The New Deal and the West*. Norman: University of Oklahoma Press, 1993.

Loy, William G., et al. "Precipitation Regimes." In *Atlas of Oregon*, 2nd ed. Eugene: University of Oregon Press, 2001.

Loy, William, Stuart Allan, Aileen Buckley, and James Meacham. *Atlas of Oregon*, 2nd ed. Eugene: University of Oregon Press, 2001.

Mackenzie, Barbara. Interviews by Katrine Barber, 27 August 1999 and 30 September 1999. OHS inv. #1936, tape recording, Oregon Historical Society Research Library, Portland, Oregon.

Mazmanian, Daniel A., and Jeanne Nienaber. *Can Organizations Change?: Environmental Protection, Citizens Participation, and the Corps of Engineers*. Washington, D.C.: The Brookings Institution, 1979.

McKeown, Martha. "The Wy-ams-pums of Celilo." *Christian Century* 77 (24 August 1960), 967–68.

McKinley, Charles. *Uncle Sam in the Pacific Northwest*. Berkeley: University of California Press, 1952.

Medhurst, Martin, Robert Ivie, Philip Wander, and Robert Scott. *Cold War Rhetoric: Strategy, Metaphor, and Ideology*. East Lansing: Michigan State University Press, 1997.

Meninick, Jay. Conversation with the author, 30 June 1998.

Minthorne, Jay. Interview by Clark Hansen, 16 August 2000, tape recording, OHS inv. #2784, Oregon Historical Society Research Library, Portland.

Moulton, Gary E., ed. *The Journals of the Lewis and Clark Expedition, Volume Five, July 28–November 1, 1805*. Lincoln: University of Nebraska Press, 1996.

Nash, Gerald. *The American West Transformed: The Impact of the Second World War*. Bloomington: Indiana University Press, 1985.

Netboy, Anthony. *The Columbia River Salmon and Steelhead Trout: Their Fight for Survival*. Seattle: University of Washington Press, 1980.

————. *Salmon of the Pacific Northwest: Fish vs. Dams*. Portland, Ore.: Binfords and Mort, 1958.

Oregon Bureau of Municipal Research and Service. *Population of Oregon Cities, Counties, and Metropolitan Areas, 1850 to 1957* (April 1958), compilation of census counts and estimates, Information Bulletin No. 106. University of Oregon, 1958.

Oregon Fish Commission. *The Indian Dip Net Fishery at Celilo Falls on the Columbia River* (November 1951), by R. W. Schoning, T. R. Merrell Jr., and D. R. Johnson. Portland, Oregon, 1951.

Oregon Historical Society. Files of Columbia Basin Fisheries Development Association. Celilo Relocation Project files. Vertical files: Bridges—Columbia River—General and Misc.; The Dalles—Oregon Cities; Dams, Columbia River—The Dalles Dam; Indians—General—Celilo Falls; Indians—General—Fishing Rights; Wasco County—Oregon Counties. Oregon Historical Society Research Library, Portland, Oregon.

Oregon State College. "Warm Springs Research Project," vol. 1–5. Corvallis: Oregon State College, 1960.

Oregon State Unemployment Compensation Commission. *A Survey of Industry and Employment in Oregon Counties*. Salem, Oregon, 1957.

Parman, Donald. "Inconsistent Advocacy: The Erosion of Indian Fishing Rights in the Pacific Northwest, 1933–1956." *Pacific Historical Review* 53 (1983), 163–89.

————. *Indians and the American West in the Twentieth Century*. Bloomington: Indiana University Press, 1994.

Philp, Kenneth R. *John Colliers Crusade for Indian Reform 1920–1945*. Tucson: University of Arizona Press, 1977.

————. *Termination Revisited: American Indians on the Trail to Self-Determination, 1933–1953*. Lincoln: University of Nebraska Press, 1999.

Pisani, Donald. *Water and American Government: The Reclamation Bureau, National Water Policy, and the West, 1902–1935*. Berkeley: University of California Press, 2002.

Pitt, Louis. Interview by Clark Hansen, 23 February 2001. OHS inv. #2791, Oregon Historical Society Research Library, Portland, Oregon.

Pitzer, Paul. *Grand Coulee: Harnessing a Dream*. Pullman: Washington State University Press, 1994.

Prucha, Francis Paul. *The Great Father: The United States Government and the American Indians*. Abridged ed. Lincoln: University of Nebraska Press, 1986.

Relander, Click. *Treaty Centennial, 1855–1955: The Yakimas*. Yakima, Wash.: The Republic Press, 1955.

Richards, Kent. *Isaac I. Stevens: Young Man in a Hurry*. Pullman: Washington State University Press, 1993.

Reisner, Marc. *Cadillac Desert: The American West and Its Disappearing Water*. New York: Viking, 1986.

Robbins, William. Comments to John Findlay, April 1997, Tacoma, Washington, at Pacific Northwest History Conference.

———. "The Indian Question in Western Oregon: The Making of a Colonial People." In *Experiences in a Promised Land: Essays in Pacific Northwest History*, ed. G. Thomas Edwards and Carlos A. Schwantes. Seattle: University of Washington Press, 1986.

———. *Landscapes of Promise: The Oregon Story, 1800–1940*. Seattle: University of Washington Press, 1997.

Ross, Alexander. *Adventures of the First Settlers on the Oregon or Columbia River, 1810–1813*. Corvallis: Oregon State University Press, 2000.

Schwantes, Carlos. *Columbia River: Gateway to the West*. Moscow, Idaho: University of Idaho Press, 2000.

———. *The Pacific Northwest: An Interpretive History*. Rev. ed. Lincoln: University of Nebraska Press, 1996.

Scott, Mel. *American City Planning Since 1890*. Berkeley: University of California Press, 1969.

Seufert, Francis. *Wheels of Fortune*. Portland: Oregon Historical Society Press, 1980.

Simpson, Louis, and Leslie Spier. *Wishram Ethnography*. Seattle: University of Washington Press, 1930.

Smith, Courtland. *Salmon Fishers of the Columbia*. Corvallis: Oregon State University Press, 1979.

Stern, Theodore. *Chiefs and Change in the Oregon Country Indian Relations at Fort Nez Percés, 1818–1855*. Corvallis: Oregon State University Press, 1996.

Suagee, Mark Allen. "The Creation of an 'Indian Problem': Niqually and Puyallup Off-Reservation Fishing." MA diss., University of Washington, 1973.

Taylor, Joseph. *Making Salmon: An Environmental History of the Northwest Fisheries Crisis.* Seattle: University of Washington Press, 1999.

Thompson, Flora Cushinway. Interview, n.d. Oregon Historical Society Research Library, Portland, Oregon.

Townsend, Kenneth William. *World War II and the American Indian.* Albuquerque: University of New Mexico Press, 2000.

Trafzer, Clifford. *Death Stalks the Yakama: Epidemiological Transitions and Mortality of the Yakama Indian Reservation, 1888–1964.* East Lansing: Michigan State University Press, 1997.

Ulrich, Roberta. *Empty Nets: Indians, Dams, and the Columbia River.* Corvallis: Oregon State University Press, 1999.

———. "Justice Delayed: A Sixty Year Battle for Indian Fishing Sites." MA diss., Portland State University, 1996.

U.S. Army Corps of Engineers. *Army Engineers and the Development of Oregon: A History of the Portland District and U.S. Army Corps of Engineers,* by William F. Willingham. Washington, D.C.: U.S. Government Printing Office, 1992.

U.S. Army Corps of Engineers, Portland District. Civil Works Project files, 1910–1983. Real Estate Division. Portland District files. All in Record Group (RG) 77, National Archives—Pacific Northwest Region, Seattle, Washington

U.S. Army Corps of Engineers. Portland District. *The Dalles Dam Indian Fishery: Minutes of Meeting with Nez Perce Negotiating Committee* (1–2 June 1955). Portland, Oregon, 1955.

U.S. Army Corps of Engineers. Portland District. *The Dalles Dam Indian Fishery: Minutes of Meeting with Yakima Negotiating Committee* (20 July 1954). Portland, Oregon, 1954.

U.S. Army Corps of Engineers. *Special Report on Indian Fishery Problem, The Dalles Dam, Columbia River, Washington-Oregon* (10 March 1952). Portland, Oregon, 1952.

U.S. Army Corps of Engineers. Portland District. *Summary of Evidence Relating to the Nez Perce Fishery at Celilo Falls, Oregon* (15 August 1955). Portland, Oregon, 1955.

U.S. Bureau of Indian Affairs. Portland Area Office. Celilo Falls files. Celilo Fish Committee files. Property and Plant Management, Celilo Relocation Records, 1947–1957. File of Edward G. Swindell, Counsel, 1947–1953, re: Celilo Matters. File 155, Spearfish Committee, 1939–1940. File 920, Conservation of Fish and Wildlife, Celilo Fisheries. Files of C. G. Davis. Files of the Area Social Worker. All in Record Group (RG) 75, National Archives—Pacific Northwest Region, Seattle, Washington.

U.S. Bureau of Indian Affairs. Portland Area Office. Files pertinent to Celilo Village 1930–1960, including records dealing with real estate, field agent correspondence, fishing rights, and the U.S. Army Corps of Engineers. Federal Building (ninth-floor metal filing cabinets), Portland, Oregon. These files were made available to the author during July 1997 by Chuck James, BIA archaeologist, who indicated that these particular records would be transferred in the near future to the National Archives—Pacific Northwest Region, Seattle, Washington.

U.S. Bureau of Indian Affairs. Yakima Agency. *Program: Celilo, Oregon, 1946–1955* (March 1955). Portland, Oregon.

U.S. Congress. House. Committee on Appropriations. *Civil Functions, Department of the Army, Appropriations for 1952 Hearings, Part 1 and 2*. 82nd Cong., 1st and 2nd sess., 1951. Report prepared by William E. Warne (Assistant Secretary, U.S. Department of the Interior). Washington, D.C.: Government Printing Office, 1951.

U.S. Congress. House. HR 5134. 86th Cong., 1st sess. *Congressional Record* 105, pt. 16 (1959), H 3178.

U.S. Congress. House. Subcommittee of the Committee on Appropriations. *Civil Functions, Department of the Army, Appropriations for 1953 Hearings, Part 1 and 2*. 82nd Cong., 1st and 2nd sess., 1952.

U.S. Department of Agriculture. U.S. Forest Service. *Prehistory and History of the Columbia River Gorge National Scenic Area, Oregon and Washington* (15 July 1988), by Stephen Dow Beckham, Rick Minor, Kathryn Anne Toepel, and Jo Reese. Washington, D.C., 1988.

U.S. Department of Commerce. Bureau of the Census. *Historical Statistics of the United States: Colonial Times to the Present, Part 1*. Washington, D.C., 1975.

U.S. Department of Health and Human Services. Public Health Service.

Indian Health Service. Office of Planning, Evaluation and Legislation. Division of Program Statistics. *Trends in Indian Health.* Washington, D.C.: U.S. Government Printing Office, 1991.

U.S. Department of the Interior. National Park Service. "Cultural Sequences at The Dalles, Oregon" (1958), unpublished report by Luther S. Cressman.

U.S. Department of the Interior. Bureau of Reclamation. *The Dalles Project, Oregon, Western Division* (November 1959). Boise, Idaho, 1959.

U.S. Department of the Interior. U.S. Fish and Wildlife Service. *Summary Report on Indian Fishery Census, Celilo Falls and Vicinity* (1951–54). Portland, Oregon, 1954.

U.S. District Court of Oregon at Portland. Civil and Criminal Case files, 1922–1943. Record Group (RG) 21, National Archives—Pacific Northwest Region, Seattle, Washington.

Vibert, Elizabeth. *Trader's Tales: Narratives of Cultural Encounters in the Columbia Plateau, 1807–1846.* Norman: University of Oklahoma Press, 1997.

Wagenblast, Joan Arrivee, and Jeanne Hillis. *Flora's Song: A Remembrance of Chief Tommy Kuni Thompson of the WyAms.* The Dalles, Ore.: The Optimist Printers, 1993.

Waldram, James. *As Long as the Rivers Run: Hydroelectric Development and Native Communities in Western Canada.* Winnipeg: University of Manitoba Press, 1988.

Walton, John. *Western Times and Water Wars: State, Culture, and Rebellion in California.* Berkeley: University of California Press, 1992.

Wasco County Planning Office. *Cherry Industry: What Does It Mean for Wasco County,* by James Snyder. Oregon State University and Wasco County Planning Office, 1974.

Weist, Katherine. "For the Public Good: Native Americans, Hydroelectric Dams, and the Iron Triangle." In *Trusteeship in Change: Toward Tribal Autonomy in Resource Management,* ed. Richmond Clow and Imre Sutton. Boulder: University of Colorado Press, 2001.

White, Richard. *"It's Your Misfortune and None of My Own": A New History of the American West.* Norman: University of Oklahoma Press, 1991.

————. *The Organic Machine: The Remaking of the Columbia River.* New York: Hill and Wang, 1995.

Wilkinson, Charles F. *Crossing the Next Meridian: Land, Water, and the Future of the West.* Washington, D.C.: Island Press, 1992.

————. *Messages from Frank's Landing: A Story of Salmon, Treaties, and the Indian Way.* Seattle: University of Washington Press, 2000.

Williams, Ira. A. *Geologic History of the Columbia River Gorge, as Interpreted from the Historic Columbia River Scenic Highway.* Portland: Oregon Historical Society Press, 1991.

Woody, Elizabeth. *Seven Hands, Seven Hearts.* Portland, Ore.: Eighth Mountain Press, 1994.

Worster, Donald. *Rivers of Empire: Water, Aridity, and the Growth of the American West.* New York: Oxford University Press, 1985.

Zucker, Jeff, Kay Hummel, and Bob Høgfoss. *Oregon Indians: Culture, History and Current Affairs, an Atlas and Introduction.* Portland: Oregon Historical Society Press, 1983.

INDEX

Pages with illustrations are indicated in boldface type.

Celilo Fish Committee (CFC), 36–37, 38–41, 47, 49, 56, 135–36, 146; conflict with white fishers, 47, 49, 56; and dam opposition, 82, 157; and intertribal conflict, 162, 168; and relocation, 146

Celilo Lake, 4, 12, 163

Celilo Village, 6, 9, 11, 14–15, 28, 30, 71, **128**, 170–71, 225n35; appearance of, 139–40; ceremonies in, 125–27, 128; *Chronicle* portrayal of, 119–24, 142; crime in, 120–21; cultural significance of, 24–25, 129; discrimination against, 135, 140–42; economy of, 129; expansion of, 130; federal purchase of, 57, 130, 201n50; governing of, 130–32, 135–36; inundation of, 127, 138, 152–53; legal status of, 129–30; modernization of, 12, 24, 136–38, 142–44; persistence of, 139, 153–54; poverty in, 138, 140–41, 154; railroad through, 122, 127; relocation of, 12, 15, 30, 116, 125, 127–28, 144–52, 226n46

Charley, Jobe (Job), 53, 57, 60

Chinese, 45–46

Chinook Indians, 21, 27; language, 22

Civil Aeronautics Administration, 109

Clark, William, 18–19, 21–22, 23, 50

Cloud, George, **148**, 151

Cold war, 13; and dam building, 32, 76–77, 85, 161, 205n20; and treaty violations, 90–91

Cole, Dave, 3

Collier, John, 62, 94, 210n92

Columbia Basin Fisheries Development Association, 70–71, 73–74

Columbia Gorge Discovery Center, 186

Columbia River, 17–18; dams on, 14, 19, 30–34, 50, 75–76, 93, 184; flooding of, 32, 33–34; islands in, 42, 235n3; management of, 7, 34; map of, 17; navigation of, 4, 5, 7, 15, 19, 26; as sacred place, 11, 25; scholarship on, 8–9; trade on, 27, 50. *See also* Celilo Falls; The Dalles Dam and Lock; Fishing sites

Columbia River Gorge, 17–18, 90

Compensation, 12, 49, 62; disbursement of, 175–79; and fish census, 159–60, 164–65; inadequacy of, 86, 172–73, 175, 182; in-lieu sites, 87, 158, 161, 163, 167, 207n37; intertribal conflict over, 41–42, 155–56, 160–66, 168; negotiations over, 80–81, 85–86, 155–58, 162–72; for personal property, 134, 149, 163; and social welfare, 173–75, 179–82, 234n55; terms of, 161, 163, 167, 168–70,

public meetings, 11, 16, 66, 67–69; and relocation, 127, 149. *See also* Compensation

United States Bureau of Indian Affairs (BIA), 12, 15–16; and compensation disbursement, 176–81; and fishing access, 36, 38–40, 57–61, 162; land purchases by, 130, 149; community management by, 133, 136–38, 143, 145–51; opposition to dam, 66, 74, 92–95, 158; reduction of, 94, 148, 171, 201n50; shortcomings of, 129

United States Congress: and compensation, 77, 80–81, 85–86, 88, 158, 170; hearings, 64, 69–70, 75–88, 229n4

United States Department of the Interior, 80, 87, 88; compensation by, 81

United States Fish and Wildlife Service: fisheries plan, 70; fish survey by, 156, 159–60, 164–65, 229n5

United States government: Indian policies of, 9, 11, 15–16, 40, 51, 63; regional funding by, 12, 98, 108–12. *See also names of agencies and departments*

United States v. Earnest F. Cramer and E. R. Cramer, 53–54, 58–59

United States v. Frank Taylor, 198n26

Van Pelt, Levi, 121
Vanport City, Ore., 34

Walla Walla treaty (1855), 41, 51–52
Wanapa Koot Koot, 10
Warm Springs Agency, 130
Warm Springs Indians, 6, 15, 38; compensation of, 81, 155–56, 158, 161–66, 172, 177–79; fishing rights of, 41, 156, 230n19; opposition to dam, 71, 75, 78, 86, 157, 161; treaty, 197n14, 228n1
Warne, William, 80–81, 87
Wasco County, 12, 15, 69, 119; bridge relocation, 113–16; population growth in, 105; and relocation, 147–48, 150; school crisis in, 106–7
Wasco County Welfare Commission, 149
Wasco Indians, 38
Webber, Ward, 30, 68–69, 98, 113–16, 149, 212n5
Welker, Herman, 170
Wellsey, Rosita, 5–6
West, Herbert, 68, 75–76, 79
Wheeler, R. L., 100–101
Whiz, John, 60, 135–36
Wilkinson, Malcolm, 134
Willamette River, 33
Williams, Lavina, 173–75, 182
Wilson, Fred, 124
Wishram Indians, 38
Women's Forum, 89–90

LIBRARY OF CONGRESS
CATALOGING-IN-PUBLICATION DATA

Barber, Katrine.
Death of Celilo Falls / by Katrine Barber.
p. cm. — (The Emil and Kathleen Sick lecture-book series
in western history and biography)
Includes bibliographical references and index.
ISBN-10: 0-295-98546-1 (pbk. : alk. paper)
ISBN-13: 978-0-295-98546-6 (pbk. : alk. paper)
1. Indians of North America—Fishing—Oregon—Celilo.
2. Indians of North America—Land tenure—Oregon—Celilo.
3. Indians of North America—Relocation—Oregon—Celilo.
4. Salmon fishing—Oregon—Celilo.
5. Fishery law and legislation—Oregon—Celilo.
6. Water rights—Oregon—Celilo.
7. Celilo Falls Indian Relocation Project—History.
8. Dalles Dam (Or. and Wash.)—History.
9. Dalles Dam (Or. and Wash.)—Environmental conditions.
10. Celilo (Or.)—Social conditions.
11. Celilo (Or.)—Environmental conditions.
12. Dalles (Or.)—Environmental conditions.
13. Columbia River—Water rights.
I. Title. II. Series.
E78.O6B37 2005 979.5'64—dc22 2005017103